Shreve's Landing

Fare for a Captain's Table

A Collection of Recipes
prepared by the
Port of Shreve - A.B.W.A.
Shreveport, La.

A Word of Thanks

The historical excerpts found throughout SHREVE'S LANDING are from the book CADDO: 1000—A HISTORY OF SHREVEPORT by Viola Carruth and published by SHREVEPORT MAGAZINE. The Port of Shreve Chapter of the American Business Women's Association would like to extend warm thanks to Graydon Smart of the SHREVEPORT MAGAZINE and Viola Carruth for endorsing our endeavor.

Title Page Photo
Shreveport was visited by many famous steamships during the height of river travel. "Plainly visible to the naked eye from the foot of Texas Street," according to the SOUTHWESTERN on August 10, 1870, was the legendary ROBERT E. LEE which made the famous steamboat race with the NATCHEZ on the Mississippi River. It arrived on August 9 from St. Louis pulling a large barge "loaded with jugs and landed below the corporate limits as wharfage would make a tremendous hole in profits on jugs." (The NATCHEZ may be seen in the left hand corner of the picture.)

International Standard Book Number — 0-918544-18-1

Printed in the United States of America
Wimmer Brothers Fine Printing & Lithography
Memphis, Tennessee 38101

"Cookbooks of Distinction"

A Message from the President

This Cook Book has been compiled as truly a work of art and the proceeds of its sale go entirely for a scholarship fund for deserving women in the pursuit and training of business careers.

The primary objective of the American Business Women's Association is to award scholarships to young women who wish to qualify for positions of importance in business and industry. In 1949, Hilary A. Bufton, Jr. founded the American Business Women's Association to establish a common ground for all business women. It quickly attracted members from all types of businesses and professions to exchange thoughts and ideas. The Association has over 1570 active chapters, members in all fifty states, and an active membership exceeding 96,000.

Port of Shreve Chapter, ABWA was organized in August, 1975 with 28 Charter Members. Since its organization, Port of Shreve Chapter has awarded five scholarships.

We reached even into the favorite recipes of our forebears in Europe to supply you with the very best. Here's hoping that you will enjoy every one of them and that you will find this book an unforgettable gift to your friends and those you love.

Marjorie C. Otto

Marjorie C. Otto
President — 1977-1978

COOK BOOK COMMITTEE

Mrs. Art A. Ogletree, Jr.
Chairman

Mrs. Court Crow
Co-Chairman

Mrs. C. D. Attaway
Treasurer

ARTIST
Mrs. Fred H. Collins

MEMBERS

Mrs. Bill Alexander
Miss Rhonda Berry
Mrs. Ronny Goodman
Mrs. Louis R. Jaudon
Mrs. Marvin Kines
Mrs. H. Russell Maddox
Mrs. A. H. Otto
Mrs. A. R. Snider
Miss Darlene Vaughn

The committee for Shreve's Landing expresses appreciation to the members of Port of Shreve Chapter and friends for their recipes, efforts and interest in this venture.

Shreveport History

Captain Henry Miller Shreve

Shreveport is named after Captain Henry Miller Shreve who undertook the immense task of clearing the Red River of a massive log jam the Caddo Indians had named the Great Raft. The Raft had turned the river out of its banks and onto thousands of acres of potentially rich agricultural and grazing lands and posed an impenetrable barrier to river travel and trade to the Mississippi and New Orleans.

Of Quaker descent, he was born in Burlington County, New Jersey, on October 21, 1785, but was reared on the Monongahela River, not far from Pittsburgh, Pennsylvania.

At the age of 21, he constructed his own barge and floated down the Ohio River to engage in fur trade at St. Louis, Missouri. In 1810 he was the first white man to go into the Illinois country and trade with the Indians for lead. He opened a barge trade from Pittsburgh to New Orleans and was responsible for breaking the Livingston-Fulton Company 18-year steamboat monopoly.

In 1817 he invented what became the typical Mississippi steamboat, with very shallow draft and decks rearing one above the other. Applying an entirely new principle in steam engines, he installed small twin engines on the lower deck and four boilers on the upper deck, instead of putting the machinery in the hold of the ship. The machinery weighed only 1/20th as much as the Fulton steamboat, but the high-pressure twin engines furnished many times the power.

In addition, Shreve added luxury to river boat travel with cabins, private rooms, and bar rooms furnished with handsome fittings, and served epicurean meals with much formality.

Captain Shreve was credited with coining the maritime term "stateroom" because he used the names of states rather than numbers to designate the cabins on his steamboats.

Then Captain Shreve turned to river safety, inventing the snagboat to clear the waterways. He accepted the post of Superintendent of Western River Improvement, paying under $5,000 a year — less than he could make on one trip to New Orleans with his steamboat.

On March 30, 1833, Shreve started his expedition to the Red River with food, clothing and medicine necessary for 160 men aboard the snagboat, ARCHIMEDES. After extensive labor and continued pleading for more funds from the government to cover the cost of the massive undertaking, Shreve completed the task in March of 1838 and the first steamboat passed up the river.

In 1834, after he had cleared the Raft to the high ground on which Shreveport is now located, he selected the site for his headquarters. Traders had long fancied the bluff as it was one of two lofty banks within a hundred miles. A high ridge with the land falling off perceptibly on both sides began at this point and meandered off toward Texas. Americans in their covered wagons moving westward invariably traveled the ridge to keep out of the mud and long before Shreveport was founded it was being called the Texas Trail.

The Shreve Town Company was organized on May 27, 1836. A village eight streets wide and eight long was laid out and each of the partners of the company agreed to buy a lot and use "all proper means to encourage the settlement of said town."

Substantial commerce was set up on Red River which was to become a Louisiana trade highway second in importance only to the Mississippi.

In 1841 Captain Shreve was recalled from his position and retired to his home in St. Louis, Missouri, where he died on March 6, 1851.

The golden age of western steamboating began when Captain Shreve cleared the Red River. The removal of the Great Raft brought trade from 1,000 miles upstream, along the Texas and Indian Territory border, and rapidly populated the drained swamplands of north Louisiana. A result was the founding and development of Shreve Town, the metropolis of the Ark-La-Tex, a living memorial to a man whose driving intention, which dominated him, was to establish safe, fast river travel and transportation.

Table of Contents

The Port of Shreve Chapter of the American Business Women's Association wishes to convey, through our cookbook, the fascinating story of the birth and growth of our "river city" to its citizens and to its future friends throughout the world. We envision our history adding that touch of old south riverboat atmosphere to each recipe you enjoy.

Appetizers

The Great Raft

Tribal legends of the Caddos often spoke of the monstrous, creeping thing which for centuries had been choking the muddy red stream miles above its confluence with the Father of Waters. Each year it crawled upriver with swampland spreading laterally, creating what eventually became perhaps the continent's biggest log jam. The Indians called it the Great Raft.

Had it not been for the tenacious ingenuity of Captain Shreve, who contributed nearly 40 years to the navigability and safety of western commerce, Shreveport would not now be the transportation hub and trade center of the Ark-La-Tex. Instead, the site might still be just a high ridge surrounded by a desolate swamp inhabited only by alligators and mosquitoes.

The Great Raft began forming where Red River flows into Louisiana from Arkansas. When Captain Shreve began removal operations in 1833 it extended to the mouth of Loggy Bayou and was roughly estimated by the government as 160 miles long, which was later changed to an estimate of 214 miles.

The Raft was a jumble of piled timbers, log jams and driftwood enmeshed in sandbars, which had accumulated in large masses in sections of the river bed. Many stretches formed solid bridges from bank to bank.

When the War Department sent Thomas Freeman, a surveyor, and Dr. Peter Custis, a naturalist, to determine the boundaries and geographic features of the Louisiana territory in 1806, the Great Raft was the most remarkable feature they had to report, and they recommended the route be improved.

PARTY CHEESE BALL

1 8-ounce package cream cheese
¾ cup (4 ounces) crumbled blue cheese
1 cup shredded sharp cheddar cheese
¼ cup minced onion
1 tablespoon Worcestershire sauce
½ cup finely snipped parsley

Place cream cheese, blue cheese, and cheddar cheese in a small mixing bowl and let stand at room temperature until softened. Blend in onion and Worcestershire on low speed of mixer. Beat on medium speed until fluffy. Cover and chill 3 or 4 hours. Shape mixture in one large ball and roll in parsley. Place on plate and chill 2 hours or until firm. Serve with crisp crackers.

Mrs. Marvin Kines (Ora)

MINI STICKS

3 pounds chicken wings
½ cup flour
½ cup Parmesan cheese
1 tablespoon monosodium glutamate
1 teaspoon salt
1 teaspoon paprika
⅛ teaspoon pepper
½ teaspoon oregano
¾ cup buttermilk
Oil or shortening

Cut wings in half. Use "drumstick" half. Blend together dry ingredients. Dip drumsticks in buttermilk, shake and roll in flour mix. Heat oil (one inch deep) to 365 degrees. Add few pieces of chicken at a time. Cook until golden brown. Drain. Serve hot or cold. Makes about 18 servings.

Mrs. Margaret Copeland

BLUE CHEESE EGG DIP

½ cup (2 ounces) crumbled blue cheese
6 hard cooked eggs
½ cup sour cream
2 teaspoons onion salt

Chop eggs finely or put through a sieve. Combine with blue cheese, onion salt and sour cream. Beat until smooth. Chill thoroughly and beat until fluffy before serving. Makes 2 cups.

Mrs. A. R. Snider (Frances)

TV SNACKS

1 cup Wesson oil
1 tablespoon Tabasco
2 teaspoons Worcestershire
1 teaspoon garlic salt
1 teaspoon celery salt
1 tablespoon chili powder
1 pound cashew nuts (salted)
½ pound almonds (salted)
½ pound pecans (salted)
½ box each — Wheat, Rice, and Corn Chex; and Cheerios
1 box pretzels

Place cereal and nuts in large pan. Mix all seasoning and oil together. Pour over cereal and nut mixture and stir well. Place in 275 degree oven for 1 hour. Stir every 20 minutes. Watch closely.
Mrs. C. D. Attaway (Margie)

MARINATED SHRIMP

2 pounds shrimp
1 cup Wesson oil
¼ cup olive oil
1 lemon, cut in thin slices
Pimiento strips
Juice of ½ lemon
⅛ teaspoon red pepper
½ teaspoon salt
Few dashes Worcestershire sauce
2 large white onions, sliced thinly in rings
½ teaspoon garlic powder
4 chopped green onions and tops

Boil shrimp in water to which salt and pepper have been added. Cool and peel. In quart jar place all the ingredients and mix very well. Put shrimp in large bowl. Pour mixture over shrimp. Cover and stir occasionally. Refrigerate for 24 hours. To serve, put lettuce on plate and use all pimiento strips, onion rings and lemon slices along with shrimp. Spear with toothpicks.
Mrs. Leonard Green, Jr. (June)

GREEN CHILI SANDWICHES

1 8-ounce package cream cheese
1 teaspoon scraped onion
½ can green chili (chopped) or more
2 drops green coloring
Sour cream or milk

Mash cream cheese until soft. Add scraped onion, salt, green chili and green coloring. Thin with sour cream or milk. Use party bread to make sandwiches.
Mrs. Margaret Copeland

TERIYAKI CHICKEN WINGS

3 to 3½ pounds chicken wings
½ cup catsup
¼ cup dry white wine
¼ cup soy sauce
2 tablespoons sugar
1 teaspoon salt
½ teaspoon ground ginger
1 clove garlic, crushed

Cut tip from each chicken wing. Separate wing from 'mini-drumstick' at joint so each wing makes two appetizers. Mix remaining ingredients and pour over chicken. Marinate in covered dish in refrigerator at least 1 hour. Turn chicken occasionally.

Barbecue over charcoal grill or cook as follows. Heat oven to 375 degrees. Bake for 30 minutes on rack in aluminum foil lined pan. Baste with reserved juice. Turn chicken and continue baking, basting occasionally. Bake until chicken is glazed about 30 to 40 minutes.

Mrs. Ronny Goodman (Janice)

GUACAMOLE DIP WITH BACON

2 cups mashed avocados (about 4 medium size)
2 tablespoons lime juice
1 teaspoon grated onion
2 teaspoons olive oil
8 drops Tabasco sauce
½ teaspoon salt
½ teaspoon monosodium glutamate
4 slices bacon, fried and crumbled

Mash avocados and add the remaining ingredients. Mix well. Serve with Doritos Chips. Yield: 2 cups.

Mrs. Leonard Green, Jr. (June)

SAUSAGE BALLS

1 pound pork sausage (either hot or mild)
½ pound mild cheddar cheese (grated)
½ pound sharp cheddar cheese (grated)
3 cups Bisquick

Crumble raw sausage. Add cheese and Bisquick and mix very well. Make into walnut size balls. Bake at 350 degrees about 10 minutes. Serve hot or cold. Can freeze the balls before baking.

Mrs. Jo Whittaker

CHEESE SPREAD

1 pound cheese
1 13-ounce can evaporated milk
1 teaspoon sugar
¼ teaspoon Tabasco

Heat milk until almost boiling. Chop cheese and put into hot milk. Add sugar, Tabasco, and heat until cheese is completely melted. Pour into container and refrigerate until it congeals. Very good!
Mrs. F. A. Kihneman (Tora)

SAUSAGE ROLLS

1 pound hot pork sausage
1 pound sharp cheese, coarsely grated
3 cups Bisquick

Melt sausage and cheese together in skillet, drain juice. Add Bisquick. Mix and chill for an hour, then roll into marble sized balls. Bake at 400 degrees for 8 to 10 minutes or until lightly brown. Drain on paper towels. Makes four dozen.
Mrs. Floyd Cunningham (Nell)

TUNA-CREAM CHEESE SANDWICHES

2 8-ounce packages cream cheese
1 7-ounce can white tuna
1 cup chopped nuts
Mayonnaise to spread
Stuffed olives
Bread

Soften cream cheese to room temperature. Combine cream cheese, tuna, nuts and mayonnaise. Add enough mayonnaise to make a good spreading consistency. Pinwheel sandwiches may be made by using a whole loaf of bread which you purchase unsliced. Using electric knife remove crust from all sides and slice bread lengthwise. Flatten each long slice with rolling pin. Spread each long slice with mixture. Before rolling the pinwheel place several small stuffed olives at end of slice where you will begin the roll. When roll is completed wrap snugly in wax paper and place in refrigerator. Leave several hours. When ready to serve, take roll and slice into pinwheels and arrange on tray. If open face sandwiches are desired without making pinwheels, just cut bread in rounds, spread with mixture and place sliced olive in center.
Mrs. Elouise Jouett

CUCUMBER-ONION DIP

1 8-ounce package cream cheese
1 package Green Onion Dip Mix (Fritos brand)
1 heaping teaspoon mayonnaise
Salt to taste
1 medium size cucumber (or ½ large cucumber)
1 8-ounce carton sour cream

Cream cheese should be at room temperature. Mash dip mix into cream cheese with fork or use electric mixer. Mix thoroughly. Add mayonnaise and salt. If seeds are large in cucumber, remove them. Mince cucumber as finely as possible — hack it. Add cucumber and sour cream to cheese mixture. Chill. Serve with corn chips or potato chips.

Variations: Add 3 or 4 drops green food coloring to make it a pale green – pretty for Christmas.

To use as sandwich spread, omit half of sour cream. The sour cream makes it much easier to spread on bread.

I have used this recipe for over 25 years and there is always a request for the recipe after a party.

Mrs. Art Ogletree, Jr. (Ann)

TINY ALOHA PINEAPPLE MUFFINS

2 cups New Bisquick
¼ cup sugar
2 tablespoons soft butter
1 egg
⅔ cup milk
½ cup well drained crushed pineapple
Thin Icing (below)
Chopped nuts

Heat oven to 400 degrees. Grease 48 tiny muffin cups. Mix Bisquick, sugar, butter, egg and milk with fork. Beat vigorously one half minute. Fold in pineapple. Fill prepared muffin cups ⅔ full. Bake 12 to 15 minutes. While warm frost with Thin Icing.

Thin Icing:

½ cup confectioners' sugar
1 tablespoon water

Blend confectioners' sugar and water until smooth. Sprinkle with nuts.

NOTE: Muffins may be baked in 12 greased medium muffin cups. Bake 15 to 20 minutes.

Mrs. Olin P. Oden (Ruth)

SATURDAY NITE EMPANADAS

2 frozen unbaked pie shells
1 zucchini
1 large tomato
½ of 4-ounce can chopped green chilies
¾ cup cheddar cheese, shredded

Trim ends and cook whole zucchini covered in boiling salted water 10 minutes. Drain. Chop tomato; combine with zucchini, chilies and cheese. Makes 2 cups. On floured surface, roll each piece of dough to a 6-inch circle. Place part of vegetable filling on each. Moisten edges with water. Fold in half, pressing edges with fork to seal. Brush with milk if desired. Slash tops in 2 or 3 places. Arrange on ungreased baking sheet and bake at 425 degrees for 15-18 minutes or until golden. Remove from baking sheet. Serve hot with Chili con Queso Dip. Garnish with parsley and cherry tomatoes. Yields 10 to 12 servings.
Mrs. Barbara Parnell

PARTY WIENERS

½ cup catsup
6 ounce jar mustard
10 ounce jar currant jelly
2 pounds wieners, sliced

Mix together catsup, mustard, and jelly. Add weiners and simmer. Serve warm in fondue or chafing dish.
Mrs. Ronny Goodman, Jr. (Janice)

AVOCADO DIP

4 fresh avocados or 3 cans frozen avocado
1 pound lean ground beef
½ cup mayonnaise
1 small onion, chopped fine
1 teaspoon Tabasco
1 small can chopped green chilies
2 teaspoons cumin
¼ pound Jack cheese finely grated
Juice of 1 lemon

Sauté onion and beef, salt to taste and add all other ingredients. Make at last minute before serving with Fritos or Doritos.
Mrs. John H. Lenard, Jr. (Carol), Lenexa, Kansas

ARTICHOKE APPETIZERS

1 15-ounce can artichoke hearts, drained and chopped
1 6-ounce jar marinated artichoke hearts, drained and chopped (save marinade)
1 small onion, chopped finely
2 cloves garlic, chopped finely
4 large eggs
1 cup Progresso Italian bread crumbs
½ pound cheddar cheese, grated

Sauté onion and garlic in reserved marinade just until onion is clear. Then, mix everything together. (To make life easier, instead of chopping the artichokes, I broke the eggs directly into my blender, then dumped in the artichokes and turned it on for a few seconds. Then, to avoid chopping the onions and garlic finely, I just chopped them up coarsely, and after I sautéed them, I dumped them into the blender with the artichokes and turned it on again. After all, you don't want big chunks of anything in this. If you don't feel like grating the cheese, just grind it up in the blender with the rest. Then all you have to do is to mix in the bread crumbs.)

Pour mixture into a greased 13x9-inch pan. Bake at 350 degrees for 30 to 40 minutes, just until the edges turn slightly brown and a knife inserted into the center comes out clean. Let cool completely, then cut into one inch squares. (These are best when made ahead and reheated when needed). To reheat, place in a warm (200 degree) oven for 15-20 minutes.

Mrs. Bruce Baker (Stacy), Baton Rouge, Louisiana

LIVERWURST BALL

1 large link liverwurst
2 3-ounce packages cream cheese
Mayonnaise
Garlic salt
Worcestershire sauce
Tabasco sauce
Parsley flakes
Caviar — black

Soften the liverwurst with mayonnaise, using an electric mixer. Add garlic salt, Worcestershire sauce, Tabasco sauce to taste. Line a small bowl or mold with foil and put liverwurst mixture into it. Refrigerate for several hours or freeze if preparing ahead. Remove mixture from mold and invert onto plate. Beat cream cheese, thinning with a little milk, until a good spreading consistency. Completely cover surface of the ball with cream cheese. Very carefully cover the cheese with caviar. The caviar may be eliminated and the cream cheese ball may be rolled in parsley flakes.

Mrs. Leonard Green, Jr. (June)

HOT CRAB DIP

4 to 6 pounds crab meat
2 sticks butter
2 onions, chopped
½ cup green onions and tops, chopped
1 small bunch parsley
Tabasco sauce to taste
4 to 6 cans cream of mushroom soup (depends on desired thickness)

Crab meat may be one half white meat and one half dark meat. Melt butter in large pan. Sauté onion until tender but not brown. Add crab meat. Cook until it begins to curl. Add green onions and parsley. Add soup until consistency for dip. Add Tabasco to taste. Cook until mixture loses mushroom taste. Serve in chafing dish with melba toast rounds, crackers or it may be served in pastry shells. If served in pastry shells it should be a thicker consistency.
Mrs. S. C. Stolzenthaler, Jr. (Betty), Baton Rouge, Louisiana

MEAT BALLS IN ALE

3 pounds ground lean beef
1 large onion, grated
1½ teaspoons salt (or more)
½ teaspoon black pepper
½ teaspoon garlic powder
¼ cup water
1 14-ounce bottle catsup
1 12-ounce can beer

Combine meat and seasoning, form into bite size balls. Heat water, catsup and beer in saucepan. Carefully drop meat balls into liquid. Boil slowly for one hour. Serve in sauce in a chafing dish. May be prepared in advance. Yield: 50-55 meat balls.
Mrs. Leonard Green, Jr. (June)

LAKE CHARLES DIP

1 pint sour cream
1 package Good Seasons Italian Dressing
3 tomatoes, chopped fine
1 cup mayonnaise
3 avocados, chopped fine

Mix sour cream, Italian seasoning, mayonnaise, tomatoes and avocados. Serve with Fritos.
Mrs. Joseph LaBarbera (Billie)

BAKED POTATO SLIMS

¼ cup water
2 tablespoons oil
½ teaspoon Tabasco
¼ cup grated cheese
1 envelope Shake 'n Bake (for chicken)
4 big potatoes (peeled and cut in large French fry size) or
1 9-ounce package frozen French fries
Foil for cookie sheet

Mix water, oil, and Tabasco. Peel potatoes and cut in ½-inch strips or use frozen French fries. Toss potatoes in water mixture. Put cheese in Shake 'n Bake. Drop potatoes in this mixture. Shake until well coated. Place foil on cookie sheet. Lay potatoes in single layers and bake in 400 degree oven 30 to 35 minutes.

Mrs. F. A. Kihneman (Tora)

DELECTABLE, DELICIOUS DIP

1 quart salad dressing
1 6-ounce can tomato paste
Fresh jalapeno peppers to taste, ground finely (the more the better)
Dash or two Tabasco sauce
Fresh garlic to taste, pressed

Chop jalapeno peppers in blender. Mix all ingredients and let stand in refrigerator overnight. This is especially good with fresh cauliflower and carrots.

Miss Rhonda Berry, Keithville, Louisiana

HARRIET'S GOOP

1 large green pepper, chopped
2 teaspoons vinegar
1 cup tomato sauce
½ pound soft butter
1 cup ripe olives, drained, chopped
4 green onions and stalks, chopped
1 2-ounce jar pimiento, chopped
1 pound sharp cheese (Tillamook or cheddar), softened
1 loaf French bread, sliced

Combine green pepper, vinegar, tomato sauce, butter, olives, onions, pimiento, and cheese. Mix well and spread on sliced French bread. Bake at 350 degrees for 20 minutes. Nice around Christmas time with mug of soup.

Mrs. John R. Clement (Martha)

CHEESE ROLL I

1 pound cheddar cheese, grated
2 cloves garlic, squeezed, or
¼ teaspoon garlic salt
Dash of cayenne pepper
Dash of salt
½ cup finely chopped nuts
2 tablespoons Worcestershire sauce
2 tablespoons mayonnaise, more or less

Mix all ingredients with about 2 tablespoons mayonnaise — just enough to be able to shape into a roll. When shaped, roll in chili powder.

Mrs. Flo Ogden
Miss Rhonda Berry

CHEESE ROLL II

1 8-ounce sharp cheddar cheese
1 8-ounce processed soft Old English cheese
3 ounces cream cheese
1 clove garlic
1 tablespoon Worcestershire sauce
Few drops Tabasco sauce
1 teaspoon paprika
1 teaspoon chili powder
Dash of red pepper

Put cheddar and processed cheese and garlic through grinder and add other seasonings (not paprika, chili powder or red pepper though). Add cream cheese and mix thoroughly. Remove your rings and work it with your hands.

Shape into balls or roll.

Coat with paprika, chili powder and red pepper mixed together. Better to chill for 24 hours before serving. Then serve at room temperature with crackers. Keeps a long time in the refrigerator.

Mrs. J. R. Collier (Mary)

CHEESE ROLL III

1 pound American cheese
2 pounds of cream cheese
1 cup pecans, chopped fine
1 button of garlic or garlic powder
Chili powder

Let cheese warm to room temperature. Use medium bowl. Crush the button of garlic and mix with the pecans. Set aside. Combine cheeses and roll into a ball. Sprinkle a sheet of wax paper with chili powder and roll the cheese ball in the chili powder . . . then roll the ball in the pecans covering the ball as well as possible.

Mrs. Court Crow (Jeanne)

SHER'S CHEESE ROLL

1 8-ounce Philadelphia cream cheese
1 8-ounce Velveeta cheese
½-1 cup finely ground pecans
Garlic powder to taste
Chili powder
Paprika

Mix cream cheese, Velveeta cheese together. Add pecans and garlic. Make into roll and sprinkle with either chili powder or paprika. Chill and serve in slices.

Ms. Sherry Anderson

EGG ROLLS A LA PHAM

7 egg roll pastry wrappers
¾ cup rice noodles
¾ cup chopped onion
1 cup oriental mushrooms, chopped fine
2 large carrots, chopped fine
1 pound ground pork (or sausage)
2 eggs
Crisco shortening
1 tablespoon fish sauce
Garlic, salt, hot pepper to taste

Take pastry wrappers out of freezer approximately 1 hour ahead of time. Place noodles in warm water and soak for 15 minutes. Pat dry. Chop onions very small and squeeze juice out (this is very important). Soak oriental mushrooms in warm water for 15 minutes; pat dry and chop fine. These are dried mushrooms and they will swell when soaked. Chop carrots very fine; pat dry. Add garlic to meat. Beat eggs 30 seconds and add to meat. Add 1 tablespoon fish sauce and hot pepper next. Put in skillet and sauté approximately 5 minutes; add onions and mushrooms. Sauté about 3 minutes, stirring constantly. Add soaked noodles; stir well. Add carrots and salt, stirring as you cook approximately 3 more minutes Let mixture cool enough to handle. Take the pastry wrappers out of package. Snip off approximately one inch of three corners of pastry. Put mixture on wrapper, rolling from cut corner *opposite* uncut corner. Fold over ends as you roll. Leave uncut pointed end down so they will not unroll. Fry in Crisco shortening. Have about 1 inch of melted shortening in bottom of skillet. Use medium to low heat. If you fry at higher temperature, the wrapper will cook too fast and may unfold. Also, the carrots will not get done.

NOTE: Pastry wrappers — buy Doll Spring Roll Shell brand if possible (made in California) — 50 pieces to package or Levil pastry wrappers (made in Philippines), 45-50 to package. Mushrooms and pastry wrappers are usually available in Oriental food stores.

A lovely lady from Viet Nam taught me to make these egg rolls.

Mrs. Robert F. Harris (Sue)

CHILI DIP I

1 can tamales
1 can chili (with or without beans)
1 pound sharp cheese (½ sharp, ½ Velveeta)
1 large onion (grated or finely chopped)
2 pods garlic or ¼ teaspoon garlic powder
4 tablespoons Worcestershire Sauce
Dash of Tabasco
Salt to taste
Dash of sugar or catsup — to taste

Mash tamales and add chili in double boiler. Add chopped cheese, then other ingredients. Stir until cheese is melted. Serve hot with Doritos or corn chips. Makes one quart.

NOTE: Thin with tomato juice or water.

Mrs. Margaret Copeland

CHILI DIP II

4 pounds ground beef
2 No. 2 cans whole tomatoes
1 3-ounce bottle chili powder
1 small (1 ounce) can cumin powder
2 large onions, chopped
4 cloves garlic, chopped
Salt and pepper
4 cups cooked pinto beans

Brown meat, onions and garlic. Add chili powder, cumin and tomatoes. Simmer until thick, one hour or longer. Add one cup cooked pinto beans for each pound of meat. Place in a chafing dish to keep warm and refill as needed. Serve with corn chips.

Makes enough for a large party — 40-50 people.

Mrs. Leonard Green, Jr. (June)

CHILI DIP III

1 large chopped onion
1½ pounds ground meat
Salt to taste
1 pound grated cheddar cheese
1 teaspoon cumin
1 teaspoon chili powder
1 large can all-meat chili

Slowly sauté onion and meat until meat is done. Add cumin, chili powder, salt, canned chili and cheese. Heat all ingredients and serve in chafing dish. Serve with Doritos or Fritos. Serves twenty.

Mrs. Jo Whittaker

SUMMER GARDEN APPETIZER

4 to 6 fresh yellow squash, quartered
3 to 4 zucchini squash, quartered
4 medium-sized carrots, cut in half lengthwise
4 to 6 green onions
3 to 4 celery stalks, halved
1 small head cauliflower, broken into flowerets
2 cups plain yogurt
3 tablespoons olive oil
3 cloves garlic, run through a press
½ teaspoon oregano
½ teaspoon dill weed
½ teaspoon thyme
½ teaspoon chives
1 tablespoon lemon juice

Combine 2 tablespoons yogurt, the olive oil, lemon juice, and all of the seasonings in a blender and blend for five minutes. Pour into a bowl and fold in remaining yogurt. Chill overnight. Arrange vegetables attractively on a large platter and place yogurt mixture in the middle so vegetables may be dipped into it. Serves 10 to 12.
Mrs. George Gekakis (Carol)

JEZEBEL SAUCE FOR CREAM CHEESE

1 18-ounce jar apple jelly
1 18-ounce jar pineapple preserves
1 4-ounce jar horseradish
1 small can (1.12-ounces) dry mustard

Mix both jelly and preserves; add horseradish and dry mustard. Mix well. Refrigerate several hours before serving. Pour over block of cream cheese, serve with Ritz crackers. This sauce will keep forever in the refrigerator.
Mrs. Joseph LaBarbera (Billie)

ANGELS ON HORSEBACK

1 12-ounce jar fresh oysters
2 tablespoons chopped parsley
½ teaspoon salt
Paprika
Pepper
8 slices bacon, cut in thirds

Drain oysters. Place an oyster on each piece of bacon. Sprinkle with parsley and seasonings. Wrap bacon around oyster and secure with a toothpick. Place "angels" on broiler rack and broil about 4 inches from source of heat for 8 to 10 minutes. Turn carefully. Broil 4 to 5 minutes longer or until bacon is crisp and oysters begin to curl at the edges. Makes approximately 20 to 25 hors d'oeuvres.
Mrs. Art Ogletree, Jr. (Ann)

YUMMY MUSHROOMS

Fresh mushrooms, sliced (I use 2 boxes)
½ cup Parkay margarine
¼ cup Worcestershire sauce
½ teaspoon onion salt

Optional:
1 green bell pepper, sliced
½ medium size onion, diced

Wash and drain mushrooms. Melt Parkay in large frying pan with Worcestershire sauce. Slice mushrooms and spread evenly in frying pan with Parkay and Worcestershire sauce. Add onion salt. Sauté on medium low heat, stirring often, until mushrooms have a rubbery texture. Serve immediately over steak or hamburger.

Variation: Add the bell pepper and the onion instead of the onion salt. Cook until onions are transparent and serve immediately.

Makes 4-6 servings.

Ms. Sherry Anderson

CURRY DIP

(for boiled shrimp)

1 pint mayonnaise
3 tablespoons catsup
1 tablespoon Lee & Perrin
3 teaspoons curry powder
2 tablespoons grated onions
Pinch salt
1 teaspoon Tabasco
Juice of ½ lemon

Rub bowl with garlic and add the above ingredients. Mix together. Let stand several hours for best flavor.

Betty Gentry

CURRY DIP

1 cup mayonnaise
1 teaspoon grated ginger
1 clove garlic
½ teaspoon salt
2 tablespoons chopped green onion
1 teaspoon curry (or more to taste)
Lemon juice to taste

Place all ingredients in blender except lemon juice. After thoroughly mixed, add lemon juice to taste. Use as dip for fresh vegetable sticks.

Mrs. Leonard Green, Jr. (June)

CHEESE BALL I

- 2 8-ounce packages cream cheese
- ¼ bell pepper, chopped finely
- 1 8-ounce can crushed pineapple, drained
- 1 tablespoon Lawry's seasoned salt
- 1 teaspoon garlic salt
- 1 cup crushed pecans
- 1 tablespoon grated onion

Soften cheese and mix all ingredients except pecans. Chill about 2 or 3 hours. Shape into ball. Roll in crushed pecans.

Mrs. R. W. Fletcher (Sue)

CHEESE BALL II

- 2 8-ounce packages cream cheese
- 1 8¼-ounce can crushed pineapple
- 1 cup chopped pecans
- ¼ cup chopped green peppers (optional)
- 2 tablespoons chopped green onions
- 1 tablespoon seasoned salt
- ¼ pound sharp cheddar cheese, grated
- Chopped parsley

Soften cream cheese and beat with a fork. Stir in well drained pineapple, pecans, peppers, onions, salt and cheese. Shape into a ball. Roll in chopped parsley or chopped pecans. Serve with Ritz crackers.

Mrs. Morris D. White (Becky)

CREOLE OYSTERS

- 1 gallon oysters and their juice
- 1 button garlic, chopped fine
- ¼ cup lemon juice or vinegar
- 1 cup vegetable oil
- 4 bunches green onions, chopped fine
- Salt and pepper to taste

Combine garlic, lemon juice, vegetable oil, green onions, salt and pepper. Add oysters and their juice to mixture. Serve with toothpick or on toasted crackers.

Mrs. Robert F. Harris (Sue)

SHRIMP DIP I

1 4½-ounce can small-size shrimp, drained
1 carton sour cream
2 tablespoons seasoned salt
1 teaspoon chopped chives

In medium size bowl, add shrimp, sour cream, seasoned salt and chives. Stir all ingredients until well mixed. Chill in covered bowl for several hours before serving. This recipe can be doubled easily for use at parties. Serve with potato chips or Doritos.
Ms.Sherry Anderson

SHRIMP DIP II

1 can shrimp
1 8-ounce carton sour cream
1 8-ounce package cream cheese
½ cup finely chopped celery
½ cup finely chopped green onions & tops
Tabasco sauce to taste
Worcestershire sauce to taste
Lemon juice to taste

Cream together the sour cream and cream cheese. Add other ingredients and blend well. Let refrigerate overnight.
Mrs. Bruce Baker (Stacy), Baton Rouge, Louisiana

SHRIMPLY DIVINE

1 3-ounce package cream cheese, softened
1 package (⅝ ounce) Italian salad dressing mix
½ cup shrimp, finely chopped
1 cup dairy sour cream
2 teaspoons lemon juice
2 tablespoons green pepper, finely chopped

Blend softened cream cheese with remainder of ingredients. Chill at least 1 hour before serving with potato chips, corn chips or various crackers. Makes 1⅔ cups.
Mrs. L. A. McKinley (Elizabeth), Magnolia Springs, Alabama

SHRIMP SPREAD

1 can shrimp (wet pack 4½ ounces)
2 packages Philadelphia cream cheese
1 onion (grated to taste)
Pinch of salt
Pepper
Garlic
Mayonnaise

Rub bowl with garlic. Mash shrimp with cream cheese, small amount of grated onion, small amount of salt, pepper. Mix with mayonnaise to spreading consistency. Serve as a dip.
Mrs. Margaret Copeland

DAZZLE DIP

6 ounces pimiento cream cheese
½ cup sour cream
½ teaspoon paprika
¼ teaspoon Tabasco sauce
½ cup chopped celery and green peppers
½ teaspoon Worcestershire sauce
½ teaspoon salt
4 tablespoons catsup

Use this dip for shrimp . . . gives two (2) cups.
Mrs. Marilyn McCrocklin

SWEET TANGY DOGS

3 pounds frankfurters
1 cup brown sugar
1 cup bourbon
1 cup chili sauce

Combine brown sugar, bourbon and chili sauce. Cut frankfurters in bite size pieces and skin. Cover these pieces with sauce. Bake, covered in 325 degree oven for three hours. Serve hot in chafing dish. This is better if made ahead of time. It can be frozen.
Mrs. Leonard Green, Jr. (June)

TUNA DIP

- 2 6½-ounce cans tuna, drained and mashed with a fork
- 1 large carton sour cream
- 1 package onion soup mix
- Lemon juice
- Salt to taste
- Tabasco sauce
- 2-3 tablespoons mayonnaise

To the tuna, add sour cream, soup mix, a little lemon juice, salt and dash of Tabasco. Add mayonnaise. If too thick, may add a little milk.
Nell M. James

MINIATURE CHEESE CAKES

- 2 8-ounce packages cream cheese
- ¾ cup sugar
- 2 eggs
- 1 tablespoon lemon juice
- 1 teaspoon vanilla
- 1 box or 1 bag of vanilla wafers

Combine cream cheese, sugar, eggs, lemon juice and vanilla; beat until fluffy. If you use regular size muffin liners, choose the larger vanilla wafers. Place one vanilla wafer in bottom of each muffin liner and place cheese mixture on top, filling about two-thirds full. Place in muffin tins and bake at 375 degrees for 15 minutes. Cool. Top with cherry or blueberry pie filling. This size cup makes 24 cakes.
For smaller size cakes, use a medium size muffin liner. You will need smaller vanilla wafers for these. Vanilla wafers which come loose in cellophane bags are usually smaller in size and will fit perfectly in these smaller liners. Recipe will make 30 or more cakes of this size.
Mrs. Olin P. Oden (Ruth)

BITE-SIZE PIZZAS

- 1 pound ground chuck
- 1 pound sausage (hot — Owen's brand)
- 1 pound Velveeta cheese
- Garlic salt to taste
- 2 loaves Pepperidge Farm party rounds

Cook ground chuck and sausage together — crumbling meats until done. Add garlic salt to taste, drain off grease. Cut up cheese and mix with meat mixture until completely melted. Spread on rye thins. Freezes very well. Take out of freezer, put in 350 degree oven 20 minutes, or until cheese melts.
Mrs. R. L. McIlwain (Linda)

Cheese · Eggs · Soups

On November 30, 1870, the Red River Packet Company was incorporated with daily departures from Shreveport to New Orleans and way landings, making close connections with St. Louis and Ohio River steamers and New Orleans railways.

(The steamboat THE RED RIVER PACKET is the third boat from the right.)

The most glorious days of steamboating in Louisiana were those between 1880 and 1898. It was the deluxe travel of the day and one which the planter made every opportunity to enjoy. It was said that most often he went to New Orleans with his harvest each year; at other times he went for any excuse he could think up, and sometimes he just went anyway.

Although river travel by steamboat was the rage of the times there were certain risks and from the earliest days steamboat operation was plagued with boiler explosions, snaggings, collisions, and fire. Two such accidents took place just outside Shreveport.

The first was the KENTUCKY, which was chartered to transport 800 Confederate troops from Camp Boggs in Shreveport. A short distance below town it struck a snag and sank so rapidly that over 200 soldiers drowned.

The second river disaster in this vicinity occurred on the night of February 5, 1869, and is said to have claimed the lives of 60 and injured many others. This was the MITTIE STEVENS, fully loaded including two kegs of gunpowder, enroute to Jefferson, Texas.

The big sternwheeler, cabins lighted with kerosene lamps and open fires of pine knots to guide it, was feeling its way through Cypress Bayou, when a pile of hay at the bow of the boat burst into flames. Soon the entire boat was ablaze. The captain immediately headed for shore and grounded the steamer, but the ground end was afire preventing escape. Many jumped into the deep water and drowned.

QUICHE LORRAINE

2 9-inch pie shells
4 slices bacon, crumbled
1 bunch green onions, chopped
1 tablespoon butter
1 4-ounce can sliced mushrooms
4 slices ham
½ pound Swiss cheese grated
4 eggs
1½ cups evaporated milk
Garlic powder to taste
½ teaspoon salt
½ teaspoon dry mustard

Bake pie shells at 400 degrees. Fry bacon until crisp. Crumble. Sauté onions in butter. Layer bacon, onions, mushrooms, ham and cheese in two shells. Mix remaining ingredients. Pour mixture in shells and bake for 35 minutes in 350 degree oven or until knife comes out clean when inserted in center.
Mrs. Ronny Goodman (Janice)

MACARONI AND CHEESE

1½ cups macaroni, cooked
3 tablespoons butter
3 tablespoons flour
2 cups milk
½ teaspoon salt
Dash pepper
¼ cup onion, minced (optional)
2 cups sharp cheese

Melt butter, blend in flour, add milk and cook, stirring, until thickened. Add salt, pepper, (onion) and cheese. Stir until cheese is melted. Mix with the macaroni. Bake in 350 degree oven for 45 minutes or until bubbly brown.
NOTE: For juicier macaroni and cheese, allow the macaroni to stand in the water cooked in until other mixture is ready to be added.
Mrs. Floyd Cunningham (Nell)

CHEESE CASSEROLE

4 slices buttered toast, cubed
¼ pound grated cheese
2 cups milk
4 eggs, beaten
2 tablespoons chopped onion
1 teaspoon salt

Arrange toast in buttered baking dish, mix eggs, cheese, onion, milk and salt and pour over toast. Bake at 350 degrees until firm, 30 to 45 minutes. Serves 4.
Mrs. James E. Williams (Yvonne)

GARLIC CHEESE GRITS

1 cup uncooked grits (not instant grits)
4 cups water
1 stick butter or margarine
1 tablespoon salt
1 roll garlic cheese
½ pound sharp cheese, cut in small pieces or grated
2 tablespoons Worcestershire sauce

Cook grits in salted water until done; add butter, garlic cheese, sharp cheese and Worcestershire sauce. Stir until butter and cheese have melted. Put in greased casserole and sprinkle with paprika. Bake in preheated 350 degree oven for 15 to 20 minutes. Bake until it bubbles.

Variation: For a main dish, add two small cans of shrimp before baking. This may be baked in a ring mold and served with center of mold filled with extra cooked shrimp.

Mrs. Olin P. Oden (Ruth)

CHEESE SOUFFLÉ

5 slices white bread (remove crusts and cube)
½ pound cheddar cheese (grated)
2 cups milk
1 tablespoon salt
1 tablespoon dry mustard (optional)
4 eggs

Layer bread in casserole and top with cheese. Sprinkle salt and mustard over this. Beat eggs with milk and pour over this layer. Refrigerate at least 1 hour or overnight. Bake 1 hour in 350 degree oven. Be sure to place casserole in shallow pan of hot water while cooking. Serve at once.

Mrs. H. W. Maddox (Charlotte)

CHEESE SOUP

½ cup chopped onion
½ cup chopped carrots
½ cup chopped celery
¼ cup butter
½ cup flour
½ cup milk
4 cups chicken broth
1 cup Velveeta cheese
Salt to taste

Cook onions in butter until tender; blend in all other ingredients except cheese. Stir until thick; reduce heat and add cheese. Simmer for 15 minutes.

Mrs. John H. Lenard, Jr. (Carol), Lenexa, Kansas

HUEVOS RANCHEROS
(Mexican Style Fried Eggs)

Hot Sauce:

½ stick oleo
1 green pepper (diced)
1 medium onion (diced)
2 jalapeno peppers
1 cup catsup

2 eggs per person
corn tortillas

Prepare sauce by melting butter and then sautéing vegetables until transparent. Add catsup and cook 5-10 minutes. Fry eggs sunny side up. Warm tortillas in oven.

Place 2 tortillas on each plate; top each with an egg. Cover eggs with desired amount of hot sauce.

Naomi C. Dugan

BAKED CELERY EGGS

4 eggs
1 10½-ounce can cream of celery soup
¼ cup milk
1 teaspoon Worcestershire sauce
⅛ teaspoon pepper
Paprika

Mix soup, milk, Worcestershire and pepper. Put half into a greased 9-inch pie pan. Break in eggs and top with remaining soup. Sprinkle with paprika. Bake at 325 degrees for 30 minutes and serve plain or on toast. Serves 4.

Mrs. A. R. Snider (Frances)

CREAM OF POTATO SOUP

2 tablespoons butter or margarine
2 tablespoons chopped onion
1½ teaspoons salt
¼ teaspoon celery salt
4 cups milk
1 package instant mashed potatoes (4 servings)
⅛ teaspoon pepper

Combine all ingredients in medium saucepan. Heat to boiling, stirring occasionally. Remove from heat and strain into serving dishes. Soup should be the consistency of heavy cream. If too thick, then add more milk. 4 to 5 servings.

Mrs. Court Crow (Jeanne)

ARTICHOKE SOUP

6 cups chicken stock or bouillon
3 cups sliced potatoes
1 bunch green onions, sliced, reserve tops
2 10-inch packages frozen artichoke hearts
1 tablespoon salt
¼ teaspoon red pepper
1 cup whipping cream
Sour cream (optional)

Bring stock to boil. Add potatoes, onions, artichoke hearts, salt and pepper. Bring back to boil and cook until tender, approximately 8 to 10 minutes. Remove from heat. Fill blender one-half full and puree. Strain to remove strings. Stir in whipping cream. Either chill or heat to serve. Garnish with a dollop of sour cream and chopped green onion tops. Delicious, but very rich!
Mrs. Richard Tally Johnson (Cathie)

EASY VEGETABLE SOUP

1 to 2 pounds stew meat, and
3 or 4 soup bones (Usually makes 2 pots at a time)
4 to 6 medium size red potatoes
1 package carrots
1 to 2 individual stalks of celery
1 medium size onion
1 to 2 tablespoons sugar
Salt and pepper to taste
2 No. 2 cans of whole tomatoes

Simmer stew meat with soup bones in big stew pan or roaster, in enough water to cover, about 20 to 30 minutes over low heat. Add cut up carrots, celery and onions, and add water within 2 inches of the top of the pot. Add sugar, salt and pepper. Simmer 30 to 40 minutes. (Add more water if necessary.) About 15 minutes before ready to serve, add the canned tomatoes, cutting up within the mixture as you are adding.
Mrs. H. Russell Maddox (Tommie Lue)

POTATO SOUP

1 tablespoon chopped onion
2 tablespoons butter or margarine
1 teaspoon salt
¼ teaspoon celery salt
⅛ teaspoon pepper
1 cup mashed potatoes or boiled potatoes
2 cups milk (hot)

Sauté onion in butter or margarine and add seasonings, potatoes and stir in the milk. Simmer slowly for 5 minutes, stir occasionally.
Mrs. Court Crow (Jeanne)

OYSTER SOUP

½ stick butter or oleo plus
2 tablespoons of same
½ cup green onions (shallots plus 1)
2 cups oysters
1 tablespoon flour
2 cups milk
Salt and pepper to taste

Place butter into a saucepan. Add ½ cup shallots. Sauté until onion is wilted. Add oysters, cook until oysters curl. Meantime melt 2 tablespoons butter in medium saucepan, add 1 tablespoon flour and blend. Add one chopped shallot, cook 2 minutes. Gradually add 2 cups milk, salt and pepper to taste. Stir, let come to scalding point. Pour mixture into pan of hot oysters. Stir gently.

Mrs. Lois Mambourg

OYSTER STEW

1 pint oysters
¼ cup chopped onion (fine)
½ cup oleo
1 quart sweet milk
1 13-ounce can evaporated milk
½ teaspoon Worcestershire sauce
1 tablespoon finely chopped parsley
½ teaspoon salt
⅛ teaspoon pepper
½ cup oyster liquid (reserved)

Sauté onions and oysters in oleo until oysters edge curls. Mix with all other ingredients and heat slowly but do not boil. Serves 6. This is tastier if the oysters are cut into pieces so seasoning will penetrate.

Mrs. F. A. Kihneman (Tora)

SPEEDY GAZPACHO

2 10¾-ounce cans condensed tomato soup
2 envelopes instant beef broth
¼ cup red wine vinegar
1 tablespoon salad oil
1 teaspoon salt
1 teaspoon Worcestershire sauce
Dash hot pepper sauce
2 medium tomatoes, chopped
¼ cup chopped green peppers
2 tablespoons minced onions
Corn chips for garnish

About 3 hours ahead or early in day: Into large bowl pour undiluted tomato soup. In small saucepan over high heat, heat 2 soup-cans water to boiling; remove from heat and stir in instant beef broth until dissolved. Add broth to tomato soup, stirring until well blended. Stir in remaining ingredients except corn chips; cover and refrigerate.

TO SERVE: Sprinkle soup with corn chips. Serve immediately. Makes about 5½ cups.

Mrs. Marvin Kines (Ora)

BEAN AND MACARONI SOUP

1½ cup dried navy beans
¼ pound bacon, in 1-inch squares
1 teaspoon salt
2 cups elbow macaroni
3 tablespoons olive oil
½ pound fresh mushrooms, sliced
1 large onion, chopped
2 cups carrots, sliced
1 cup celery, chopped
1 clove garlic, crushed
3 cups tomatoes, peeled and cut up
1 teaspoon dried sage
½ teaspoon thyme
½ teaspoon oregano
1 bay leaf
Salt and pepper to taste
Grated Parmesan cheese

Cook beans with bacon and salt until beans are tender. (Bring to a boil and simmer for two hours.) Cook macaroni according to label directions. In a large skillet heat olive oil and sauté the mushrooms, onion, carrots, celery, and garlic with cover on until vegetables are soft, about 20 minutes. Do not brown. Add tomatoes, sage, thyme, oregano, bay leaf and salt and pepper to taste. Cover again and cook over medium heat for 15 minutes. Add to beans. Add macaroni to bean mixture. Bring to a boil, then reduce heat. Cover and simmer 35 to 40 minutes, stirring occasionally. Sprinkle each serving with Parmesan cheese. Serves 8.
Mrs. Richard Schreiner (Lois)

OLD FASHIONED BEAN SOUP

1 pound (2 rounded cups) Great Northern beans soaked in 3 quarts of water overnight
Meaty ham bone or ham hocks
1 cup finely chopped onion
2 cloves of garlic, minced
1 small bay leaf
Salt and pepper to taste
1 cup thin sliced celery
1 cup thin diced carrots
1 cup instant mashed potatoes (Usually use about 2 cups of leftover creamed potatoes)
Light cream or undiluted evaporated milk

Combine in heavy cooking pot or dutch oven the beans and soaking water, ham bone, onion, garlic, bay leaf. Bring to boiling point; reduce heat to simmer, cover tightly and cook about 2 hours or until beans are tender. Add celery and carrots. Stir in the mashed potatoes which serves to thicken the soup without sieving the beans. Taste for need of salt, add if necessary, along with coarse ground pepper, simmer covered about 1 hour. Remove ham and cut off the meat, dice it and add to the soup. Reheat to just boiling, stirring to prevent scorching. Light cream or undiluted milk may be stirred into the soup just before serving. Serves 10 generously. (Party Idea!)
Mrs. Nell B. Guilliams, Springhill, Louisiana

Salads · Salad Dressings

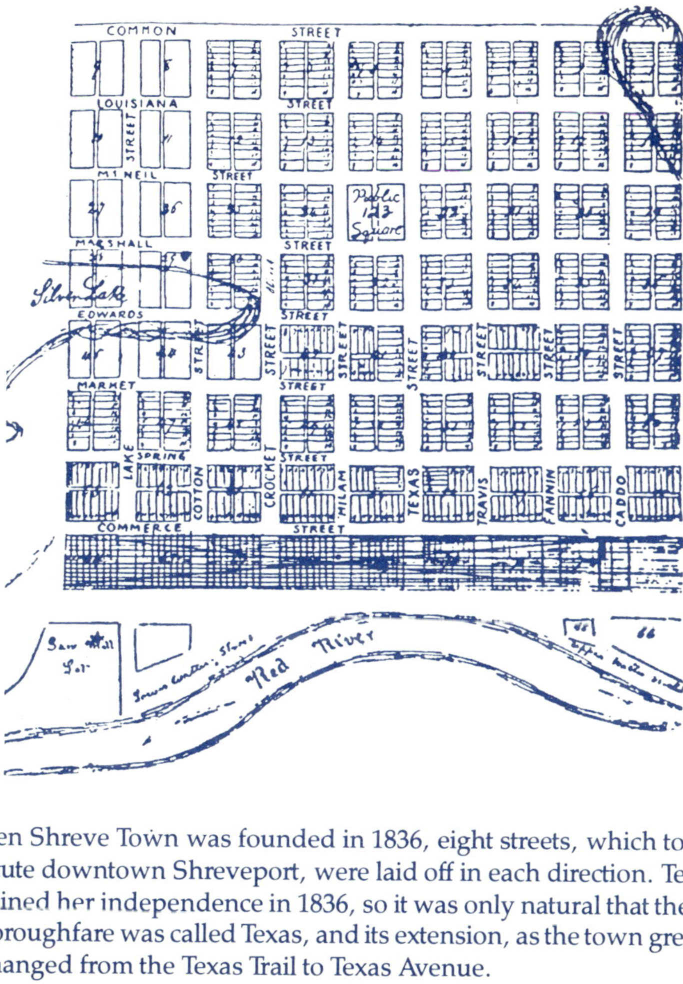

When Shreve Town was founded in 1836, eight streets, which today still constitute downtown Shreveport, were laid off in each direction. Texas had just gained her independence in 1836, so it was only natural that the principal thoroughfare was called Texas, and its extension, as the town grew into a city, changed from the Texas Trail to Texas Avenue.

After naming the northernmost street Caddo in honor of the original owners, the Indians, the streets paralleling it were named for the heroes who lost their lives at Goliad, the Alamo and San Jacinto. They were Fannin, Travis, Milam, and Crockett. King Cotton was honored in the naming of Cotton Street, and the southernmost was called Lake because it was interrupted by the broad expanse of Silver Lake, which was later drained by the further opening of the Red River.

The street paralleling the river was called Commerce with the hope it would develop into a busy levee. Spring Street received its name from the nearby springs, and Market was in anticipation of the town market. Edwards Street honored Larkin Edwards, who owned the land where Shreve Town originated; Marshall was for Colonel Henry Marshall, who had recently settled near Gloster; and McNeil for the president of the company.

The phenomenal part of their planning was that the founders not only planned for Shreveport of 1837 but for the Shreveport of today. Nearby cities like Dallas and Baton Rouge envy Shreveport's 100-foot Texas Street bisected by the 86-foot Market Street in the heart of town; they have none so wide.

Bossier City, our neighbor across the river, originated as Cane City, being named after James Huntington Cane, one of the two owners of the first trading post located on the bluff which later became Shreveport. His partner, William Smith Bennett, was originally from New Hampshire and had accumulated land in Tennessee, Alabama and Mississippi. Bennett's wife, who was probably the first white woman in the area, was separated from him and married Cane. The Canes built a handsome four-story brick home on the Bossier side of Red River near the Texas Street traffic bridge, and up until 1905, Bossier City was known as Cane City.

CARROT SALAD

2 bunches carrots
1 onion, chopped
1 bell pepper, chopped
1 10¾-ounce can tomato soup
½ cup vinegar
½ cup sugar
½ cup oil
1 tablespoon Worcestershire sauce
1 teaspoon salt
Dash red pepper

Peel or scrape carrots, cut into slices or strips and boil in salted water until just tender. Drain. Mix all other ingredients. Add cooked carrots. Refrigerate at least 12 hours before serving. Keeps for days.
Mrs. Margaret Copeland

SPINACH SALAD

1 pound fresh spinach
6 slices crumbled bacon
1 pound fresh mushrooms
1 large can artichoke hearts
2 boiled eggs

Dressing:
½ cup sugar
2 tablespoons oil
½ cup vinegar
1 tablespoon green onion, chopped
1 teaspoon Worcestershire sauce
1 teaspoon mustard
1 ice cube

Mix dressing ingredients in container. Shake well. Place in refrigerator. At serving time, pour dressing over spinach. Garnish with bacon, mushrooms, artichoke hearts and eggs.
Mrs. Ronny Goodman (Janice)

CABBAGE SALAD

1 medium cabbage (shredded)
1 large green pepper
1 large onion
1 cup sugar
1 cup vinegar
¾ cup oil
1 teaspoon celery seed
1 teaspoon mustard seed
1 tablespoon salt

Place ingredients by layers in large salad bowl. Pour oil and vinegar over salad, cover, and place in refrigerator for several hours. *NOTE: By using a combination of purple and green cabbage, the salad is more colorful.*
Mrs. H. Russell Maddox (Tommie Lue)

VEGETABLE SALAD MAGNIFIQUE

8-10 medium carrots
3 1-pound cans Blue Lake sliced green beans
1 7-ounce can black olives sliced in half lengthwise
Seasoned salt
6 ribs celery, chopped
2 16-ounce cans sliced beets
2 14-ounce cans artichoke hearts
4 green onions with tops, sliced
French Dressing

May add, in like proportions, asparagus, broccoli, avocado, or hard-boiled eggs.

Drop sliced carrots in boiling water. After 5 minutes add chopped celery. Cook 5 minutes more. Drain well. Mix all ingredients together and let stand overnight in refrigerator. Serves 16.

NOTE: To make it a meal-in-a-dish, add 1 small can of Spam cut in julienne strips.

Mrs. A. R. Snider (Frances)

LAYERED SALAD

1 small head lettuce, chopped
¼ to ½ chopped bell pepper
1 tablespoon sugar
Parmesan cheese
½ to ¼ cup chopped onions
1 15-ounce can tiny green peas, drained
Hellmann's mayonnaise

In a 9x12-inch Pyrex dish place the head of chopped lettuce in the bottom of dish. Place onions, peppers and drained peas in layers, sprinkle with sugar, spread with Hellmann's mayonnaise and spread ¼-inch of Parmesan cheese on top. Refrigerate. Serve cold, cut in squares.

Mrs. Louis Braun, Lafayette, Louisiana

KRAUT SALAD

1 No. 2½ can shredded sauerkraut
¾ cup sugar
¾ cup finely chopped celery
½ cup grated carrots
½ cup finely chopped onions
1 green pepper, chopped
4 tablespoons mayonnaise

Drain sauerkraut well. Blend all ingredients well and place in a glass dish and chill at least 24 hours. The longer it is chilled, the more the flavors blend and the tastier it is. Serves 6 to 8.

Mrs. Mary Wells

GREEK SALAD

1 large head iceberg lettuce, cored and cut into cubes
3 tomatoes, cored and diced
1 onion, thinly sliced
1 green pepper, seeded and chopped
1 cup pitted black olives, cut into halves
1 cucumber, peeled and sliced
½ cup olive oil
¼ cup red wine vinegar
½ teaspoon oregano
salt and pepper to taste
Feta cheese, crumbled (optional)

Combine all vegetables in large salad bowl and chill. When ready to serve, beat olive oil and vinegar until smooth. Pour over salad. Add oregano and salt and pepper to taste. Add Feta cheese. Toss salad until all particles are coated. Serve at once. Serves 8.

Mrs. Art Ogletree, Jr. (Ann)

SPINACH SALAD

Dressing:

1 cup salad oil
5 tablespoons red wine vinegar
4 tablespoons sour cream
1½ teaspoons salt
½ teaspoon dry mustard
⅛ teaspoon garlic salt
2 tablespoons sugar
¼ teaspoon black pepper

Salad:

2 10-ounce packages fresh spinach, washed & dried
4 hard-boiled eggs, chopped
8 strips bacon, fried and crumbled

Prepare dressing 6 hours prior to serving. Toss spinach with desired amount of dressing before serving. Top with eggs and bacon.

Mrs. Naomi C. Dugan

MEXICAN SLAW

3 cups shredded cabbage
1 12-ounce can Mexi-Corn
2 tablespoons sugar
¾ teaspoon salt
¼ cup vinegar
¼ cup salad oil

Combine cabbage and drained corn in bowl. Dissolve sugar and salt in vinegar. Add salad oil. Mix in covered jar or use electric blender. Pour over cabbage and corn and toss lightly.

This can be made a day in advance and keeps well for several days in refrigerator. Great with fried fish!

Mrs. Theo Hutches (Jennie)

MARINATED COLE SLAW

4 cups shredded cabbage
1 large onion, sliced thin and separated
½ cup sugar
½ cup cider vinegar
⅓ cup salad oil
1½ teaspoons salt
1 teaspoon celery seed
1 teaspoon dry mustard

Combine sugar, vinegar, oil, salt, celery seed and dry mustard. Pour over cabbage and onions. Toss. Marinate overnight. Keeps well in the refrigerator for days.
Mrs. O. F. Matthews (Elise)

COLE SLAW

4 cups cabbage, grated or shredded
½ cup salad dressing
1 teaspoon powdered mustard
1 teaspoon wet horseradish
1 teaspoon salt
½ teaspoon pepper
3 tablespoons white vinegar
¼ teaspoon paprika
2 tablespoons minced onion
1 tablespoon milk
½ teaspoon celery seeds
½ cup sliced stuffed olives (optional)

Dressing:
Mix all ingredients except milk, adding milk last. Heat, but do not boil. Cool slightly before pouring over cabbage.
Mrs. Floyd Cunningham (Nell)

CABBAGE SLAW

1 medium size cabbage (grated)
1 carrot (grated)
1 medium size onion (grated)
1½ tablespoons salad oil
¾ cup mayonnaise
½ cup sugar
2 tablespoons vinegar
½ tablespoon celery seed
1½ tablespoons mustard
¼ tablespoon salt

Grated items are to be grated in a blender. Mix all other ingredients and add to cabbage, carrots, and onions. Serve cold. Will keep for a long time in the refrigerator.
Mrs. Billie Ford

KOREAN SALAD

1 pound fresh spinach
1 8-ounce can water chestnuts, drained, sliced and chilled
4 hard-boiled eggs, chopped and chilled
6 slices bacon (or ½ pound bacon), crumbled
1 16-ounce can bean sprouts, drained and chilled

Wash spinach thoroughly and dry well; tear into bite size pieces. Combine just before serving, the spinach, water chestnuts and bean sprouts in a large salad bowl. Sprinkle with bacon.

Dressing:
½ cup sugar
⅓ cup catsup
⅓ cup vinegar
1 cup salad oil
5 tablespoons Worcestershire sauce
1 small onion, quartered

Combine all ingredients in container of electric blender. Blend well. When ready to serve, pour over salad. Garnish with the hard-boiled eggs.
Mrs. James Allen Fisher (Reba)

MARINATED ZUCCHINI SALAD

4 fresh zucchini squash, sliced paper thin
2 4-ounce cans sliced mushrooms or fresh mushrooms
2 14-ounce cans artichoke hearts, sliced
2 cans bamboo shoots
2 cans black olives, pitted and sliced
1 small bottle Wishbone Italian dressing
1 envelope Hidden Valley Ranch dressing mix

Combine all ingredients and marinate in refrigerator for several hours.
Mrs. Joe Kelly (Reba), New Orleans, Louisiana

DIET SALAD

1 can tropical fruit
1 9-ounce Cool Whip
1 pint small curd cottage cheese
Diet toast or crackers

Mix fruit, cottage cheese and Cool Whip. Serve with diet toast or crackers.
Mrs. Louis Braun, Lafayette, Louisiana

MACARONI SALAD I

1 8-ounce package small macaroni
2 quarts boiling water
1 tablespoon salt
1 can California pitted ripe olives
¾ cup sliced celery
¾ cup diced green pepper
1 4-ounce jar chopped pimientos
3 green onions, chopped
¾ cup mayonnaise
2 tablespoons tarragon vinegar
2 teaspoons prepared mustard
1 teaspoon salt
⅛ teaspoon white pepper

Cook macaroni in boiling water with 1 tablespoon salt, for 10 minutes or till tender. Drain and rinse with cold water. Add olives, celery, green pepper, pimientos, and onions. Blend in mayonnaise with vinegar, mustard, salt and pepper. Pour over salad mixture and mix well. Makes about 1½ quarts.
Mrs. Louis R. Jaudon (Betty)

MACARONI SALAD II

1 12-ounce package macaroni twirls
1 cup chopped celery
1 cup chopped onion
½ bell pepper, chopped
2 medium size dill pickles, chopped
6 ounces sharp cheese, diced
1 cup mayonnaise
6 tablespoons chili sauce
3 tablespoons salad oil
3 tablespoons wine vinegar
1 2-ounce jar sliced pimiento, drained
Salt and white pepper to taste
5 hard-boiled eggs, chopped

Cook macaroni twirls according to package directions; drain, rinse with cool water; drain well. Use large mixing bowl to combine macaroni, celery, onion, bell pepper, pickles and cheese. Combine mayonnaise, chili sauce, salad oil and vinegar; mix well. Add to macaroni mixture and blend. Add salt and white pepper, drained pimiento and chopped hard-boiled eggs and mix again. (I add the pimiento and eggs last so they will not break too much with all the mixing.) Chill. This makes a lot of macaroni salad!
Mrs. Art Ogletree, Jr. (Ann)

TACO SALAD I

1 head of lettuce, chopped
2 medium size tomatoes, chopped
1 small onion, chopped
1 green bell pepper, chopped
1 bag Doritos, crushed (but not too fine)
½ pound Longhorn cheese, shredded
1 bottle Catalina salad dressing
2 cans Ranch Style and/or kidney beans (I prefer to mix one can of each)

In large bowl, mix lettuce, tomatoes, onion, bell pepper, cheese, beans and salad dressing. Refrigerate in covered bowl for at least 3 hours. Directly before serving, pour bag of Doritos over salad. This salad is good with any meat or as a meal by itself.
Mrs. Sherry Anderson

TACO SALAD II

1 pound ground beef
1 onion, chopped
1 cup grated Jack cheese
½ head lettuce, chopped
3 medium tomatoes, chopped
1 bag taco flavored Doritos
2 No. 2 cans pinto beans
Taco sauce as desired

Combine ground beef and onions and brown over slow flame, Meanwhile, prepare cheese, lettuce, tomatoes and beans and combine in large salad bowl. Serve meat/onion mix as a side dish and finely crushed Doritos as another. Allow guests to mix own as desired, as well as taco sauce as desired. If you have a warming dish available it is well to serve the meat/onion dish in this to keep it hot until the meal is all served. Garlic buttered French bread goes well with this one-dish meal.
Mrs. Ted Jordan (Frances)

CORNED BEEF SALAD

1 7 or 12-ounce can corned beef (Libby's)
1½ cups chopped celery
1 tablespoon minced onion
1 cup mayonnaise
½ cup Snappy Tom or tomato juice
1 envelope Knox unflavored gelatin

Dissolve gelatin by heating in the Snappy Tom or tomato juice. Add all other ingredients and mix well. Chill overnight. May be garnished with chopped boiled eggs.
Mrs. Jo Whittaker

CALIFORNIA CHICKEN SALAD

3 cups diced chicken
1½ cups chopped celery
3 tablespoons lemon juice
1 cup almonds
Dash black pepper
1½ cups white seedless grapes
1 cup mayonnaise
½ cup light cream
1½ teaspoons salt

Pour the lemon juice over diced chicken; add celery, grapes and almonds. Combine cream with mayonnaise and add salt and pepper. Mix with chicken mixture. Serve on crisp lettuce.
Mrs. Claude Cummins, Bossier City, Louisiana

ORIENTAL CHICKEN SALAD

1 pint cooked chicken breasts, diced
1 can water chestnuts, sliced
1½ cups seedless white grapes
½ cup toasted slivered almonds
½ cup sliced celery

Dressing:
⅔ cup mayonnaise
¼ teaspoon curry powder (or less)
¼ teaspoon salt
1 teaspoon soy sauce

Combine diced chicken, water chestnuts, grapes, almonds and celery. In separate bowl combine mayonnaise, curry powder, salt and soy sauce; mix well. Add dressing to other mixture. This is excellent for luncheons served on lettuce leaf or sliced cantaloupe.

NOTE: This salad may be made a day ahead, but do not add grapes and almonds until a few hours before serving.
Mrs. A. L. Hennersdorf (Evelyn), Fort Worth, Texas

CRAB MEAT SALAD

1 pound blue crab meat, lump grade
2 tablespoons sweet pickle, chopped
2 hard-boiled eggs, chopped
½ teaspoon salt
Lettuce leaves
1 cup celery, chopped
2 tablespoons onion, chopped
Dash of pepper
½ cup mayonnaise

Combine all ingredients, except lettuce. Chill 1 hour in refrigerator. Serve on lettuce leaves. 4 to 6 servings.
Mrs. A. R. Snider (Frances)

TUNA SALAD

1 6½-ounce can light tuna
½ cup green pepper, chopped
2½ teaspoons Worcestershire sauce
½ cup celery, sliced thin
1 can pimiento, drained and chopped
1½ tablespoons India Relish
⅓ cup chopped onion
3 tablespoons vinegar
¼ teaspoon black pepper
3 heaping tablespoons mayonnaise
Dash cream style mustard
2 hard-boiled eggs, chopped
8 stuffed olives, sliced thin
Salt to taste
½ cup apples, diced (optional)

Mix all ingredients gently with fork, adding apple last. Chill one to two hours. Crab meat or shrimp may be substituted for tuna. Serves 4-6 persons.

Mrs. Margaret Copeland

CONGEALED TUNA SALAD

1 6-ounce package lemon Jello
2 cups boiling water
1 9¼ or 12½-ounce can tuna
½ cup chopped sweet pickles
½ cup sliced Spanish olives
3 boiled eggs (chopped)
1 cup diced celery
1 cup mayonnaise
1 tablespoon lemon juice
½ cup chopped pecans

Dissolve Jello in water. Let set in refrigerator until it begins to congeal. Mix mayonnaise and lemon juice together. Fold all ingredients together and pour into gelatin mold. Let set until firm. Unmold onto chilled plate. Garnish as desired and serve.

Mrs. Robert L. Snead (Shirley)

SHRIMP SALAD

¾ pound cooked shrimp
1 cup celery, chopped
1 tablespoon grated onion
2 tablespoons sweet pickle relish
½ teaspoon salt
Dash of pepper
¼ cup mayonnaise or salad dressing
3 hard-boiled eggs, chopped
1 medium apple, chopped (leave peel)
½ cup English walnuts, chopped

If shrimp is large, cut them in half. Mix all ingredients and sprinkle lemon juice over top. Chill. Serves 6.

Mrs. John E. Ewing (Helen)

SHRIMP AND MACARONI SALAD

2 cups shrimp, cooked
2 cups cooked macaroni
2 hard-boiled eggs, chopped
½ cup celery, chopped
¼ cup halved ripe olives, pitted
1 tablespoon pimiento, chopped
1 tablespoon onion, chopped
Juice 1 lemon
Salt to taste
Mayonnaise
1 tablespoon horseradish

Mix all ingredients. Chill one hour; then add mayonnaise just before serving.
Mrs. Margaret Copeland

TOMATO SOUP SALAD

1 can tomato soup
1 8-ounce package cream cheese
2 envelopes unflavored gelatin
1 cup cold water
1 cup mayonnaise (do not substitute salad dressing)
4 dashes Tabasco
1 teaspoon Worcestershire sauce
½ teaspoon garlic salt
Seasoned pepper
¾ cup celery, chopped fine
¼ cup bell pepper, chopped fine
3 green onions with tops, chopped fine
½ cup stuffed olives, sliced

Allow cream cheese to soften to room temperature. Using electric mixer, beat it until smooth. Bring soup to boil. Add soup to cheese. Blend. Dissolve gelatin in ½ cup cold water. Add to soup and cheese mixture. Blend; stir in mayonnaise, seasonings, celery, olives, onions and bell pepper. Mix well. Pour into a one-quart mold or a 9-inch x 9-inch (or a longer dish) glass dish. Chill until it sets well. Serves 12.

Variation: Cooked, peeled small shrimp or pieces of shrimp are good in this salad. If you use shrimp, use a larger mold. This will gel in an hour. To serve, cut into squares and sprinkle with paprika – very colorful! Do not add mayonnaise to top!
Mrs. Art Ogletree, Jr. (Ann)

HOLIDAY JEWEL SALAD

1 3-ounce package gelatin — either lemon, lime or pineapple
1 cup hot water
½ teaspoon salt
½ cup canned crushed pineapple, drained
1 cup cold liquid (drained pineapple juice plus water to equal 1 cup)
1 cup raw cranberries, chopped
½ cup diced celery
½ cup chopped walnuts

Dissolve gelatin in hot water. Add salt and cold liquid. Chill until slightly thickened. Fold in remaining ingredients. Turn into a one quart mold and chill until firm. Unmold on a bed of crisp lettuce. Decorate with additional walnut pieces. Serves 8.

If desired, serve with a dressing made of 1 3-ounce package cream cheese, ¼ cup sour cream, ¼ teaspoon salt and 2 tablespoons honey whipped together, or serve with a dressing of your choice.
Mrs. Leonard Green, Jr. (June)

RED HOT SALAD

1 package apple Jello
2 cups boiling water
1 16-ounce can applesauce
1 package lime Jello
1 cup Red Hots (red candy)

Topping:
1 3-ounce package cream cheese
Milk
1 tablespoon sherry or rum

Completely dissolve Red Hots in water, then add Jello and applesauce. Stir and pour into greased pan or mold. For topping, beat cream cheese, sherry or rum, adding milk as needed so it spreads easily. Put a little on each serving. Serves 6.
Mrs. John G. Grant (Madelyn), Dallas, Texas

CRANBERRY SALAD I

4 winesap apples
3 oranges
1 pound cranberries
2 cups sugar

Grind ingredients together and add sugar. Will keep for weeks. Very tasty.
Mrs. John Hoppe (Jo)

CRANBERRY SALAD II

2 3-ounce packages red Jello
1 No. 2½ can whole cranberry sauce
1 No. 2½ can crushed pineapple
1 cup chopped nuts
2 cups boiling water

Add Jello and cranberry sauce to boiling water; let cool, add pineapple and nuts. Chill.
Mrs. H. Russell Maddox (Tommie Lue)

BLUEBERRY SALAD I

1 6-ounce package black raspberry gelatin
2 cups boiling water
1 15-ounce can blueberries, drained
1 15-ounce can crushed pineapple, drained
1 cup liquid from fruit
1 8-ounce package cream cheese
1 cup sour cream
1 teaspoon vanilla
¾ cup sugar
½ cup chopped nuts

Allow cream cheese to soften to room temperature. Dissolve gelatin in boiling water; using liquid from fruit, add enough cold water to make 1 cup. Add to hot mixture and stir well. Add drained blueberries and pineapple, mix well and pour into oblong baking dish or pan and congeal in refrigerator until firm.

Mix cream cheese, sour cream, vanilla and sugar; mix thoroughly and spread over top of congealed mixture. Sprinkle with chopped nuts. Keep refrigerated until ready to serve. Cut in squares.
Mrs. Ralph Garrett (Dottie)

BLUEBERRY SALAD II

1 6-ounce package black cherry Jello
2 cups hot water
½ cup nuts (finely chopped)
1 16-ounce can blueberries (drained)
1 8-ounce can crushed pineapple (drained)

Put all juice in a cup except for ½ cup blueberry juice. Reserve this for topping. Add enough water to juice to make the 2 cups liquid for Jello. Dissolve the Jello in the 2 cups hot liquid. Add juice, fruit and nuts to Jello. Chill until firm.

Topping:
Whip 1 3-ounce package Dream Whip as directed. Add the ½ cup blueberry juice. Pour over Jello. Chill for 2 hours in refrigerator before serving.
Mrs. Jo Whittaker

CHERRY SALAD

1 No. 2 can red cherries, drained
1 20-ounce can crushed pineapple, drained
Juice of 2 oranges and 1 lemon
½ cup sugar
2 3-ounce packages cherry Jello
1 cup pecans, chopped

Add water to all juices to equal 3½ cups. Boil three minutes. Pour over Jello which has been dissolved in ½ cup cold water. Add fruit and nuts. Chill.
Mrs. Margaret Copeland

MANDARIN ORANGE SALAD

1 3-ounce package orange gelatin
1 cup hot water
Pinch of salt
½ envelope unflavored gelatin
1 11-ounce can mandarin orange slices
¼ cup cold water
½ of 6-ounce can frozen orange juice, undiluted
1 pint orange sherbet

Dissolve orange gelatin in hot water. Add salt. Soften unflavored gelatin in cold water, mix with the orange gelatin and hot water and dissolve. Add orange juice. Whip sherbet with electric mixer. Add gelatin mixture to sherbet. Blend thoroughly and refrigerate until slightly thick (stir once during this time). When thickened, add oranges. Mold. Good with sour cream topping. Makes a one quart mold.
Mrs. Leonard Green, Jr. (June)

ORANGE CHEESE SALAD

1 No. 3 can crushed pineapple
½ cup sugar
1 large box orange Jello (13½-ounce)
1 cup water
1 13½-ounce carton Cool Whip
1 cup grated cheddar cheese
½ cup pecans

Bring pineapple and sugar to boil. Remove from heat and add orange Jello. Mix in cold water and place in refrigerator until mixture begins to gel. Then fold in Cool Whip, 1 cup cheese, and pecans. Refrigerate until well set.
Mrs. Lurline Wilson

LEMON CHEESE SALAD

2 3-ounce packages lemon flavored gelatin
3¾ cups hot water
1 8-ounce package cream cheese
1 teaspoon salt
½ pint cream, whipped
1 8-ounce can crushed pineapple, drained
1 cup chopped nuts
1 cup chopped celery

Dissolve gelatin in hot water, let cool. Cream the cheese and salt together. Then add gelatin mixture. Add pineapple, nuts and celery. Fold in cream. Pour in large Pyrex dish and chill till firm.
Mrs. Claude Cummins, Bossier City, Louisiana

QUICKIE FRUIT SALAD

1 3-ounce package strawberry Jello
1 9-ounce carton Cool Whip
1 No. 2 can fruit cocktail
1 8-ounce carton cottage cheese

Mix Jello with Cool Whip. Drain fruit cocktail and save 2-3 tablespoons juice. Add fruit cocktail, juice and blend in cottage cheese. For larger servings use the 16-ounce Cool Whip and 16-ounce cottage cheese.
For variety, substitute lime Jello and pineapple chunks or slices cut up for the strawberry Jello and fruit cocktail.
Mrs. H. Russell Maddox (Tommie Lue)

CONGEALED FRUIT SALAD

1 8-ounce package cream cheese
¾ cup mayonnaise
1 cup miniature marshmallows
2 3-ounce packages orange gelatin
1 No. 2 can fruit cocktail
1 8-ounce can crushed pineapple

Beat cream cheese and mayonnaise in electric mixer until well blended. Dissolve orange gelatin with heated juice from fruit cocktail and pineapple, adding water to make 4 cups liquid. Add fruit and marshmallows. Stir in cheese mixture. A cup of chopped nuts may be added.
Mrs. Leonard Green, Jr. (June)

PINEAPPLE CONGEALED SALAD

1 package Knox unflavored gelatin
1 cup cold water
1 cup crushed pineapple
1 cup sugar
1 cup salad dressing or mayonnaise
1 cup whipped cream or Cool Whip
1 cup Velveeta cheese (grated)

Soak gelatin in cold water. Put crushed pineapple and sugar on stove and bring to a boil. Pour over gelatin. Place in refrigerator. When it begins to congeal add salad dressing, whipped cream, and cheese. Return to refrigerator to congeal.
Mrs. John Hoppe (Jo)

APRICOT-PINEAPPLE SALAD

1 No. 2½ can apricots
1 20-ounce can crushed pineapple
2 3-ounce packages orange gelatin
2 cups boiling water
1 cup combined apricot and pineapple juice
¾ cup miniature marshmallows

Topping:
½ cup sugar
3 tablespoons flour
1 egg, slightly beaten
1 cup combined apricot and pineapple juice
2 tablespoons butter
1 cup heavy cream, whipped
¾ cup cheese, grated

Drain and chill apricot and pineapple, dicing apricots and reserving the juices. Dissolve gelatin in boiling water. Add 1 cup reserved juice, save rest for topping. Chill until slightly congealed. Fold in fruit and marshmallows. Pour into 9-inch x 10-inch shallow pan. Chill until firm. Spread with topping.

Topping: Combine sugar and flour; blend in egg and juice. Stir over low heat until thickened. Remove from heat, stir in butter; cool. Fold in whipped cream and spread over gelatin mixture. Sprinkle with grated cheese. Chill and cut into squares. Serves 10-12.
Mrs. Leonard Green, Jr. (June)

APRICOT JELLO SALAD

1 8-ounce package of dried apricots
1 cup water
½ cup sugar
1 3-ounce package orange Jello
2 cups water (hot)
1 3-ounce package cream cheese
1 8-ounce can crushed pineapple
Chopped nuts for topping

Cook apricots in water using a heavy pan with lid. Cook on low flame until apricots are soft and water is absorbed. Mash apricots with a potato masher until very mushy. Add sugar and mix well. Mix the Jello with the 2 cups hot water stirring until dissolved. Add apricot mixture to Jello stirring until very well blended. Refrigerate. When ready to serve, mix the cream cheese (room temperature) with the pineapple (drained). Spread cheese and pineapple mixture over Jello and sprinkle with chopped nuts.

Mrs. Francis A. Zonkel (Helen)
Mrs. Jo Whittaker

APRICOT CONGEALED SALAD

1 3-ounce package apricot Jello
1 cup orange juice
1 cup buttermilk

Heat orange juice. Pour into Jello and stir until Jello is dissolved. Cool and pour buttermilk into mixture. Pour into individual molds or double recipe and pour into large single mold. This is a tasty salad and good for low calorie diet.

Mrs. John L. Hoppe (Jo)

STRAWBERRY JELLO SALAD

2 boxes strawberry Jello (regular)
1 20-ounce can crushed pineapple
1 cup miniature marshmallows
2 cups boiling water
2 10-ounce boxes frozen strawberries
½ cup pecans
1 cup sour cream

In 2 cups of boiling water, add strawberry Jello. When dissolved, remove from heat, add frozen strawberries, crushed pineapple (juice and all), nuts and marshmallows. Pour ½ mixture in mold, congeal. Spread sour cream over congealed part, add remaining Jello mix and refrigerate.

Tastes great on angel food cake.

Mrs. Charles Cook (Darleen)

STRAWBERRY JELLO MOLD

- 2 3-ounce packages strawberry Jello
- 2 10-ounce packages frozen strawberries
- 1 20-ounce can crushed pineapple
- 1 cup water (boiling)
- 2-3 bananas (mashed)
- 1 cup nuts (chopped)
- 1 8-ounce carton sour cream

Dissolve packages of strawberry Jello in the boiling water. Add to the Jello, the strawberries (with juice), the pineapple (with juice), the bananas, and the pecans. Put half of Jello mix in large Pyrex dish. Chill. Spread sour cream over this and chill. Pour rest of Jello mix on top. Chill at least 1½ hours. Slice in squares. Very pretty salad.

Mrs. John Hoppe (Jo)

STRAWBERRY COTTAGE CHEESE SALAD

- 1 No. 3 can crushed pineapple
- ½ cup sugar
- 1 6-ounce box of strawberry Jello
- 1 cup water
- 1 large 13½-ounce carton Cool Whip
- 1 8-ounce carton cottage cheese (drained)

Bring pineapple and sugar to boil. Remove from heat and stir in strawberry Jello and water. Place in refrigerator until mixture begins to gel. Then fold in Cool Whip and cottage cheese (drained). Refrigerate until well set. Refrigerate until well set.

Mrs. Lurline Wilson

FROZEN FRUIT SALAD

- ½ cup Royal Anne cherries cut in halves and pitted
- ½ cup Bing cherries, cut in halves and pitted
- ½ cup pears, diced and drained
- ½ cup peaches, diced
- ½ cup pineapple, diced
- ⅛ cup powdered sugar
- ½ cup pineapple juice
- ½ cup mayonnaise
- ¼ teaspoon lemon rind, grated
- ½ cup marshmallows, diced or use small ones
- 1 cup whipping cream, whipped

Mix diced fruits and set aside to drain. Mix sugar, pineapple juice, mayonnaise and lemon rind until sugar is dissolved. Fold in whipped cream, fruit, and marshmallows. Put in molds and freeze.

Muriel Bundrick

FRUIT SALAD

1 15 or 16-ounce can mixed fruits for salads
1 16-ounce can pears
1 16-ounce can peaches
1 20-ounce can pineapple chunks
1 11-ounce can mandarin oranges
6 fresh peaches
6 bananas
Any other fresh fruits may be added
5 cups watermelon
4 cups cantaloupe
2 cups green grapes
8 ounces sour cream
6½ ounces Cool Whip
¾ cup mayonnaise
3 ounces or 2 cups miniature marshmallows

Drain all canned fruits before putting into large, large bowl. Cut all fruits into small pieces, fresh and canned. Thoroughly drain again. Add marshmallows, sour cream, Cool Whip and mayonnaise and mix well. Good to eat immediately — better after it has been refrigerated 8 to 12 hours. Will keep indefinitely in refrigerator if you can keep it there. After several days you may add more watermelon and bananas as it will get soggy. Very rich but "delicious."
Mrs. Lois Mambourg

FIVE WAY SALAD

1 20-ounce can pineapple chunks
1 11-ounce can mandarin oranges
1 8-ounce carton sour cream
1 cup small marshmallows
1 cup coconut (optional)

Drain fruit well. Mix fruit, marshmallows, sour cream and coconut. Chill. Serve on lettuce leaf.
Mrs. C. G. Peyton (Nelle)

FRUIT SALAD TERES'

No. 2 size can grapefruit sections
No. 2 size jar cherries
No. 2 size can pineapple tidbits
1 tablespoon Karo syrup
No. 2 size can mandarin oranges
3-4 bananas
3 shredded apples
½ small can concentrated orange juice

Mix orange juice concentrate with bananas (sliced) and shredded apples. Partially drain canned fruit. Add to orange juice mixture.
Mrs. Russell Smith (Liz)

FRUIT SALAD QUICKIE

1 16-ounce can fruit cocktail
2 cups miniature marshmallows
1 large container sour cream
2 11-ounce cans mandarin oranges
1 7-ounce can angel flake coconut

Mix all ingredients. Cover and chill over night. Serve in lettuce cups.
Mrs. A. R. Snider (Frances)

CARROT AMBROSIA

4 cups grated carrots
1 cup diced oranges or pineapple
1 cup coconut
1 cup miniature marshmallows
½ cup sour cream
½ cup mayonnaise
2 tablespoons honey
2 tablespoons lemon juice
¼ teaspoon salt

Mix carrots, oranges (or pineapple), coconut, marshmallows. Combine sour cream, mayonnaise, honey, lemon juice and salt; toss with carrot mixture. Serve in lettuce cup. Serves 6 to 8.
Mrs. Lawrence A. McKinley, Magnolia Springs, Alabama

MRS. LBJ'S AMBROSIA

4 oranges
1 8-ounce can crushed pineapple (drained)
1 cup freshly grated coconut or ½ can grated coconut

After peeling and removing seeds from oranges, cut sections into bite size pieces. Add crushed pineapple and grated coconut to oranges and let stand for several hours so that they will be well blended. If desired, add sugar for extra sweetening and/or lemon juice for tartness. Miniature marshmallows also give ambrosia a "little something special."
Mrs. C. D. Attaway (Margie)

MILLION DOLLAR RICE SALAD

1 10½-ounce package miniature marshmallows
1 8-ounce can crushed pineapple (drained)
1 8-ounce package cream cheese
2 tablespoons sugar
2 tablespoons mayonnaise
2 cups cooked rice
12 or more maraschino cherries
1 cup whipped cream
1 cup pecans (if desired)

Mix marshmallows, drained pineapple, cream cheese, sugar, and mayonnaise together until smooth. Add rice and cherries. Fold in the whipped cream and nuts.
Mrs. C. E. Clawson (Frances)

POPPY SEED DRESSING

¾ cup sugar
1 tablespoon dry mustard
⅓ cup vinegar
1½ tablespoons poppy seed
1 cup salad oil
1 teaspoon salt
1½ tablespoons grated onion

Mix sugar, salt, mustard and vinegar in small mixing bowl. Add grated onion and stir well. With mixer on medium speed, add oil slowly, beating until thick. Add poppy seed and beat a little longer. (If you do not have dry mustard, use prepared mustard.) Makes one pint — keeps well in refrigerator.
Mrs. L. A. McKinley (Elizabeth), Magnolia Springs, Alabama

SALAD DRESSING FOR FRUIT

2 eggs
6 tablespoons sugar
½ cup lemon juice
2 teaspoons butter
⅛ teaspoon salt
2 tablespoons light cream

Beat eggs very well. Add to eggs the sugar, lemon juice, butter and salt. Cook over direct heat (low), stirring constantly until sauce is thick and fluffy. Cool before serving and add the light cream. Makes 1 cup.
Mrs. Art Ogletree, Jr. (Ann)

SESAME CITRUS DRESSING

- 2 tablespoons sesame seeds, toasted
- 2 tablespoons honey
- 1 teaspoon grated orange rind
- 1 teaspoon grated lemon rind
- 1/8 teaspoon salt
- 1 cup plain yogurt
- For garnish: slivered orange rind, optional

Toast sesame seeds by spreading on a pie tin and placing in oven heated to 350 degrees for 4 to 5 minutes. Then combine seeds with honey, orange and lemon rinds and salt. Fold in yogurt. Use this for any fruit salad. Garnish with slivered orange rind, if desired.

Mrs. Floyd Cunningham (Nell)

SPECIAL DRESSING FOR LETTUCE

- 1 egg
- 1 clove garlic
- 1/2 cup olive or salad oil
- 1 small container Parmesan cheese
- 1/4 teaspoon red pepper
- 1/4 teaspoon salt
- 1 tablespoon vinegar

Mince garlic or put through garlic press. Mix together the egg, garlic and oil with rotary beater or electric mixer. Mix well. Add Parmesan cheese, red pepper, salt and vinegar

Serve dressing over torn pieces of lettuce and croutons. Add croutons just before serving.

Variation: Sliced red onion rings are good with lettuce and dressing.

Mrs. Art Ogletree, Jr. (Ann)

EASY 1, 2, 3 SALAD DRESSING

- 2 or 3 small cloves garlic
- 1 tablespoon sugar
- 2 tablespoons vegetable oil
- 3 tablespoons vinegar

Cut up cloves of garlic in small pieces, mix with sugar and oil. Pour in vinegar stirring constantly to mix oil with vinegar and to melt sugar. Ready to pour over green salad. Better to let dressing set in refrigerator to marinate before using.

Mrs. H. Russell Maddox (Tommie Lue)

HOME MADE MAYONNAISE

1 egg
1 teaspoon prepared mustard
Dash of salt and pepper
1 teaspoon lemon juice or vinegar
Oil (desired thickness determines amount)

Beat together egg, mustard, salt, pepper. Add oil gradually in thin stream. Beat until desired thickness, depending on amount of oil used. Add lemon juice or vinegar at end of beating. I have used electric blender when mixing this.
Mrs. Art Ogletree, Jr. (Ann)

THOUSAND ISLAND DRESSING I

1½ cups mayonnaise
½ cup chili sauce
1 tablespoon onion, grated
2 tablespoons green pepper, chopped
2 tablespoons celery, finely chopped
2 tablespoons stuffed olives, chopped
1 hard-boiled egg, chopped

Beat or stir at mix speed until well blended. Makes about two cups dressing.
Mrs. Margaret Copeland

THOUSAND ISLAND DRESSING II

1 cup mayonnaise
½ cup chili sauce
⅓ cup pickle relish

Combine the mayonnaise, chili sauce and pickle relish; chill.
Mrs. R. W. Fletcher (Sue)

Meats

It seems the early settlers of the South were poor road builders. Streams were not bridged but were forded, and "corduroying" of wet places was just about the extent of improvements. Travel was mostly on horseback or in heavy wagons drawn by oxen, but even these could be used only in dry weather.

Mud was one of the biggest handicaps during the wet seasons, and it plagued the early wagon trains on Texas Street from Common to the river during the busy cotton seasons. There were times when it was impassable and a corduroy road was constructed with two-by-four oak planks. A city ordinance was passed requiring property owners on the street to build plank sidewalks two feet wide.

Modern conveniences were unheard of during this period. Streets were unpaved, houses were unscreened, there was no sewerage and the supply of drinking water was inadequate.

R. N. McKellar is credited with taking Shreveport out of the mud. He began his administration as mayor and city judge in 1896. While city judge he began his paving program by issuing a popular fine, "$7.50 or 1,000 bricks." Both went into the paving project, and those who could not pay laid the bricks. Milam Street was the first to be paved in this fashion.

BEEF-MUSHROOM WITH PORT WINE

- 1 pound beef, top round steak
- 2 tablespoons butter
- 1 cup sliced fresh mushrooms
- 1 teaspoon salt
- 1/8 teaspoon pepper
- 1/2 teaspoon grated lemon rind
- 1/4 teaspoon marjoram leaves
- 3/4 cup Port wine
- 1/4 cup water
- 2 teaspoons cornstarch

Cut beef into 1-inch cubes. Sauté lightly in butter until browned. Push to one side of pan; add mushrooms and brown lightly. Add all remaining ingredients except cornstarch. Stir to blend. Cover and simmer over low heat until beef is tender, about 50 or 60 minutes. Remove cover, blend in cornstarch, mixing with an additional tablespoon of Port. Cook, stirring until sauce boils and thickens. Serve over noodles or rice. Serves 4.
Mrs. Leonard Green, Jr. (June)

MARINATED BRISKET

- 1 brisket, approximately 8 pounds
- 3 teaspoons salt petre
- 5 teaspoons sugar
- 5 scant tablespoons salt
- 5 tablespoons allspice
- Dash of cinnamon
- 2 or 3 cloves garlic

Rub garlic over meat well. Combine seasonings and rub into brisket. Sliver garlic and work into meat. Wrap brisket in foil securely and refrigerate for 3 or 4 days. Cook in 350 degree oven for 2 to 2½ hours. Delicious!
Mrs. H. H. Andrews (Joyce)

HUNGARIAN GOULASH

- 2 pounds round steak (cut in bite size pieces)
- 4 tablespoons oil
- 1 cup onion (chopped)
- 1 clove garlic
- 2 teaspoons salt
- 3¼ cups water (reserve ¼ for thickening)
- 2 tablespoons flour
- 3/4 cup catsup
- 1/4 cup plus 2 tablespoons Worcestershire sauce
- 1 teaspoon vinegar
- 1 tablespoon brown sugar
- 2½ teaspoons paprika
- 1 teaspoon mustard

Brown steak in the oil with onions and garlic. Mix all the other ingredients, cook 2½ hours. Thicken with flour and the ¼ cup water that has been reserved.
Mrs. Clara Cummins, Bossier City, Louisiana

BEEF CURRY

2 pounds beef stew meat, cubed
Butter, salt, pepper
2 onions, chopped
2 cloves garlic
2 tablespoons flour
1 tomato, cut up
1 cup celery, chopped
½ cup green pepper, chopped
1 apple, chopped
1 can bouillon, plus whatever amount needed
Curry powder to taste
Rice

Sear meat in pot until brown. Remove. Add butter, onions and garlic — brown. Add flour to make good paste and brown. Add can bouillon, pouring little at a time, stirring constantly; add can water and curry powder. Return meat to pan and add tomato, celery, green pepper and apple. If meat is not covered, add ½ to 1 can bouillon. Boil briskly for forty-five minutes with lid off. Add any necessary seasoning. Cover and cook slowly for one hour. Serve over rice.
Mrs. Margaret Copeland

CORNED BEEF AND CABBAGE CASSEROLE

3 tablespoons butter
3 tablespoons flour
1½ cups milk
Salt and pepper
1 teaspoon mustard
1 small onion, chopped
4 cups cabbage, chopped
1 cup corned beef, chopped

Make white sauce with butter, flour, milk, salt and pepper. Stir in mustard, onion, cabbage and corned beef. Place in a 2-quart baking dish and bake at 375 degrees for 45 minutes. Serves 6.
Mrs. Marvin Kines (Ora)

CHIPPED BEEF ON TOAST

1 stick of margarine
2 cups milk
1 2½-ounce jar dried beef
4 hard boiled eggs
½ to 1 cup flour
1 cup water (for soaking dried beef)
Salt and pepper to taste
6 slices of toast cut in small squares

Melt margarine in skillet, add flour to form paste, using only enough to make smooth paste. Add milk to make a white gravy; add salt and pepper. Separate the dried beef slices that have been soaking in the 1 cup of water. Add beef to white gravy. As gravy thickens, add as much of the water as necessary to get the consistency you prefer. Serve over the toasted squares and top with slices of hard boiled egg.
Mrs. Louis R. Jaudon (Betty)

OLD FASHIONED BEEF STEW

2 pounds lean beef (cut in 1-inch cubes)
4 medium size potatoes
4 carrots
2 medium size onions
1 16-ounce can tomatoes
1 tablespoon sugar
1 teaspoon salt
½ teaspoon thyme
¼ teaspoon black pepper
½ teaspoon glutamate
2 bay leaves
1 clove garlic (chopped)
½ cup flour
2 tablespoons oil
½ cup water
2 beef bouillon cubes

Use a fry pan, add the oil and lightly brown the beef after it has been dusted with the flour. Using a large pot add diced potatoes, sliced carrots, chopped onions, garlic, tomatoes and all other seasoning. Cook on low heat until all ingredients are tender. If more liquid is needed add the water with the dissolved bouillon cubes. A large soup bone cooked ahead of time makes good stock for cooking all the vegetables and seasoning. This can be frozen and used at a later time.

Mrs. F. A. Kihneman (Tora)

FOUND MONEY CASSEROLE

2 slices bread, cubed
2 tablespoons bacon drippings
3 tablespoons flour
½ cup milk
1 medium chopped onion
½ cup sharp cheese, grated
1 cup left over peas or beans
2 tablespoons drippings
1 cup left over meat, cut up
1 tablespoon bacon drippings

Mix bread cubes, grated cheese and 2 tablespoons drippings. Put ½ the bread and cheese mixture in a greased 2 quart casserole. Add 1 cup of left over peas or beans. Add a cream sauce made of 2 tablespoons drippings, 3 tablespoons flour and ½ cup milk. (Melt drippings, stir in flour. Add milk and stir until thickened.)

Brown 1 cup cut-up left over meat and 1 medium chopped onion in 1 tablespoon drippings and add to casserole. Add the remaining bread and cheese mixture and bake at 350 degrees until hot through.

NOTE: If left over chicken is used, cream of mushroom or cream of chicken soup may be substituted for the cream sauce.

Mrs. L. A. McKinley (Elizabeth), Magnolia Springs, Alabama

BEEF JAMBALAYA

2 pounds cubed beef
2 tablespoons oil
Salt to taste
Pepper to taste
Garlic to taste
½ cup onion, finely chopped
2 beef bouillon cubes
1 cup water
2 cans cream of mushroom soup
1 teaspoon parsley
6 drops of Tabasco sauce
2 cups uncooked rice

In skillet sauté meat in oil until brown. Add salt, pepper, garlic, and onion. Continue cooking until onion becomes transparent. Add beef bouillon cubes, dissolved in hot water and both cans of soup. Sprinkle in parsley and Tabasco. Cook rice. Blend rice into the other ingredients and simmer for 15-20 minutes. Serves 4..

Mrs. Kenneth Braswell (Debbie)

VITOCHKI

(Sour Cream Meat Balls)

3 slices white bread
1 pound ground beef
1 teaspoon salt
Dash of pepper
1 onion, chopped very fine
1 cup water
1 pint sour cream
1 cup fine dry bread crumbs
2 sticks margarine
2 10¾-ounce cans cream of mushroom soup
½ cup milk

Crumble bread in small pieces (the bread can be several days old); soak in ½ cup water. Squeeze out excess liquid with hands. Add bread to ground beef and season with salt, pepper and chopped onion; mix thoroughly with hands. Add at least 2 generous tablespoons of the sour cream to mixture and mix well. Shape in small balls about size of fresh apricot and roll in bread crumbs. Melt margarine in skillet; fry meat balls in margarine until nicely browned all over. Remove from skillet. Drain and place in baking casserole. Add 2 tablespoons margarine to skillet with ½ cup water. Bring to a boil, scraping all browned solids from sides and bottom of pan. Stir in 1 can of mushroom soup and ½ cup milk; mix thoroughly. Add remaining can of soup and heat, stirring constantly. Last, mix in remaining sour cream and heat through. Do not boil or sauce will curdle. Pour sauce over meatballs. Reheat in covered casserole in 300 degree oven until hot or bubbly. Serve over rice or noodles.

This recipe can easily be doubled and frozen. When freezing, do not reheat after meatballs and sauce are combined.

Mrs. S. C. Stolzenthaler, Jr. (Betty), Baton Rouge, Louisiana

PARMESAN MEAT BALLS

1 pound ground meat
½ cup grated Parmesan cheese
½ cup dry bread crumbs
2 eggs
½ teaspoon garlic salt
½ teaspoon salt
All purpose cooking oil
3 cups water
2 beef bouillon cubes
2 tablespoons cornstarch

Combine meat, cheese, bread crumbs, eggs and seasoning. Shape into balls. Brown in oil and drain. Add 1½ cups water, bouillon cubes, cover and simmer 10 minutes.

Combine cornstarch and 1½ cups water stirring constantly until well blended. Add cornstarch mixture to meat balls. Stir until mixture boils and thickens. Simmer 5 minutes. Serve over noodles.

Kraft recipes submitted by Mrs. R. L. McIlwain (Linda)

SWEDISH MEAT BALLS

1 pound hamburger meat
½ cup cracker crumbs
1 egg
1 teaspoon salt
1 teaspoon pepper
¼ cup milk
1 package Lawry's spaghetti sauce mix
1 8-ounce can tomato sauce
2 tablespoons brown sugar

Mix together the hamburger, cracker crumbs, egg, salt, pepper, and milk. Roll mixture into individual meat balls, a little larger then marble size. Brown in skillet. In separate sauce pan combine the sauce mix, tomato sauce, and brown sugar. Put browned meat balls in sauce mix and simmer for 30 minutes. Serve over cooked spaghetti. Serves 4.

Mrs. Faye Braswell

MEAT BALLS

1 pound ground chuck
1 egg
1 cup bread crumbs (soak in ¼ cup milk)
1 package onion soup mix
½ bell pepper, chopped
1 can tomato sauce (8 ounces)
1 can water (use tomato sauce can)

Mix the ground chuck, egg, bread crumbs, onion soup mix, bell pepper and form into meat balls. Brown in skillet, then add tomato sauce and the can of water. Let simmer about 45 minutes. Serve over spaghetti. Serves 4 or 5 people.

Mrs. Sybil Braswell

STELLA'S MIXED UP CASSEROLE

1 pound ground round steak (or hamburger)
2 tablespoons fat
1/3 cup chopped onions
1 10-ounce can condensed tomato soup
1 1/2 cups water
Parsley
1/2 8-ounce package noodles
1 17-ounce can creamed corn
1 cup grated American cheese
1/4 cup chopped ripe olives
Salt and pepper

Brown meat in hot fat, add onions, cook in fat until golden. Add tomato soup, water and noodles. Cook until noodles are tender, stirring frequently. Season to taste. Add corn, olives, and one half cup grated cheese. Pour into greased 2-quart casserole. Sprinkle with remaining cheese. Bake in moderate oven (350 degrees) for approximately 45 minutes. Garnish with olives and parsley.
Mrs. Gene Hallman (Stella)

HAMBURGER/NOODLE CASSEROLE

1 pound ground lean hamburger
2 medium onions, chopped
1 can enchilada sauce
1 can tomato puree (medium)
Garlic salt to taste
1 package (small) egg noodles

Put Wesson oil in skillet and sauté onions — add hamburger and cook until done. Pour off excess grease. Add onions and hamburger to the enchilada sauce and tomato puree. Add garlic to taste. Cook egg noodles until tender and drain well. Mix everything together and put in casserole. Top with grated "rat" cheese. Cook at 350 degrees until cheese is melted.
Mrs. Jo Whittaker

SALISBURY STEAK

2 pounds ground chuck or round
1 13-ounce can evaporated milk
3 tablespoons beef bouillon
2 cups ground crackers
3 eggs
Pepper to taste

Mix thoroughly and make into large serving size. Cook on medium heat and brown on each side until done.
Mrs. F. A. Kihneman (Tora)

HOKEM POKEM

2 pounds ground meat
5 1-pound cans pork and beans
1 large onion, chopped
1 bell pepper
½ box brown sugar
½ bottle Kraft's hot barbecue sauce

Slice 5 rings from bell peper and chop the remaining portion. Reserve the rings. Combine the ground meat, chopped onion and bell pepper and cook until meat has browned. Drain fat from mixture. In large casserole combine the meat mixture, pork and beans, brown sugar and barbecue sauce. Cook in 350 degree oven for 1½ hours. This is a large casserole and will serve approximately 10 people, or more if prepared for a covered dish meal where there is more food served.

Variation: Sweet pickle relish added to above ingredients is good.

Mrs. Louis R. Jaudon (Betty)

SAUSAGE RICE CASSEROLE

1 pound bulk hot sausage
1 cup chopped celery
1 cup chopped onion
1 cup chopped green pepper
2 10¼-ounce cans chicken broth
1 cup uncooked regular rice
1½ teaspoons salt
¼ teaspoon pepper

Brown sausage in skillet, add celery, onion, and green pepper and simmer until tender. Add broth, rice and seasonings. Mix well. Pour into a two quart casserole. Cover and bake in a 325 degree oven for 1 hour. Serves 6 to 8.

Mrs. G. G. Sharp

HAMBURGER CASSEROLE

1½ pounds ground beef
1 onion, chopped
1 bell pepper, chopped
1 can chicken noodle soup
1 can cream of mushroom soup
½ cup uncooked rice
½ cup Parmesan cheese
Salt
Pepper
1 tablespoon Worcestershire sauce
Rice Krispies (for topping)

Cook beef, onion, and bell pepper together until meat changes color. Add the remaining ingredients except the Rice Krispies. Put mixture in greased casserole, top with Rice Krispies, and cook for one hour at 350 degrees.

Variation: Chopped celery may be sautéed with onion, bell pepper and meat. Also, a 4-ounce can of mushroom stems and pieces may be added.

Mrs. Robert C. King (Theresa)

DIRTY RICE DRESSING

3 tablespoons cooking oil
2 medium onions, chopped
4 toes garlic
2 ribs celery
3 shallots
2 tablespoons parsley
½ pound lean ground beef
2 cups cooked rice
Salt and pepper to taste
¼ pound chicken livers, chopped or ground
2 tablespoons dry sherry (if available)
1 tablespoon Worcestershire sauce
1 beef bouillon cube dissolved in ½ cup hot water or ½ cup beef bouillon soup

To heated cooking oil, add chopped onions, celery, shallots. Sauté until soft, at least ten minutes. Add chopped or ground livers, ground beef, parsley and garlic. After browning meat thoroughly, add dry sherry and other liquids. Cover and simmer over low heat for 30 minutes. Remove from heat, add to rice and mix well. Good with beef or fowl.
Mrs. C. D. Attaway (Margie)

FANCY PANTS HAMBURGERS

12 prepared hamburger patties
6 slices thin sliced cheese
Salt and pepper to taste
Garlic powder to taste
1 8-ounce can tomato sauce
Hamburger buns

Place hamburger, patties on waxed paper and flatten them out until larger in diameter and very thin, as two patties will be used for one hamburger. Cut cheese slices with large biscuit cutter or drinking glass in smaller circle than the pattie. Place slice of cheese on single pattie and place another pattie on top. Seal the edges by crimping all around the edge with fingers —this will prevent the cheese from running out of hamburger while cooking. When patties are completed, brown in skillet on medium fire on both sides. Remove them from skillet and drain juice. Return them to skillet and pour the can of tomato sauce over the hamburgers. Cover and cook over slow to medium heat for approximately 15 to 20 minutes. Do not cook the juice away entirely. Serve with regular hamburger trimmings. Big and juicy!
NOTE: This should make 6 large hamburgers. It will require a very large skillet or two smaller skillets. An electric skillet is excellent for this.
Mrs. Art Ogletree, Jr. (Ann)

BARBECUE SANDWICHES FOR LARGE CROWD

3 pounds ground meat
1 large onion, chopped
1 small bottle catsup
2 tablespoons Worcestershire sauce
1 tablespoon sweet pickle relish
2 tablespoons prepared mustard
¾ can chili powder
Salt and pepper to taste

Sauté onion in small amount of oil until soft (not brown). Combine catsup, Worcestershire sauce, relish, mustard and chili powder; mix thoroughly, and set aside. Brown meat with onion, season well with salt and pepper. Then gently place sauce mixture over meat. Cook in moderate oven until thickened and tastes good. Fill hot buns with this mixture — serve with baked beans and potato salad. If any is left, it freezes well. Half the recipe for a smaller amount.
Mrs. Hal Johnson, Jr. (Shirley)

SPOON BURGERS

1 pound ground chuck
½ cup chopped green pepper
½ cup chopped celery
½ cup chopped onion
1 tablespoon flour
½ teaspoon salt
1 cup barbecue sauce
8 big buns split and toasted

Mix all ingredients together and simmer until done. Spoon onto buns and can be topped with a slice of cheese. Serves 8.
Mrs. F. A. Kihneman (Tora)

STOVE TOP MEAT LOAVES

1½ pounds ground beef
½ cup dry bread crumbs
1 10¾-ounce can tomato soup
¼ cup finely chopped onion
1 egg, slightly beaten
1 teaspoon salt
Generous dash of pepper
1 tablespoon shortening
¼ cup water
½ teaspoon prepared mustard
2 slices process cheese, cut in half

Mix thoroughly the ground beef, ¼ cup of the soup, onion, egg, salt and pepper. Shape the mixture into two loaves. Melt shortening in skillet and brown the loaves in skillet on both sides. Cover; cook over low heat for 25 minutes. Spoon off fat and pour remaining soup which has been mixed with water and mustard, on loaves; top with cheese. Cook 10 minutes uncovered. 4 to 6 servings.
Mrs. Charles D. Brown (Kaye)

ROLL-IN-ONE MEAT LOAF WITH VEGETABLE

1 10¾-ounce can tomato soup
1½ pounds ground beef
½ cup fine dry bread crumbs
¼ cup minced onion
2 tablespoons chopped parsley
1 egg, slightly beaten
1 teaspoon salt and dash of pepper
1 9-ounce package frozen cut beans*

Cook frozen green beans until tender and drain well. Combine ½ cup soup with all ingredients except beans. Mix well. Place meat mixture on waxed paper and pat into a 12x9-inch piece. Spread beans to within 1 inch of edges. Pat them into meat. With aid of waxed paper, roll meat tightly (jelly roll fashion), starting at long edge. Seal ends. Use waxed paper to transfer to baking dish. Bake at 350 degrees for 40 minutes. Spoon off fat. Pour remaining soup over loaf. Bake 10 minutes longer. Yield: 6 to 8 servings.

*Canned Blue Lake green beans may be used in place of frozen beans. It is not necessary to cook them prior to using in meat loaf — just drain them well.

Mrs. M. J. Hodges (Mary)

MEAT LOAF WITH POTATOES

3 pounds ground chuck
4 eggs
⅔ cup evaporated milk
2 teaspoons salt
1 cup onion (coarse ground)
1 cup celery (coarse ground)
2 cups grated potato
1 cup catsup

Mix all ingredients thoroughly except the catsup. Put the catsup in bottom of loaf pan. Press meat mixture into pan. Bake for 1½ hours in 325 degree oven.

Mrs. F. A. Kihneman (Tora)

ANN LANDERS MEAT LOAF

2 pounds ground round or chuck
1½ cups bread crumbs
1 teaspoon Accent
1 package Lipton's onion soup mix
3 strips bacon
2 eggs
¾ cup catsup
½ cup warm water
8-ounce can tomato sauce

Mix everything thoroughly, except bacon and tomato sauce. Put in loaf pan — cover with bacon strips — pour tomato sauce over all. Bake 1 hour at 350 degrees.

Mrs. Jo Whittaker

MEAT LOAF PATTIES

1 pound ground meat
Salt and pepper to taste
1 egg
½ cup corn flakes
1 5.33-ounce can evaporated milk
1 tablespoon Worcestershire sauce
1 small onion (chopped)
1 10¾-ounce can cream of mushroom soup

Mix all ingredients together except mushroom soup. Shape into patties. Spoon undiluted mushroom soup on each one. Bake at 300 to 350 degrees for approximately 40 minutes.
Mrs. Lois Mambourg

MEXICAN STYLE MEAT LOAF

1½ pounds lean ground chuck
½ pound ground pork
Salt and pepper to taste
¼ of large onion (chopped fine)
½ small bell pepper (chopped fine)
1 clove garlic
3 tablespoons Parmesan cheese
1 tablespoon chili powder
1 tablespoon liquid smoke
1 6-ounce can tomato paste
2 tablespoons cooking oil
Flour for dusting
Water for cooking
Dash of Louisiana hot sauce (optional)

Mix meats, salt, pepper, onion, garlic, bell pepper, chili powder, hot sauce and cheese thoroughly. Shape into loaf and dust good with flour. This gives you a quick browning. Put oil in cast iron skillet on medium flame and when hot place loaf in pan and brown on both sides. Drain off excess grease. Be sure loaf is centered in skillet. Fill skillet ½ capacity with water. Place this in 325 degree oven and cook for 1 hour. Remove from oven and add tomato paste to liquid and mix well. Dash the liquid smoke on top of loaf. Raise temperature to 350 degrees and cook for 30 more minutes, basting two or three times during this period. This makes a nice tomato gravy and can be eaten over rice or with baked potato.
Mrs. C. D. Attaway (Margie)

MEXICAN CASSEROLE I

1 pound ground beef
1 large onion, chopped
Grated cheddar cheese
1 10¾-ounce can mushroom soup
1 11-ounce can cheddar cheese soup
1 15-ounce can Ro-tel tomatoes
6 to 8 corn tortillas

Brown ground beef. Mix soups and tomatoes. Layer tortillas, ½ ground beef, ½ onion, ½ cheese on bottom of casserole. Pour ½ soup mixture over top. Repeat. Bake at 350 degrees 1 hour.
Mrs. Ronny Goodman (Janice)

MEXICAN CASSEROLE II

1 can hot tamales (6 tamales), save juice
1 can chili (without beans)
1 small bag Fritos
1 cup grated cheese
1 small onion, chopped

Break hot tamales into fourths and layer them in 2 quart baking dish. Sprinkle chopped onion over tamales, then a layer of Fritos. Spoon chili and juice from tamales over this. Sprinkle cheese on top last. Bake 1 hour at 300 degrees. Serves 4 to 6.
Mrs. Hubert L. Joyner (Virginia)

GREEN CHILIES CASSEROLE

1 pound ground beef
½ cup chopped onion
½ teaspoon salt
¼ teaspoon pepper
2 4-ounce cans green chilies
1½ cups shredded sharp cheese
1½ cups milk
¼ cup all purpose flour
½ teaspoon salt
Pepper to taste
4 beaten eggs
Several dashes hot pepper sauce

Cut the green chilies in half crosswise and seed. In skillet, brown onion and beef; drain off fat. Sprinkle meat with the first ½ teaspoon salt and ¼ teaspoon pepper. Place half the chilies in a 10x6x1½-inch baking dish; sprinkle with cheese. Top with meat mixture. Arrange remaining chilies over meat. Combine flour, milk, salt, pepper, eggs and pepper sauce. Beat until smooth. Pour over meat-chilies mixture. Bake in moderate oven, 350 degrees, 50 to 60 minutes, or until knife inserted just off center comes out clean. Let cool 5 minutes and cut into squares to serve. Makes 6 servings.
Mrs. Olin P. Oden (Ruth)

MEXICAN DINNER

1 pound ground beef
1 can cream of chicken soup
1 can chopped green chilies
1 7½-ounce package cheese flavored Doritos
1 medium onion, chopped
1 10¾-ounce can cream of mushroom soup
1 jar (8-ounce) taco sauce
Cheese to taste

Brown meat and onions, drain. Add soups, chilies and taco sauce. Simmer for 15 to 20 minutes. Pour over Doritos in 9x12-inch baking dish. Top with cheese. Place in 350 degree oven only until cheese melts. Serves 4-5 people.

Mrs. Louis R. Jaudon (Betty)

MEXICAN STYLE BEEF CASSEROLE

1 10¾-ounce can cream of mushroom soup
1 10¾-ounce can cream of chicken soup
1 pound lean chuck (ground)
1 soup can of water
2 tablespoons cooking oil
1 4-ounce can chilies-tomato sauce
1 4-ounce can green chilies
½ pound grated cheese
Large package of Dorito chips

Use skillet and add the oil and chuck. Cook until chuck is brown. Add soups, tomato sauce, chilies and water together. Crunch part of Dorito chips into buttered baking dish. Add meat mixture. Top with grated cheese and balance of Dorito chips. Bake in 350 degree oven until cheese is melted and hot through out.

Mrs. Lois Mambourg

MEXICAN ROLL UPS

1 package corn tortillas
1 No. 2 can refried beans
1½ to 2 pounds barbecued beef (may use steak or brisket)
¼ medium onion, chopped fine
1 tablespoon lime or lemon juice
½ teaspoon salt
2 ripe avocados

Warm tortillas in oven, if they seem dry, sprinkle with water. Heat beans in skillet. Slice barbecued beef into strips 2 inches long by ½ inch wide. Prepare guacamole by mashing avocados and adding onion, lime juice and salt. Make rollups by placing 2 tablespoons beans in center of a tortilla; add 2 strips meat, then top with 1 tablespoon guacamole. A prepared green or red sauce may be added for extra seasoning. Roll up and eat with your hands.

Naomi C. Dugan

TAMALE PIE

⅔ cup yellow corn meal
2 tablespoons margarine
1 small onion, chopped
½-¾ pound ground beef
1 6-ounce can tomato paste
¼ cup sliced stuffed olives
½ cup sliced ripe olives
¼ cup chopped green pepper
Paprika
1 teaspoon chili powder
½ cup beef bouillon or consommé
½ 17-ounce (No. 2) can whole kernel corn
Dash of cayenne pepper
½ teaspoon salt
½ cup shredded cheese

Stir corn meal into rapidly boiling water. Cook and stir until thick. Remove from heat. In a heavy skillet melt margarine and brown onion in it. Add ground beef. Stir and cook until meat is no longer red. Add tomato paste, olives, green pepper, chili powder, bouillon, corn, cayenne and salt. Taste to be sure this is enough salt. Stir well. Line a shallow well-margarined baking dish or individual bakers with corn meal mush, reserving some for top. Pour meat-vegetable mixture into lined dishes. Drop remaining corn meal mush by spoonfuls around edge of meat, or cover entire top, if preferred. Sprinkle shredded cheese over top. Dash paprika liberally over all. Bake in moderate oven (350 degrees F.) 1 hour. Serve piping hot. (Makes 8 servings.)

Mrs. C. D. Attaway (Margie)

BEAN CHALUPA

1 pound pinto beans
3 pounds pork roast
7 cups water
½ cup chopped onion
2 cloves garlic, minced
Corn chips
1 tablespoon cumin
1 tablespoon salt
1 teaspoon oregano
1 can (4-ounces) chopped green chilies
1 tablespoon chili powder

Place beans, pork roast, water, onion, garlic, seasonings and green chilies in heavy kettle or dutch oven. Cover and simmer about 5 hours, or until roast falls apart. Break up roast. Uncover and cook until thick, about ½ hour. Serve over corn chips. Pass condiments for choice of toppings. Serves 10-12.

Condiments: Chopped tomato. chopped avocado, chopped onion, shredded lettuce, grated cheddar cheese, taco sauce or hot sauce.

NOTE: Bean Chalupa may be made ahead and reheated. Freezes well.

Mrs. L. A. McKinley (Elizabeth), Magnolia Springs, Alabama

LASAGNA

1 medium onion, chopped
1 garlic clove
1 pound ground beef
1 small can tomato paste
1 16-ounce can tomatoes
½ cup catsup
Salt
Pepper
2 teaspoons Italian seasoning
½ package lasagna noodles
1/6 cup butter
¼ cup flour
1 cup milk
Grated Romano, Parmesan, & Mozzarella cheese

Brown onion, beef and garlic. Add tomato paste, tomatoes and catsup. Salt and pepper to taste. Add Italian seasonings. Let simmer. Cook noodles per package directions. Make white sauce by mixing butter, flour and milk. Layer in oblong casserole: ½ noodles, ½ meat sauce, all white sauce, cover with grated cheeses. Repeat noddles, tomato sauce. Top with Mozerella. Cover with foil and bake at 350 degrees for 1 hour. Freezes well. Can be made day ahead.
Mrs. Ronny Goodman (Janice)

RIGATONI WITH ITALIAN SAUSAGE

1 pound rigatoni (pasta)
1 pound Italian pork sausage
3 tablespoons olive oil
1 onion (chopped)
1 pound fresh mushrooms
1 bay leaf
1 15-ounce can tomato puree
½ cup grated Parmesan cheese
1 clove garlic
Salt and pepper to taste

Cut sausage in 1 inch pieces. Place in hot skillet with olive oil and brown slightly for about 10 minutes. Add onion, mushrooms, garlic, salt and pepper. Simmer for 15 minutes, add tomato puree and bay leaf. Cover pan and cook slowly for 1 hour. Remove bay leaf. Cook rigatoni about 20 minutes in 5 quarts rapidly boiling salted water. When tender, drain and place in baking dish. Add sausage and sauce mixture. Sprinkle with grated Parmesan cheese. Bake in moderate oven about 10 minutes. Serve it very hot. Serves 6.
Mrs. W. A. Doyle (Frances)

ITALIAN MEAT BALLS AND SAUCE

3 pounds ground chuck
3 slices bread
2 eggs
Enough milk to soak bread
1 12-ounce package spaghetti
1 small onion, chopped
4-5 cloves garlic, chopped
1 rib celery, chopped
1 tablespoon sweet basil
Salt and pepper to taste

Sauce:
½ medium size onion, chopped
5 cloves garlic, chopped
1 rib celery, chopped
Bell pepper if desired
2 12-ounce cans tomato paste
2 15-ounce cans tomato sauce
4-5 whole cloves
4 12-ounce cans water
2 tablespoons sweet basil
1 tablespoon fennel seed
1 tablespoon anise seed
Sugar enough to remove tartness
2 tablespoons Parmesan cheese
Salt and pepper to taste

Mix all meat ball ingredients well. Form into balls and fry until lightly browned. Drop into sauce and cook for 1 hour. Can be frozen until needed. Cook spaghetti according to directions on package for proportions. Shortly before serving mix in a large bowl: the spaghetti, meat balls, and enough sauce to saturate all ingredients.
Sauce: Sauté onions, garlic, celery, pepper (if desired) in a dutch oven. Add tomato paste, tomato sauce, and water. Add sweet basil, fennel seed, salt, pepper, anise seed, cloves, and the sugar to remove tartness. Add the Parmesan cheese shortly before dropping the meat balls in for cooking the one hour. Yields 8 large servings. Sauce left over can be frozen for later use.
Mrs. C. Don Attaway (Frances), Blanchard, Louisiana

SPAGHETTI SAUCE I

3 20-ounce cans tomatoes
1 8-ounce can tomato sauce
1 6-ounce can tomato paste
2 large chopped onions
Salt and pepper to taste
1½ to 2 pounds lean chuck
1 8-ounce can sliced mushrooms
Italian seasoning to taste

Blend tomatoes (chopped), tomato sauce, tomato paste, salt and pepper together. In separate skillet sauté onions. Set aside. Sauté chuck in same skillet until brown. Combine first mixture with chuck and onions. Cook several hours, simmering. Stir occasionally. One half hour before done add mushrooms and Italian seasoning.
Mrs. Lois Mambourg

SPAGHETTI SAUCE II

1½ pounds lean ground beef
½ cup chopped onion
½ teaspoon garlic
2 8-ounce cans tomato sauce
¼ cup crushed parsley
1 teaspoon salt
1½ teaspoons oregano
¼ teaspoon thyme
1 tablespoon brown sugar
Dash of pepper
1 whole bay leaf
3 drops Tabasco sauce
Grated Parmesan cheese

Brown the meat, garlic and onion in skillet. Remove fat. Add all other ingredients in the order listed. Simmer uncovered for one hour. Remove bay leaf and serve over cooked spaghetti. Top with grated Parmesan cheese. Serves 4.

Mrs. Kenneth Braswell (Debbie)

STUFFED GRAPEVINE LEAVES

(Greek Dolmades)

1 jar grapevine leaves (1 pint)
1½ pounds ground beef
2½ teaspoons salt
Pepper
2 tablespoons vegetable oil
2 onions, grated
1 cup long grain rice
Juice of 1½ lemons
½ cup chopped parsley
¼ cup dill
¼ cup mint
¼ cup butter

Rinse leaves in cold water. Let stand in warm water as Dolmades are being prepared. Combine ground meat and remaining ingredients, except butter, adding ¾ cup water to soften mixture. Place 1 teaspoon filling in the center of grapevine leaf (ribbed side) and shape a narrow roll. Line a deep saucepan with the grape leaves and arrange Dolmades in layers. Add butter and 2 cups water and cover with inverted plate. Simmer covered for about 45 minutes or until rice is tender. Prepare Egg Lemon Sauce and pour over Dolmades. Serve at once. Makes 8 servings.

Egg-Lemon Sauce for Stuffed Grapevine Leaves:

3 eggs, well beaten
¼ cup water
Juice of 2 lemons

In mixing bowl, beat the eggs until light and fluffy. Add lemon juice and water blending well. Gradually add hot liquid of Dolmades a little at a time until eggs are lukewarm, beating constantly. Remove saucepan from heat. Pour egg sauce slowly over Dolmades. Shake saucepan to spread sauce evenly. Serve at once.

Mrs. Fran Lorant Moore

GREEK PASTITSO ME KIMA

(Baked Macaroni and Meat)

1 pound cooked macaroni
2 pounds ground lean beef
6 tablespoons butter
1 cup chopped onion
1 tablespoon salt
½ cup grated Romano or Parmesan cheese
½ teaspoon pepper
½ teaspoon ground cinnamon
4 tablespoons tomato paste
2 eggs

Melt the butter in skillet and sauté the onions for about 5 minutes. Add the ground meat, stirring well to brown a little. Cover and cook for about 20 minutes. Add the salt, pepper, cinnamon, and tomato paste and continue to cook for another 10 minutes, stirring to keep from sticking. Combine this mixture with the cooked macaroni. Add the grated cheese and the 2 unbeaten eggs. Blend well using hands to mix and pour into a lightly greased 9x12-inch baking dish, about 4 inches deep. Cover evenly with the following cream sauce.

Cream Sauce for Pastitso:
8 tablespoons butter
¾ cup flour
4 eggs
½ teaspoon salt
1 quart warm milk

Melt the butter and add the flour. Remove from heat and stir in warm milk slowly to keep the mixture smooth. Beat eggs slightly and add the hot mixture to the eggs to keep from curdling. Add salt and cook until thickened. Pour and spread evenly on the meat and macaroni. Bake in 375 degree oven for 30 minutes until custard is set. Watch so as not to brown too quickly. Cut into serving pieces.
Mrs. Fran Lorant Moore

LEMON VEAL

16 veal scallops
Salt and pepper to taste
2 tablespoons olive oil
2 tablespoons melted oleo
1 cup beef stock
Juice of two lemons
2 lemons, thinly sliced

Sprinkle veal with salt and pepper; dredge in flour. Heat olive oil and oleo in skillet; brown veal slowly on both sides.

Remove veal from skillet, drain off excess fat. Add stock and lemon juice; heat thoroughly. Add veal and top with lemon slices; cover. Simmer slowly until stock is reduced by ⅔, about 20-30 minutes. Yield: 8 servings.
Mrs. Carter Graham (Jackie), Tulsa, Oklahoma

STUFFED YELLOW SQUASH

6 medium sized yellow squash
¾ pound ground chuck
1 cup bread crumbs
¾ cup celery, chopped
½ cup onion, minced
½ teaspoon garlic salt
Pepper to taste
⅓ cup Parmesan cheese
Dash of sweet basil
⅓ cup minced parsley

Scrub squash with vegetable brush. Cut them in half lengthwise and parboil. Do not cook them too long as they need to be firm to hold stuffing. When partially cooked, scoop out pulp and set aside to drain. Sauté celery, onion and parsley. Add seasoning, then ground meat; brown. Remove from fire. Add to mixture the pulp, bread crumbs and cheese; mix well. Stuff the squash shells. Place in baking dish or pan and bake for 35 to 40 minutes in 350 degree oven. Cover while cooking for the first 30 minutes.
Mrs. Hal Johnson, Jr. (Shirley)

HAM STUFFED SQUASH

2 medium squash
2 tablespoons margarine
½ cup chopped celery
⅓ cup chopped onion
1½ cups chopped cooked ham
2 tablespoons light brown sugar
⅛ teaspoon ground allspice

Cut squash in half lengthwise and remove seed. Place cut side down in a greased baking dish; add ½ inch water. Cover and bake at 350 degrees for 30 minutes. Melt margarine in a small saucepan, add celery and onions. Cook until tender. Add ham, sugar and allspice. Stir to mix and cook over medium heat until heated through. Stuff squash with ham mixture. Cover and bake at 350 degrees for 15 minutes. Remove cover and bake an additional 15 minutes. Serves 4.
Mrs. Jean Jaster, Texarkana, Arkansas

GREEN NOODLES AND HAM

1 8-ounce package green noodles
2 cups cooked ham cut in 1-inch pieces
1 pint sour cream
1 cup grated Parmesan cheese

Cook noodles in boiling salted water for 10 minutes. Then drain. Combine all ingredients. Pour into a covered baking dish. Bake at 350 degrees about 40 minutes. Yield 6 servings.
Mrs. William Perry (Mattie), Haughton, Louisiana

CARBONARA

1 cup chopped green onions and tops
1 can Hormel's chunky ham
6 tablespoons melted oleo
4 tablespoons all purpose flour
1 quart half and half
¾ to 1 cup Parmesan cheese
1 12-ounce package vermicelli or spaghetti

Sauté onion in oleo. Add ham; blend in flour. Gradually add half and half; cook and stir until smooth and thickened. Gradually stir in Parmesan cheese and cooked vermicelli.

This makes a very large recipe. Serve with green salad.

Mrs. Carter Graham (Jackie), Tulsa, Oklahoma

DIRTY RICE

3 tablespoons of oil
2 medium onions, finely chopped
2 stalks celery, finely chopped
2 tablespoons water
Chopped parsley leaves
1 tablespoon flour
1 clove minced garlic
½ cup finely chopped bell pepper
3 tablespoons fresh pork sausage
2 cups of raw rice
Chopped green onion tops

In an iron skillet, make a golden brown roux using the 3 tablespoons of oil and the flour. Add the onion, garlic, celery, and bell pepper and cook slowly until the vegetables are clear (about 10 minutes). Add the chicken livers and sausage and cook until the meats are brown. Add about 2 tablespoons water and simmer a few minutes. Stir in raw rice. Put the dirty rice in a big double boiler and keep hot over hot water for at least an hour or put in a tightly covered casserole and place in a low heat oven for the same time. About 15 minutes before ready to serve stir in a small handful of chopped parsley leaves and the same amount of chopped green onion tops. Serves 8.

Mrs. Jo Whittaker

7-UP PORK CHOPS

6 pork chops, 1-inch thick
1 12-ounce bottle 7-Up
1 package onion soup mix

Put chops in shallow pan. Pour 7-Up over them and sprinkle with onion soup mix. Bake at 350 degrees for 1 hour. Serves 6.

Mrs. A. R. Snider (Frances)

PORK CHOP MEAL-IN-ONE CASSEROLE

Salt
Pepper
Flour
1 stick oleo
4 or 5 pork chops
4 or 5 medium size potatoes
1 medium onion

Salt, pepper and flour pork chops. Brown in skillet in oleo. Put a layer of chops in a casserole and top with a layer of sliced onions and a layer of sliced potatoes. Salt. Repeat layers of chops, onions and potatoes until chops are used. Pour drippings over the top. May add a small amount of water. Cover tightly and bake in oven one hour at 350 degrees.
Mrs. H. Russell Maddox (Tommie Lue)

PORK CHOP CASSEROLE

4 pork chops
¾ cup raw rice
1 tomato, sliced
1 bell pepper, sliced
1 onion, sliced
1 can beef bouillon
Salt
Pepper

Place raw rice in bottom of casserole. Salt and pepper pork chops, brown in skillet and place on top of rice. Place slice of tomato, onion and pepper ring on top of each pork chop. Pour can of bouillon over all. Cover casserole and bake in 375 degree oven for about 1 hour. Add water as needed. This casserole can be prepared ahead of time and baked when ready for it.
Mrs. James E. Williams (Yvonne)

The tendency to brood and fret has never solved a problem yet. Worry is a rocking chair that never gets us anywhere.

MY KITCHEN PRAYER

Bless my little kitchen, Lord
I love its every nook
And bless me as I do my work
Wash pot, pans and cook.

And may the meals that I prepare
Be seasoned from above
With Thy great blessing and Thy grace
But most of all, Thy Love.

As we partake of earthly food;
The table thou hast spread,
We'll not forget to thank thee, Lord,
For all our daily bread.

So bless my little kitchen, Lord
And those who enter in;
May they find naught but joy and peace
And happiness therein. Amen.

Seafood

One of the earliest stores in Shreveport was the Buckelew's Hardware Store. Selling harnesses, farming equipment, and buggies when it began it later grew into a lively business offering sporting goods, stoves, ranges and gas supplies as well as hardware.

INTERESTING FACTS ABOUT SHREVEPORT

As early as 1924 Shreveport was designated as a stop on an air line from New York to Dallas and a field to accommodate the airway was prepared off the Mansfield Road.

Two local aviators pioneered the mid-air refueling method now used by the U.S. Air Force. July 1929 marked the attempt of William Currey Sanders and Van Lear Leary to establish an endurance record on a continuous flight above Shreveport. They succeeded in establishing two important firsts; maintaining telephone communication between planes during refueling; and close contact flying during refueling operations. This method was later perfected by the U.S. Air Force to enable jet bombers to fly non-stop to any point on the globe.

One of the planes was named the KWKH and backed by W. K. Henderson.

William Curry Sanders held the distinction of being the first Louisiana pilot licensed by CAA, in 1926.

Barksdale Air Force Base was officially dedicated on February 2, 1933, being named in commemoration of the bravery of Lieutenant Eugene Hoy Barksdale, Air Corps, U.S. Army. Lieutenant Barksdale, a native of Goshen Springs, Mississippi, and World War I veteran, lost his life on August 11, 1926, while flight-testing an observation type airplane near Wright Field, Dayton, Ohio.

STUFFED CRAB

2 teaspoons onions, minced
2 cups crab meat
½ cup bread crumbs (dried)
¼ pound oleo or butter
¼ cup water
½ cup lemon juice
1 tablespoon parsley
2 hard cooked eggs (chopped)
Extra bread crumbs (mashed fine)

Brown onion in butter, add crab meat, ½ cup bread crumbs, lemon juice and water. Cook 15 to 20 minutes. Add parsley and eggs. Stir well. Put into shells or baking dish. Sprinkle with the extra bread crumbs. Bake at 350 degrees until warm and crumbs are brown.

Mrs. Lois Mambourg

CRAYFISH ELEGANT

1 pound crayfish tails, peeled
1 small bunch green onions
1 cup parsley, chopped
1 stick butter
3 tablespoons flour
1 pint half and half cream
3 tablespoons cooking sherry (wine may be substituted)

Sauté crayfish tails in ½ stick butter. In separate skillet sauté onions, parsley, in ½ stick butter. Add 3 tablespoons flour and stir until smooth. Combine sautéed crayfish and seasonings. Cook a little while. Add 1 pint half and half cream slowly; then add sherry. Season with red pepper and salt to taste. Serve over rice.

Variation: Boiled shrimp are also good.

Mrs. David L. Richardson (Nancy), Baton Rouge, Louisiana

CRAB-SPINACH SOUFFLE

1 10-ounce package frozen chopped spinach souffle, defrosted
2 pounds small curd cottage cheese
6 tablespoons flour
6 eggs
Worcestershire sauce
½ stick butter, diced
½ pound sharp cheddar cheese diced
1 7-ounce can crab meat
Salt to taste

Mix all ingredients well. Pour into greased 9x13-inch pan or a 2 quart soufflé dish (2 of them). Bake at 350 degrees for 1 hour. Can be prepared ahead of time. Serves 10 to 12.

Mrs. John G. Grant (Madelyn), Dallas, Texas

GOURMET CRAB RING

1 teaspoon unflavored gelatin
¼ cup cold water
2 8-ounce packages cream cheese, softened
2 tablespoons cooking sherry (optional)
¾ teaspoon seasoned salt
1 2-ounce jar sliced pimientos, drained and chopped
1 6-ounce package frozen king crab meat, thawed, drained, cut-up*
⅛ teaspoon ground black pepper
¼ cup snipped parsley

Sprinkle gelatin over water to soften; stir over hot water until dissolved. Beat into cream cheese until smooth. Stir in sherry, salt, pimientos, crab meat, pepper and 2 tablespoons of parsley. Pour into a 3 cup ring mold. Refrigerate at least 4 hours, or until set. To serve, turn out on plate; garnish with remaining parsley. Place parsley sprigs in center. Crackers may be placed around outside of plate.

*NOTE: Tuna may be substituted for crab meat. It is very good.

Mrs. Art Ogletree, Jr. (Ann)

EGGPLANT STUFFED WITH CRAB

1 large eggplant (round)
4 tablespoons melted butter
1 teaspoon minced onion
1 tablespoon dried parsley
½ pound lump crab meat
Dash cayenne pepper

Topping:
Fine dry bread crumbs
Grated Parmesan cheese
Paprika

Cut eggplant in half from stem end and slash flesh in a crisscross pattern, being careful not to cut through to skin. Bake, flesh side down, in preheated oven, 350 degrees, until tender; about 25 minutes. Scoop pulp from skin (leave ¼ inch thick shell) and reserve shells. Purée pulp or whir in blender. Add remaining ingredients, folding crab in carefully, and season to taste. Fill shells lightly and sprinkle with topping ingredients in order listed. Return to oven and bake until browned, about 20 minutes. Makes two hearty servings.

Mrs. Leonard Green, Jr. (June)

SEAFOOD CASSEROLE

- 1/3 cup chopped onion
- 1/4 cup melted margarine
- 1/4 cup all-purpose flour
- 1 teaspoon salt
- 1/2 teaspoon white pepper
- 1 cup half and half cream
- 1 cup milk
- 1 cup shredded cheddar cheese
- 2 cups cooked regular rice
- 2 tablespoons lemon juice
- 1 6-ounce package frozen crab meat (thawed and flaked)
- 1 cup cooked, peeled, and deveined shrimp
- 1 5-ounce can water chestnuts (drained and sliced)
- 2 tablespoons chopped pimiento

Sauté onion in margarine until tender. Add flour, salt, and pepper. Cook until bubbly. Gradually add half and half and milk. Stirring constantly; cook over low heat until smooth and thickened. Remove from heat. Add remaining ingredients, except 1/2 cup cheese. Stir to blend. Spoon mixture into a lightly greased 2 quart casserole dish. Sprinkle with reserved cheese. Bake at 325 degrees for 30 minutes. Serves 6 to 8.

Ms. Polly Sharp

SEAFOOD GUMBO

- 3 pound hen or fatty fryer
- 1/2 cup chopped celery
- 1/2 cup chopped onion
- 1/8 teaspoon black pepper
- 1 teaspoon salt
- 1/2 cup oil
- 1 clove garlic
- 6 ounces raw crab meat (claw or white)
- 1/2 pint raw oysters
- 1 teaspoon gumbo filé
- 2 tablespoons tomato paste
- 1 pound peeled shrimp
- 1/2 to 1 cup flour
- 1 package (8-ounce) frozen okra

Boil chicken until done, having lots of broth; bone chicken and put back in broth. Add chopped celery and onion, black pepper and salt. Brown 1/2 to 1 cup flour in oil in pan. Add to chicken broth. Cut up onion and piece of garlic and package of frozen okra in frying pan and sauté rather brown. Add to broth. Add raw crab meat and oysters; add filé, tomato paste and shrimp. Boil over medium heat for one hour.

FOR CHICKEN GUMBO, OMIT ALL SEAFOOD.

Mrs. Betty Gentry

SHRIMP CHEVEL CASSEROLE

⅓ cup rice
2 tablespoons shortening
1¼ cups water
½ teaspoon salt
½ pound fresh shrimp
½ cup water
½ teaspoon salt
1 tablespoon margarine or butter
1½ tablespoons flour
½ cup cooked tomatoes
2 teaspoons grated onion
½ cup grated carrots
¼ teaspoon Worcestershire sauce
4 ounces Shefford Chevel, sliced

Melt shortening, add rice and cook, stirring constantly until golden brown. Add 1¼ cups water and ½ teaspoon salt; cover and simmer 20-25 minutes or until tender. Remove shells and vein from shrimp, rinse well; add ½ cup water and ½ teaspoon salt. Simmer 3 minutes. Drain and reserve liquid. Melt margarine or butter in saucepan; add flour; stir until well blended. Gradually add ½ cup shrimp liquid and the ½ cup tomatoes. Cook, stirring constantly until thickened. Add the grated onion and grated carrots, Worcestershire sauce and shrimp. Heat through. Place hot rice in casserole and cover with hot shrimp mixture. Arrange 4 ounces sliced Shefford Chevel on top. Heat under broiler 2-3 minutes or until browned.
Mrs. L. A. McKinley (Elizabeth), Magnolia Springs, Alabama

SHRIMP MOLD

1 10¾-ounce can cream of mushroom soup
1 8-ounce package cream cheese
1 cup mayonnaise
Juice of one lemon
Few dashes Tabasco sauce
1 pound boiled shrimp, chopped
1 cup chopped celery
1 bunch chopped green onions
1 envelope Knox unflavored gelatin
3 tablespoons cold water

Heat mushroom soup and gradually add cream cheese to it, blending well. Remove from fire and add mayonnaise, lemon juice, Tabasco, shrimp, celery and green onions. Quickly mix gelatin in cold water and dissolve. Stir into soup mixture. Pour into mold and refrigerate overnight. Dip mold in hot water to unmold.
Mrs. Bruce Baker (Stacy), Baton Rouge, Louisiana

SHRIMP BARBECUE

4-5 pounds large shrimp
1¾ pounds butter
¼ cup black pepper
2 cloves garlic, minced or pressed
1 cup lemon juice

Wash and clean shrimp well, but do not shell. Place shrimp in large pan that is at least 2 inches deep. Melt butter; add to it the pepper, garlic and lemon juice. Pour this over shrimp. Cover with foil if pan does not have cover.

Bake at 250 degrees for 2 hours. Turn oven off and let shrimp marinate in warm oven until ready to serve. Serve shrimp in liquid mixture with green salad and French bread. (Have a good supply of napkins available.) Be sure and dip your bread in butter sauce!

NOTE: Reduce cooking time ½ hour if shrimp is to marinate in oven.

Mrs. Arlis C. Hinson, Jr. (Georgia)

EGGS AND SHRIMP BAKE

1 cup chopped boiled shrimp
¼ cup stuffed green olives, sliced
1 teaspoon salt
4 teaspoons butter
1 cup sour cream
1 tablespoon chopped chives
⅛ teaspoon pepper
8 eggs

Mix all the above ingredients in a large bowl. Put 1 teaspoon of butter into each of 4 10-ounce individual casseroles. Place in 400 degree oven until butter melts. Break 2 eggs into each casserole. Top with shrimp and sour cream mixture. Bake at 400 degrees for 15 minutes or until eggs are cooked as you like.

Mrs. A. R. Snider (Frances)

BROILED SHRIMP

2 pounds shrimp
1 stick oleo
1 bunch chives
1 cup sauterne wine

Put cleaned shrimp in ovenproof dish. Salt and pepper shrimp and add chives. Melt butter and pour over it. Put under broiler and cook until shrimp turn pink. Then broil on other side. Add sauterne wine and cook 2 or 3 minutes. Serves 4 people.

Mrs. Jean K. Rice

SHRIMP CREOLE

1 pound shrimp (shelled and deveined)
1 medium size onion
1 small green bell pepper
4 tablespoons margarine
1 teaspoon salt
¼ teaspoon whole oregano
¼ teaspoon paprika
1 16-ounce can tomatoes
1 8-ounce can tomato sauce

Chop onions and pepper. Sauté in margarine until tender, not brown. Add rest of ingredients and bring to a boil. Add shrimp last and simmer until shrimp is tender. Serve over cooked rice.
Mrs. F. A. Kihneman (Tora)

FRIED SHRIMP

10 pounds fresh large shrimp
6 eggs
1 large can evaporated milk
3 to 4 cups flour
1 large box Italian bread crumbs
Crushed red pepper
Oil

Shell and devein shrimp. Split down back for form "butterfly." Sprinkle shrimp generously with red pepper. Beat eggs and add milk. Coat shrimp with flour and dip in egg and milk mixture. Then roll in bread crumbs and fry in hot oil until brown. Serves 12 to 14.
Mrs. George Gekakis (Carol) submitted by Rhonda Berry

SHRIMP ETOUFFEE

2 pounds shrimp (peeled and deveined)
¼ pound oleo
1 cup onions (chopped fine)
½ cup celery
Salt
Pepper
½ cup bell pepper
4 cloves garlic
1 tablespoon cornstarch
1½ cups water
Paprika

Split shrimp and season generously (I leave shrimp whole and season.) Set aside. Melt oleo and add onions, celery, bell pepper and garlic. Cook slowly in electric skillet until onions are wilted. Add seasoned shrimp and let simmer, stirring occasionally for 20 minutes. Add paprika heavily. Dissolve cornstarch in water and add to mixture. Cook another 15 minutes on simmer, covered, stirring occasionally. Serve over cooked rice. Serves 4.
Mrs. Fran Lorant Moore

FAT MAN'S SHRIMP

2 10-ounce packages frozen chopped spinach
1 cup sour cream
2 10¾-ounce cans cream of mushroom soup
1 8-ounce can browned-in-butter mushrooms, drained (or ½ pound fresh ones, sautéed in butter)
½ cup grated Parmesan cheese
½ teaspoon dry mustard
2 cups cooked shrimp (fresh, canned or frozen)
Grated coconut for top

Cook spinach according to directions on package and let drain in a colander while combining sour cream with both cans of soup. Add to this the mushrooms, Parmesan cheese and dry mustard. Heat it through; then add cooked shrimp. Put a layer of the spinach in a baking dish, then a layer of the shrimp mixture, and so on, hopefully ending with the shrimp mixture. Sprinkle some grated coconut on top for a gala note. The coconut will toast as you bake the dish later, uncovered, at 350 degrees for half an hour.

If you're out of coconut, you can use very coarse buttered crumbs, though it isn't so gala.

Mrs. Bruce Baker (Stacy), Baton Rouge, Louisiana

SHRIMP AND RICE CASSEROLE

1 pound fresh shrimp or 12 ounce package of peeled and deveined frozen shrimp
1 cup cooked rice
1 cup grated cheese
2 ounce can mushrooms (and juice)
1 10¾-ounce can cream of mushroom soup
Lea and Perrin sauce to taste
Tabasco sauce to taste
½ stick butter
1 cup celery, diced
½ cup chopped onion
½ cup chopped green pepper
Thin slices lemon

Cook shrimp with shrimp seasoning. Combine shrimp, rice, cheese, mushrooms and juice, and mushroom soup. Add Lea and Perrins and Tabasco sauces. Sauté in butter the celery, onion and green pepper; add to mixture. Place in baking dish and top with thin slices of lemon. Heat at 350 degrees until hot and bubbly. Serves 5 to 6.

Mrs. Ralph Garrett (Dottie)

BARBECUED SHRIMP

5-6 pounds medium size shrimp, rinsed well, but not peeled
1 package onion soup mix
1 package Good Seasons garlic dressing mix
2 tablespoons Worcestershire sauce
2 tablespoons lemon juice
1 tablespoon parsley flakes
1 tablespoon paprika
½ small box black pepper
5 to 6 sticks margarine

Use a large flat baking pan covered with foil — seems to work best. Put shrimp in pan and mix all the other ingredients except the butter and put over shrimp. Cut the butter in squares and lay over the top of the shrimp. Bake covered at 375 degrees until done — approximately 40 minutes. Stir every ten minutes. Serve French bread with this for dunking in the juice and a tossed salad.
Mrs. Francis A. Zonkel (Helen)

DEVILED SHRIMP

2 pounds boiled, deveined shrimp
1 pint barbecue sauce
1 jar (about 10 ounces) dill pickles, chopped
1 jar (about 10 ounces) hamburger relish
1 jar (about 10 ounces) hot dog relish
½ of 10-ounce bottle of Worcestershire sauce

Mix together all the ingredients and chill 12 to 24 hours. Serve with crackers.
Mrs. Leonard Green, Jr. (June)

SHRIMP IN BEER

2 pounds fresh shrimp (in shells)
Flat beer
2 tablespoons peppercorn
3 bay leaves
1 teaspoon hot sauce

Cover shrimp with flat beer. Add peppercorns, bay leaves and hot sauce. Bring to a boil and then simmer 15 minutes. Remove from heat. Let shrimp stand for one hour in juice. Drain. Peel and serve on crushed ice.
Mrs. Lois Mambourg

GEORGIA'S SHRIMP SALAD

1 pound shrimp cooked or 2 5-ounce cans, cleaned
1 cup celery, coarsely chopped
2 hard boiled eggs, chopped
3 tablespoons dill pickles, diced
½ cup mayonnaise or salad dressing
1 tablespoon lemon juice
1 tablespoon catsup
½ teaspoon Worcestershire sauce
¾ teaspoon salt
¼ teaspoon pepper

Chill shrimp and if large, cut in halves or quarters. Toss together shrimp, celery, eggs, and pickles with mayonnaise which has been combined with lemon juice, catsup, Worcestershire sauce and seasonings. Serve on crisp lettuce and salad greens. Garnish top with shrimp and egg. Makes 4 servings.

Mrs. Arlis C. Hinson, Jr. (Georgia)

SHRIMP CURRY

3½ ounces shredded coconut
3 cups water
½ cup butter, melted
1 cup chopped onions, browned
½ cup flour
2 cups milk
1 tablespoon curry powder
4 pounds fresh, deveined shrimp
2½ teaspoons salt
1 teaspoon ginger root, finely chopped
2 tablespoons lemon juice
Chutney
Chopped scallions
Crumbled bacon
Chopped hard boiled eggs
Shredded coconut
Chopped nuts
Steamed raisins

Simmer coconut in water for 20 minutes; strain through cheesecloth and reserve 2 cups liquid. Combine butter and onions; mix in flour smoothly. Add reserved liquid and milk blended with curry powder. Cook, stirring until thickened. Add shrimp, salt and ginger root. Simmer for 30 minutes. Stir in lemon juice and additional curry to taste before serving. Serve over rice with remaining ingredients as condiments. Yield: 12 to 15 servings.

Mrs. Leonard Green, Jr. (June)

REAL NEW ORLEANS GUMBO

1½ pounds hot smoked sausage, cut into bite size pieces
1 stalk celery, cleaned and diced
2 green peppers, diced
3 medium onions, chopped
5 tablespoons bacon fat
½ pint oysters
1½ pounds cleaned and deveined shrimp
1 can crab meat
2 No. 2 cans tomatoes
1 15-ounce can tomato paste
5 tablespoons bacon fat
4 tablespoons flour
2 tablespoons gumbo filé
2 packages whole baby okra

In a large sauce pan, cover sausage with water, bring to a boil and boil 5 minutes. Pour off and discard greasy water. In a heavy iron skillet, sauté celery, peppers and onion in 5 tablespoons bacon fat until clear but not browned. Put smoked sausage and vegetable mixture in a 10-quart boiler and bring to a slow simmer. Add tomatoes and tomato paste, crab meat and oysters. Simmer 45 minutes. In an iron skillet, make a roux with 5 tablespoons bacon fat, flour and gumbo filé, stirring constantly, browning mixture to a very dark brown. Add to gumbo mixture very carefully and in small quantities to prevent steaming over. Add shrimp and okra. Cook until shrimp is pink and okra is a bright green. Do not over cook. More filé and salt may be added to taste.

Serve over fluffy white rice and accompany with a green salad and garlic buttered french bread.

Mrs. Marvin Kines (Ora)

SHRIMP CASSEROLE

1 6-ounce box of Uncle Ben's wild rice
1 10¾-ounce can mushroom soup
1 package frozen cooked shrimp
4 slices American cheese

Cook rice according to package directions. Add soup and blend thoroughly then add shirmp. Place one half of the mixture in a 2 quart loaf shaped casserole and cover with cheese slices. Add the last half and cover with remaining cheese. Bake at 350 degrees for 30 minutes. (If you prefer a larger shallow baking dish, just use additional cheese slices to cover and reduce baking time to 20 minutes.)

NOTE: If casserole is sprayed with Pam, the servings are easier to remove from the dish.

Mrs. Ike Cullick (Barbara)

SHRIMP NEWBURG

1 pound packaged (raw, frozen), fully peeled, deveined shrimp
¼ cup butter or margarine
2½ tablespoons flour
¾ teaspoon salt
2 egg yolks, beaten
Dash cayenne pepper
Dash nutmeg
1 pint coffee cream
2 tablespoons sherry
Toast points

Boil shrimp. Cut large shrimp in half. Melt butter; blend in flour and seasonings. Add cream gradually and cook until thick and smooth, stirring constantly. Stir a little of the hot sauce into egg yolks; add to remaining sauce, stirring constantly. Add shrimp; heat. Remove from heat and slowly stir in sherry. Serve immediately on toast points. Serves 6.
Mrs. Arlis C. Hinson, Jr. (Georgia)

SEAFOOD NEWBURG

¼ cup butter or margarine
½ pound fresh mushrooms, trimmed and sliced (or 8-ounce can)
1 cup chopped scallions
⅓ cup flour
1 cup dry white wine
1 cup (½ pint) light cream
½ teaspoon curry power
Salt and pepper
⅓ cup grated Parmesan cheese
1 pound shrimp, cooked, shelled and deveined
1 pound flounder filets cut into 1-inch strips
1 pound scallops, cleaned
½ cup corn flake crumbs
2 tablespoons melted butter or margarine

In a saucepan, melt butter and sauté mushrooms until wilted. Add scallions and sauté for a few minutes. Stir in flour. Gradually stir in white wine and cream. Add curry powder and cheese. Stir over low heat until sauce bubbles and thickens. Add shrimp, flounder and scallops. Season to taste with salt and pepper. Pour mixture into a 2½ quart glass-ceramic casserole. Mix crumbs and melted butter. Sprinkle mixture evenly over casserole. Bake in a preheated moderate oven, 350 degrees, for 40 to 60 minutes or until top is golden brown. Serve in casserole dish.
Mrs. Art A. Ogletree, Jr. (Ann)

SHRIMP 'N SAUCE

4-5 pounds boiled, deveined shrimp
1 pint mayonnaise
1 bottle catsup
1 teaspoon mustard
½ onion, chopped
1 button garlic, minced
1 cup chopped celery
1 bell pepper, chopped
Juice of ½ lemon
1 tablespoon vinegar
1 teaspoon olive oil
1 tablespoon Lea & Perrin sauce
Louisiana Hot Sauce or Tabasco to taste
Salt and pepper to taste
Paprika to taste

Combine all ingredients for sauce and serve along with cooked, chilled shrimp. The sauce is a pretty color and is very attractive when shrimp is placed on a lettuce leaf and sauce is poured over them. This sauce will keep well when refrigerated and may be used later.
Mrs. Larry Ogletree (June), Houston, Texas

FISH FILETS

1 package fish filets (number desired)
Flour
1 tablespoon baking powder
Salt and pepper to taste
1 egg
⅛ inch oil for skillet
1 tablespoon water

Beat egg, add water. Dip filets in flour and baking powder mixture, then egg and flour again. Fry in oil.

Sauce: (if desired)
½ cup lemon juice
½ cup oil
1 teaspoon oregano mix

Mix well and pour over cooked fish.
Mrs. Lois Mambourg

FISH FRY SEASONING

4 cups corn meal
1 cup flour
Red pepper
Lemon pepper
Salt

Combine ingredients and use to coat fish for frying.
Mrs. David Richardson (Nancy), Baton Rouge, Louisiana

SCALLOPED OYSTERS

1 pint oysters
2 cups medium coarse cracker crumbs
¾ cup light cream
½ teaspoon salt
Pepper to taste
½ cup butter, melted
¼ teaspoon Worcestershire

Drain oysters, reserving ¼ cup liquid. Combine crumbs and butter. Spread ⅓ of crumbs in greased pan. Cover with half the oysters. Use ⅓ of the crumbs for second layer and cover with remaining oysters. Combine cream, oyster liquid and seasonings. Pour over oysters and top with remaining crumbs. Bake 40 minutes at 350 degrees. Serves 4.
Mrs. John Grant (Madelyn), Dallas, Texas

SCALLOPED CORN AND OYSTERS

1 No. 303 can cream style corn
½ pint oysters
1 egg
¼ cup milk
1 tablespoon butter
Crackers
Seasoning to taste

Mix corn, egg, milk and butter. Alternate layers of corn and oysters in baking dish with crushed cracker in between, top layer being cracker crumbs. Do not top with butter. Bake at 350 degrees for 30 minutes.
Mrs. C.D.Attaway (Margie)

OYSTERS GABRIEL

3 12-ounce jars oysters
½ teaspoon thyme
¾ teaspoon oregano
3 teaspoons garlic powder
1 stick butter or margarine
1 cup chopped artichoke hearts
Parmesan cheese
1 large onion, chopped
¼ teaspoon red pepper
2 teaspoons parsley
2 tablespoons dry vermouth
1 cup Italian seasoned bread crumbs
Salt and pepper to taste

Sauté onions, butter and seasonings, add oysters. When edges curl, add the oyster juice; fold in bread crumbs and artichoke hearts. Pour in buttered 2 quart casserole and cover with cheese. Bake 15 to 20 minutes at 350 degrees.
Mrs. Louis Braun, Lafayette, Louisiana

SALMON CROQUETTES I

1 large can salmon, reserve juice
1 heaping tablespoon baking powder
1 egg
1 cup flour
Pepper
Onion salt

Drain juice from salmon and add baking powder to juice. Mash salmon; add egg, flour, pepper, onion salt and juice. Mix well. Drop by spoonfuls into hot grease. Brown and drain.
Mrs. Hal Johnson, Jr. (Shirley)

SALMON CROQUETTES II

1 No. 2 can pink or red salmon (drain off liquid and reserve)
1 egg
½ cup flour
1 teaspoon soda
2 tablespoons corn meal

Drain salmon and add egg and flour. Mix well with fork. To ¼ cup of reserved liquid add the soda and corn meal. Mix this with salmon mixture. Drop in deep hot fat by using two iced teaspoons. Fry until golden brown. These are good hot or cold.
Mrs. F. A. Kihneman (Tora)

QUICK 'N EASY SALMON PATTIES

1 can (15-16 ounces) pink salmon
1 egg
⅓ cup minced onion
½ cup flour
1½ teaspoons baking powder
1½ cups Crisco

Drain salmon; set aside 2 tablespoons of the juice. In a medium mixing bowl, mix salmon, egg and onion until sticky. Stir in flour. Add baking powder to salmon juice; stir into salmon mixture. Form into small patties and fry until golden brown (about 5 minutes) in hot Crisco. Serve with tartar sauce. Serves 4-6.
Mrs. Louis R. Jaudon (Betty)

TUNA-BROCCOLI CASSEROLE

- 2 7-ounce cans tuna, drained
- 2 pounds fresh broccoli or
- 2 10-ounce packages frozen broccoli
- 4 tablespoons butter or oleo
- 4 tablespoons flour
- 1 cup light cream (or half and half)
- 1 cup chicken broth
- Salt and pepper
- 1 tablespoon chopped parsley
- 2 hard cooked eggs, chopped
- ¼ cup Parmesan or cheddar cheese

If the broccoli is fresh, trim off almost all of the stem part. Whether fresh or frozen, cook in boiling salted water until barely tender and arrange in single layer in baking dish. Melt butter, blend in flour; stir in cream and broth to make a smooth sauce. Season to taste with salt and pepper. Stir in gently the parsley, tuna and chopped egg. Pour carefully over the broccoli and top with cheese. Bake for 15 to 20 minutes in a moderate oven, 350 degrees, then put under the broiler for a minute or two to brown well. Serves 4-5.

Mrs. John E. Ewing (Helen)

CHOPSTICK TUNA

- 1 10¾-ounce can cream of mushroom soup
- 1 3-ounce can (2 cups) chow mein noodles
- 1 7 or 9¼-ounce can tuna
- 1 cup sliced celery
- ½ cup salted toasted cashews
- ¼ cup chopped onion
- 1 11-ounce can mandarin orange sections

Combine soup and ¼ cup water. Add 1 cup chow mein noodles, the tuna, celery, cashews, onion and toss lightly. Place in ungreased 10x6x1½-inch baking dish. Sprinkle remaining noodles over top. Bake at 375 degrees for 15 minutes or heated through. Garnish with mandarin orange sections. Serves 4-5.

To double recipe, bake in 11½x7½x1½-inch baking dish for 25 minutes or until hot through.

Mrs. L. A. McKinley (Elizabeth), Magnolia Springs, Alabama

TUNA CASSEROLE I

1 10¾-ounce can cream of mushroom soup
1 9¼-ounce can tuna
1 medium onion (chopped)
1 5-ounce package egg noodles (cooked)
⅓ cup milk
Cracker crumbs

Mix all ingredients together except cracker crumbs. Put in buttered casserole. Top with cracker crumbs. Bake in 375 degree oven for 30 minutes or until bubbly.
Mrs. Lois Mambourg

TUNA CASSEROLE II

1 2½-ounce can mushrooms (drained)
1 tablespoon margarine
¼ cup onion
½ cup milk
1 10¾-ounce can mushroom soup
1 cup grated cheese
1 9¼ or 12½-ounce can tuna
2 cups cooked macaroni

Add onion to margarine and sauté. Add cheese, milk, soup, add tuna last. Bake in greased casserole dish at 350 degrees until cheese browns.
Mrs. Clara Cummins, Bossier City, Louisiana

TUNA MOUSSE

1 tablespoon unflavored gelatin
¼ cup cold water
2 7-ounce cans tuna
2 tablespoons lemon juice
½ cup mayonnaise
2 tablespoons grated onion
Salt and pepper to taste
1 cup sour cream
1 small jar stuffed olives, sliced
Cherry tomatoes

Dissolve gelatin in cold water — melt over hot water. Combine tuna which has been drained and flaked, lemon juice, mayonnaise, onion, salt and pepper. Beat until smooth. Stir into tuna mixture the gelatin, sour cream and sliced olives. Spoon into a 3 cup mold and chill. Unmold and garnish with cherry tomatoes. Serves 4 to 5.
Mrs. Hubert L. Joyner (Virginia)

TUNA RICE

2 9¼-ounce cans tuna (drained)
3 cups cooked rice
1 cup celery (chopped fine)
½ cup onion (chopped fine)
Croutons or chow mein noodles for topping
3 tablespoons pimiento (chopped)
1 10¾-ounce celery soup
⅓ cup milk
1 cup grated cheese

Mix all ingredients together. Place in 2 quart buttered casserole dish. Top with your favorite topping. I sometimes use crushed buttered toast. Bake approximately 15 to 20 minutes in a 350 degree oven or until hot through and through.
Mrs. F. A. Kihneman (Tora)

BAKED RED FISH

1 pound red fish filets
1 cup flour
Salt and pepper
1 stick butter or oleo
Lemon juice

Combine flour, salt and pepper. Coat filets with flour mixture and cook in butter in skillet slowly until light brown. Carefully turn over with egg turner and brown lightly on other side. Remove from skillet and place in baking dish. Combine melted butter with lemon juice and pour over fish. Place in 350 degree oven for about 10 minutes.
Mrs. James A. Richardson (Margie), Baton Rouge, Louisiana

TROUT AMANDINE

Trout filets
Sweet milk
Flour
Salt
Wesson oil
Almonds, lightly toasted
Butter sauce

Soak filets in sweet milk. Roll in salted flour and sauté in ¼-inch Wesson oil. Serve with lightly toasted almonds and a butter sauce.
Mrs. W. G. Alfred (Anna)

BAKED RED SNAPPER

1 4-5 pound red snapper
1 lemon
½ cup cooking oil
2 8-ounce cans tomato sauce
3 cloves garlic (minced)
Green onion tops, parsley, to taste, chopped
Salt, black pepper and cayenne (red) pepper to taste
⅔ cups chopped onion
⅓ cup chopped celery
2 cups cold water
1 16-ounce can whole Italian tomatoes
¼ teaspoon oregano
1 7½-ounce can Progresso Egg Plant Appetizer (caponata) (optional)

Put oil in heavy pot with celery, garlic and chopped onion. Cook until onions are wilted, stirring constantly. Add whole tomatoes and tomato sauce. Cook for approximately 40 minutes or until oil separates from tomatoes. Add cold water and season to taste with salt, black pepper and cayenne. Cook in uncovered pot for 20 minutes. Season fish with black pepper, cayenne, salt and oregano and place in baking dish. Before pouring sauce mixture over fish add caponata if desired. Pour sauce mixture over fish and place in a 325 degree oven for 35 to 45 minutes continually basting fish with sauce. When fish is done garnish with thin slices of lemon, green onion tops and parsley. Serve with rice. Serves 5-7.
Don Attaway

Thank God for dirty dishes. They have a tale to tell, while others go hungry we are eating very well. With home, health and happiness we shouldn't want to fuss. For by this stack of evidence God is really good to us.

Poultry · Game

The homes of the early pioneers were hurriedly and crudely built of logs which were usually two single log rooms connected by a gallery or "dog run" which made the most of the breeze and was also used for storage.

When sawmills arrived and smoother lumber was available, homes were built more spacious and columns were added across the front. Kitchens were seldom included under the same roof.

Food consisted of game, corn and wild honey. Corn was easily raised and left in the field until needed. Each home had a spinning wheel and loom, and clothing was made of home-spun cloth. Calico, which cost 50 cents a yard, was used for party dresses, and many men wore buckskin suits which were durable, warm and cheap. Moccasins were worn instead of shoes and only a few of the pioneers wore "store bought" clothes.

Located on the river highway to New Orleans and only 20 miles from the Republic of Texas, Shreveport flourished. The lure of the west kept a steady stream of Americans and European immigrants flowing through the city.

Every covered wagon, flatboat, barge and steamboat brought business, as did every hunter and every trapper with packs of pelts from the wilderness. Deer hides, buffalo robes, smoked buffalo tongue, venison hams, wild honey, beeswax, and even bear oil were important cargo in the very early days.

Settlers around the present site of Dallas and northward to the Red River looked to Shreveport for supplies and a market for their cotton, cattle, hides and furs.

PAULET MAISON

4 to 5 whole fryer chicken breasts
4 tablespoons butter or margarine
1 envelope instant chicken bouillon mix or 1 cube
¾ cup water
1 teaspoon salt
⅛ teaspoon pepper
2 tablespoons cut chives (fresh or freeze dried)
1 tablespoon chopped parsley
¼ teaspoon dried leaf thyme
¼ teaspoon rosemary
½ cup cream (heavy)
¼ cup sauterne
¼ cup toasted slivered or sliced almonds

Halve breasts. Brown slowly in butter in large skillet over low heat, about 20 minutes. Dissolve chicken bouillon in water; add with all remaining ingredients except heavy cream, wine and almonds. Blend well, cover; simmer 15 minutes or until chicken is tender. Remove chicken; keep warm. Add heavy cream to pan liquid; stir and heat to serving temperature. (Do not boil.) Stir in wine. Serve in rice ring pouring sauce over chicken or serving separately. Scatter almonds over all.
Mrs. Ronald E. Pitkin (Phyrne), Alexandria, Virginia

SPICY CHICKEN BAKE

3 cups chicken, cut in bite-size pieces
1 package Pepperidge Farm cornbread stuffing mix
½ cup butter or margarine
½ cup flour
½ teaspoon pepper
½ teaspoon salt
Dash of cayenne pepper
4 cups chicken broth
6 eggs, slightly beaten

Make stuffing by directions on package. Spread stuffing in 13x9x3-inch baking pan and top with chopped chicken. Melt butter saucepan; add flour, seasonings and cool broth. Cook on low heat, stirring until thick. Stir a small amount of hot mix into the beaten eggs. Mix all together and pour over chicken. Bake at 325 degrees for 45 minutes. Let stand for 5 minutes before serving. Serve with the following sauce:

Sauce:
1 10¾-ounce can cream of mushroom soup
¼ cup milk
1 cup sour cream
¼ cup chopped pimiento

Combine all ingredients, heat over low flame until hot.
Mrs. Charles L. Ogletree (Linda)

BAKED CHICKEN CASSEROLE

- 1 5-ounce can boned chicken
- 1 can condensed cream of chicken soup
- 1 cup diced celery
- 2 teaspoons minced onion
- ½ cup chopped walnuts or pecans
- ½ teaspoon salt
- ¼ teaspoon pepper
- ¾ cup mayonnaise
- 3 hard cooked eggs, chopped
- 2 cups crushed potato chips

Dice boned chicken. Combine chicken and juices in a 9-inch baking dish with soup, celery, onion, nuts, salt, pepper, mayonnaise and eggs. Top with potato chips. Bake in hot oven (450 degrees) about 20 minutes. Makes six to eight servings.

Mrs. W. D. Sandifer, Jr. (Evelyn)

BAKED CHICKEN 'N NOODLES

- 1 10¾-ounce can cream of mushroom soup
- ½ cup milk
- 2 cups diced cooked chicken
- 2 cups cooked noodles
- 2 tablespoons diced pimiento
- 1 tablespoon chopped parsley
- ½ cup buttered bread crumbs

Blend soup and milk; add chicken, noodles, pimiento and parsley. Spoon into a 1 quart casserole; sprinkle crumbs on top. Bake at 375 degrees for about 25 minutes.

Mrs. Ralph Garrett (Dottie)

PARMESAN CHICKEN

- ½ cup Parmesan cheese
- ¼ cup flour
- 1 teaspoon salt
- Dash pepper
- ¼ cup butter
- 2 chicken breasts, split
- 1 egg, slightly beaten
- 1 tablespoon milk

Heat oven to 350 degrees. Combine cheese, flour, and seasonings. Dip chicken in combined egg and milk. Coat with cheese mixture. Pour butter over chicken. Bake 1 hour or 15 minutes on high in a microwave oven.

Mrs. Ronny Goodman (Janice)

HOT CHICKEN SALAD I

2 cups cooked chopped chicken
½ cup chopped almonds
1 cup mayonnaise
2 tablespoons lemon juice
2 cups thinly sliced celery
2 teaspoons grated onion
1 teaspoon salt
¼ teaspoon curry powder
1 cup crushed potato chips
½ cup grated cheese

Mix all ingredients except potato chips and cheese. Put into baking dish and cover with chips and cheese. Bake at 400 degrees for 25 minutes.
Mrs. Ralph Garrett (Dottie)

HOT CHICKEN SALAD II

4 cups cooked chicken, chopped
4 cups celery, chopped
2 cups seasoned croutons
2 cups mayonnaise
1 cup slivered almonds
4 tablespoons lemon juice
4 tablespoons chopped onion
1 teaspoon salt
1 cup grated cheese
2 cups crushed potato chips

Mix all ingredients except cheese and potato chips. If ingredients are to be mixed in advance and not cooked immediately, wait until ready to put in oven to add croutons, as they need to remain crisp. Place in large baking dish. Sprinkle with layer of cheese, then potato chips on top. Cook about 15 minutes or until bubbly at 400 degrees. (Potato chips will burn easily.)
Mrs. John E. Ewing (Helen)

BAKED CHICKEN CAMILLE

2 pounds chicken drumsticks or thighs
½ cup flour
2 teaspoons salt
⅛ teaspoon pepper
3 tablespoons butter or other fat
1 can condensed cream of mushroom soup
⅔ cup water

Mix flour, salt and pepper. Roll chicken in seasoned flour. Sauté chicken in hot fat in skillet, turning to brown. Remove chicken to 2-quart baking dish. Combine soup and water with drippings in skillet, blending well. Pour over chicken. Cover and bake in moderate oven (350 degrees) for 45 minutes; then uncover and bake until tender — 15 to 30 minutes. Serves 6.
Mrs. W. D. Sandifer, Jr. (Evelyn)

CHICKEN SOUFFLÉ

1 small hen (4-5 pounds)
8 slices bread
4 eggs, beaten
1 cup chicken broth
1 can cream of mushroom soup
1 pint milk
1 stick butter
1 onion, grated
1 can cream of celery soup

Sauce:
1 can mushroom soup
½ stick butter
½ can (soup can) water
1 small jar pimiento

Cook chicken until tender, cool, slice meat from bone. Butter large baking dish and place chicken in bottom. Heat soups, milk, broth and butter to boiling point. Pour over bread, cover and let steam a few minutes. Mash bread well, add onions and eggs, salt and pepper. Mix well and pour over chicken. Bake at 400 degrees until light brown.

Mix and heat to boiling point the mushroom soup, water, butter and pimiento for the sauce mix. Pour over casserole.

Mrs. Joseph LaBarbera

EGG FOO YUNG

1 can Chinese mixed vegetables
1 cup chopped chicken
½ teaspoon salt
1 tablespoon butter or oleo
6 eggs, well beaten
1 medium onion, chopped
¼ teaspoon monosodium glutamate
Salt and pepper to taste

Chinese Brown Gravy:
4 tablespoons bacon drippings
2½ tablespoons soy sauce
Dash of pepper
4 tablespoons flour
1 teaspoon brown gravy sauce

Drain vegetables; reserve 1⅔ cups liquid for gravy. Combine eggs, vegetables, chicken, onion and seasonings. Melt butter in skillet. Pour one-half of mixture into skillet; cook until set and brown on edges. Turn; brown other side. Repeat with remaining mixture. Serve with Chinese brown gravy.

Chinese brown gravy: Melt drippings; blend in flour, add soy sauce, brown gravy sauce, pepper and reserved vegetable liquid. Stir constantly, until smooth and thickened. Serves 6.

Mrs. Eileen LaBarbera

YORKSHIRE CHICKEN

⅓ cup enriched flour
2 teaspoons salt
1½ teaspoons sage
¼ teaspoon pepper
1 2½ to 3-pound fryer, cut up
¼ cup fat
1 cup sifted enriched flour
1 teaspoon baking powder
1 teaspoon salt
3 well beaten eggs
1½ cups milk
¼ cup butter or margarine, melted
¼ cup snipped parsley

Combine ⅓ cup flour, 2 teaspoons salt, sage and pepper; coat chicken with this mixture. Brown in hot fat; place in 2 quart casserole. Sift together the 1 cup flour, baking powder and salt. Combine eggs, milk, butter, and parsley; add to flour mixture; stir until smooth. Pour over chicken. Bake in moderate oven (350 degrees) about one hour. Yield: 4 servings.
Mrs. W. D. Sandifer, Jr. (Evelyn)

CHICKEN POT PIE

1 4 or 5-pound hen
2 ribs of celery
2 bay leaves
⅛ teaspoon nutmeg
1 medium onion
¼ cup flour
2 or 3 boiled eggs
2 tablespoons margarine

Boil hen with celery, bay leaves, and nutmeg. Remove meat from bone and strain broth. Sauté onion in margarine. Add flour, then add 2½ cups of broth, cook until thick. Add cut-up chicken and cut-up boiled eggs. Put in casserole. Make pie crust and put over top and bake in 400 degree oven until brown. If you like, brush top with beaten egg yolk. You may also add green peas and pimiento to mixture before topping.
Mrs. W. S. Bynum (Curla)

STACY'S CHICKEN BREASTS

6 chicken breast halves
1 package dry onion soup mix
1 small jar apricot preserves
½ bottle red Russian dressing

Place chicken breast halves in shallow baking pan. Combine the onion soup mix, preserves and dressing; pour over chicken. Bake covered in 350 degree oven for one hour.
Mrs. Bruce Baker (Stacy), Baton Rouge, Louisiana

CHICKEN ENCHILADAS

1 3-pound chicken
2 6-ounce frozen tortillas
1 pound Monterey Jack cheese, grated
1 onion, minced fine
1 10¾-ounce can cream of chicken soup
2 tablespoons Crisco oil
2 No. 2 cans Rotel tomatoes (drained)
1 carton sour cream
1 tablespoon cumin powder
Salt and pepper to taste
2 cups sharp cheese, grated

Boil chicken in well seasoned water until tender; debone and cut up in small pieces. Sauté chopped onion in small amount of Crisco oil until clear. Add soup and tomatoes (cut up tomatoes). Add seasonings. Blend in sour cream, heat well, and remove from heat.

Tortillas — preheat ¼ inch oil in skillet. Fry each tortilla about 3 seconds, drain on paper towels.

In an oblong casserole dish, layer as follows: tortillas, chicken, and Monterey Jack cheese. Two layers of all this is plenty. Pour sauce over this and top with grated sharp cheese. Bake in 350 degree oven for about 45 minutes or until it is hot all the way through and bubbly, and the cheese is well melted.

Mrs. Dale Ward (Renee)

MEXICAN CHICKEN CASSEROLE

1 whole chicken, boiled
1 medium bag Doritos
1 can Ro-tel tomatoes with chilies
½ cup onion
¼ teaspoon garlic
Salt to taste
Pepper to taste
2 10¾-ounce cans cream of chicken soup
1 cup grated cheddar cheese

Boil chicken until done and debone. Save broth. Soak Doritos in the broth until tender but not limp. Line a baking dish (9x4-inches) with these Doritos. In separate bowl mix together the chicken, tomatoes, onion, garlic, salt and pepper, Mix thoroughly. Spread this mixture over the Doritos. Spoon the soup (undiluted) over the chicken mixture and top with grated cheese. Bake at 350 degrees for 30 minutes. Serve with cornbread and salad. Serves 4 very well. (For the left over turkey at Thanksgiving, use it in this casserole for a different flavor.)

Mrs. W. Glen Mangham (Betty)

MEXICAN STYLE CHICKEN CASSEROLE

- 1 chicken (boiled)
- 1 10¾-ounce can cream of mushroom soup
- 1 10¾-ounce can cream of celery soup
- 1 10-ounce can Ro-tel tomatoes and chilies
- 1 medium onion (chopped)
- 2 tablespoons butter
- 1 8½-ounce bag dip size Fritos
- ½ pound cheese (grated)

Debone chicken and cut in bite size pieces. Set aside. In sauce pan heat butter and sauté onion. Add mushroom soup, celery soup and Ro-tel tomatoes. Stir and heat until mixed well. Add chicken and Fritos. Stir until well coated. Pour in casserole dish. Top with cheese and heat in 400 degree oven for 20 minutes.

Mrs. R. L. McIlwain (Linda)

CHICKEN AND ARTICHOKE CASSEROLE

- 2 3-pound fryers
- 1 cup butter
- ½ cup flour flour
- 3 ounces Gruyere cheese
- ½ tablespoon Tabasco
- 2 large cans (8-ounce) mushrooms drained
- 2 large cans (14-ounce) artichokes, drained and quartered
- 3½ cups milk
- 1 tablespoon Accent
- 2 cloves garlic, mashed
- ⅛ pound rat cheese

Boil chicken in seasoned water. Remove skin and bone and cut meat into large pieces. Set aside. Melt butter, stir in flour until well blended. Slowly add milk and stir until the sauce is smooth and thick. Add cheeses and seasonings. Stir until cheese melts and sauce bubbles. Add chicken, mushrooms, and artichokes to the sauce. Pour into casserole. Bake at 350 degrees for 30 minutes. Serves 12.

Mrs. Fran Lorant Moore

CHICKEN CONTINENTAL

- 6 chicken breasts
- 1 2½-ounce jar dried beef
- 1 can cream of mushroom soup
- 6 slices bacon
- ½ pint sour cream

Place slices of beef in bottom of casserole. Wrap chicken breasts in bacon slices and secure with toothpicks. Mix sour cream and soup. Put chicken in casserole on top of beef and pour soup mixture over same. Bake in 300 degree oven for one and a half hours. (Do not salt chicken.)

Mrs. Mary Wells

CHICKEN WITH DROP DUMPLINGS

1 3½ to 4-pound chicken
1 teaspoon salt
1½ cups all purpose flour
3 teaspoons double acting baking powder
½ teaspoon salt
1 cup milk
1 teaspoon minced parsley
¼ teaspoon celery seed
½ teaspoon yellow food coloring

Cook chicken with teaspoon salt in enough water to have 3 pints broth when chicken is done. Bring to a boil and simmer gently — 1 to 1½ hours or until chicken can be easily removed from bone. Remove chicken from broth and bring broth to a rolling boil. Then combine flour, baking powder, salt, milk and parsley, celery seed and food coloring and blend thoroughly. Drop dumpling batter by the teaspoonful into the boiling broth. Drop dumplings as quickly as possible into pot, lower heat and simmer lightly covered for about 12 minutes. Then add deboned chicken to dumplings and serve in a large tureen.
Mrs. Marvin Kines (Ora)

CHICKEN WITH CASHEW NUTS, MANDARIN STYLE

3½ pounds chicken breasts
2 tablespoons cornstarch
Peanut or corn oil
1 green pepper cut in ½-inch slices
1 onion or ½ bunch green onions, very thinly sliced
1 4-ounce can bamboo shoots (not sliced) cut in ½-inch slices
1 4-ounce can water chestnuts, sliced
Salt, freshly ground pepper, garlic salt
½ pound whole cashew nuts

Bone and skin chicken breasts. Cut chicken into 1-inch pieces and mix with cornstarch, then 4 tablespoons oil. Heat 1½ inches oil in a large skillet and fry chicken over high heat for 40 seconds. Remove chicken to a strainer to drain off excess oil. Heat 7 tablespoons oil in skillet and fry green pepper and onion for 1 minute; then add bamboo shoots and water chestnuts and cook ½ minute. Add chicken; season to taste with garlic salt, salt and pepper and toss together for 2 minutes. Turn off heat and mix in cashew nuts. Serves 8.
Mrs. Robert L. Snead (Shirley)

CHICKEN GUMBO I

1 large chicken
1 bell pepper, chopped
3 green onions, chopped
½ teaspoon filé
Tabasco to taste
2 tablespoons soy sauce
2 chicken bouillon cubes
2 tablespoons shortening or bacon grease
2 medium onions, chopped
5 stalks celery, chopped
2 packages frozen cut okra
2 tablespoons cumin
Salt & pepper to taste
2 bay leaves
½ cup flour

Brown flour in shortening or bacon grease, in large pot. When smooth, fill pot with boiling water; add chicken, bell pepper, onions, celery, okra, soy sauce, bouillon cubes, cumin, Tabasco, bay leaves, salt and pepper. After 30 minutes remove chicken and debone. Replace chicken and cook at slow boil for 1 hour. After cooking, turn out fire and add filé. Serve with rice.
Mrs. Louis R. Jaudon (Betty)

CHICKEN GUMBO II

1 large fryer
1 pound okra
2 medium size onions (chopped)
2 cups celery (chopped)
1 clove garlic (chopped)
1 tablespoon margarine
½ pound cooked carrots
1 cup rice (cooked)
2 tablespoons bouillon (chicken)
Pepper and salt to taste

Cook chicken until tender. Reserve broth. Remove bone and skin from chicken and cut into bite size pieces. Boil okra and drain into colander. Sauté celery, onions, and garlic in margarine until tender. Set broth in refrigerator for a few minutes until fat settles on top. Remove fat and add bouillon and all the rest of the ingredients. Simmer for about 25 minutes. Can be frozen.
Mrs. F. A. Kihneman (Tora)

CHICKEN CHESTS

4 whole chicken breasts
1 3½-ounce bottle chipped beef
8 strips bacon
1 pint sour cream
2 cans cream of chicken soup

Put chipped beef in bottom of baking dish; wrap bacon around chicken breasts. Cover chicken with soup and sour cream. Bake three hours uncovered in 300 degree oven. Great to serve when you have in-laws over! Serves 4.
Mrs. J. R. Rader (Judy)

CURRIED CHICKEN DIVAN

4 large boiled, deboned chicken breasts
2 10-ounce packages frozen, chopped broccoli
1 can condensed cream of chicken soup, undiluted
⅓ cup evaporated milk
⅔ cup mayonnaise or salad dressing
1 teaspoon salt
¾ cup grated sharp cheddar cheese
2 teaspoons lemon juice
½ teaspoon curry powder
2 tablespoons melted butter
½ cup dried bread crumbs

Cut boiled chicken breasts into bite size pieces. Boil broccoli until almost tender; drain well. In bowl mix the soup, milk, mayonnaise, salt, cheese, lemon juice and curry powder. Mix separately the melted butter and bread crumbs.

Grease well a two quart baking dish. Arrange broccoli in bottom and cover with ⅓ of sauce mixture. Add chicken and cover with remaining sauce. Sprinkle the mixture of butter and bread crumbs and sprinkle over top. Place under 550 degree broiler for a few minutes to brown.

Mrs. W. D. Sandifer, Jr. (Evelyn)

CHICKEN WITH RICE

1 3-pound fryer
Salt to taste
3 tablespoons corn oil
1 medium onion (chopped fine)
1 clove garlic (chopped fine)
1 bell pepper (chopped)
1 16-ounce can stewed tomatoes
¼ teaspoon pepper
½ teaspoon paprika
2 whole cloves
1 bay leaf
1 cup water
1¼ cups uncooked rice
1 cup small English peas
1 2-ounce jar pimiento

Cut up fryer in serving pieces and salt. Use dutch oven and heat corn oil. Put chicken in pot and brown. Add onion, garlic, bell pepper, and brew for 5 minutes. Add tomatoes, pepper, paprika, cloves, bay leaf, water, peas and ½ of the pimiento. Cover and bring to a boil. Lower flame and simmer 15 minutes. Add rice, boil and stir until well mixed. Cover and simmer 30 more minutes. Garnish with the reserved pimiento and a few of the peas.

Mrs. F. A. Kihneman (Tora)

CHICKEN AND WILD RICE CASSEROLE

2 3-pound fryers
1 cup dry cooking sherry (Chablis)
1½ teaspoons salt
½ teaspoon curry powder
1 medium onion, sliced
1 cup sliced celery
1 pound fresh mushrooms or 2 6-ounce packages frozen in butter
¼ cup oleo
2 6-ounce packages long grain rice with seasoning
1 cup sour cream
1 10¾-ounce can cream of mushroom soup

Place whole chicken in deep kettle with water, sherry, salt, curry powder, onion and celery. Bring to a boil. Reduce heat and simmer for one hour, covered. Remove from heat. Strain broth. Refrigerate chicken and broth at once. When chicken is cool, remove from bones and cut into bite sized pieces. Wash mushrooms and pat dry. Sauté in oleo until golden brown or follow package directions if using frozen mushrooms. Reserve enough to make a circle on top of casserole. Slice other mushrooms in half. Measure chicken broth and use as part of liquid for cooking rice. Follow package directions for firm rice (25 minutes). Combine chicken, rice and mushrooms in 3½ to 4-quart casserole. Blend sour cream with undiluted soup. Toss together with chicken mixture. Arrange reserved mushrooms in circle on top. Cover and refrigerate. To heat, bake at 350 degrees for 1 hour. This can be made ahead — or frozen. Serves 8 to 10 people.
Mrs. Ralph Garrett (Dottie)

CHICKEN 'N RICE CASSEROLE

¾ cup long grain rice (uncooked)
1 envelope onion soup mix (dry)
1 10¾-ounce can cream of mushroom soup and 1 can water
1 fryer cut up in serving pieces
¼ to ½ cup Italian salad dressing

Grease an 8x12-inch casserole dish, mix dry onion soup mix with rice and pour in casserole. Combine mushroom soup and water, pour ½ of the mixture over the rice and stir. Dip chicken in Italian dressing and place on top of rice. Pour remaining soup mixture over chicken (you may pour the remaining salad dressing over also) and bake 1½ hours at 300 degrees.
Mrs. Dale Ward (Renee)

EASY CHICKEN AND RICE CASSEROLE

3-4 strips bacon
1 box Uncle Ben's wild rice
1 chicken (uncooked) (or pork chops)
1 10¾-ounce can mushroom soup (or chicken)
1 soup can of boiling water

Line bottom of 10x13-inch Pyrex casserole dish with raw bacon strips. Pour layer of rice. Place pieces of chicken around on rice. Spoon can of soup on top of chicken. Pour can of boiling water in between the chicken (so soup will not be washed off). Cover tightly with foil and bake in oven at 325 degrees for 2 hours or until most of liquid is cooked out.
Mrs. Roy F. Brabham (Jean)

What is patience? Patience is when you idle your motor when you feel like stripping your gears.

Unknown

CHICKEN ELEGANTE

6 chicken breasts, skinned
Salt
Pepper
Paprika
1 stick melted margarine
¼ teaspoon basil
¼ teaspoon rosemary
½ cup chopped onion
1 4-ounce can mushrooms with liquid
½ cup slivered almonds
½ lemon, juiced
¼ cup cooking sherry
1 can mushroom soup
1-1½ cups uncooked rice

In large pan sprayed with Pam, lay chicken breasts and sprinkle with salt, pepper and paprika. Mix the 9 next ingredients and pour over chicken breasts. Preheat oven to 350 degrees. Cook 1 hour. Cook rice; put in middle of platter, place chicken around and pour part of the gravy over the rice. Serve remaining gravy in sauce dish. Serves 6.
Mrs. L. A. McKinley (Elizabeth), Magnolia Springs, Alabama

ESCALLOPED CHICKEN AND AVOCADO

1 small white onion, finely chopped
3 tablespoons butter
3 tablespoons flour
½ teaspoon salt
1 cup cream
¾ cup milk
¼ cup dry sherry
2 cups diced cooked chicken
1 3-ounce can whole or sliced mushrooms
1 cup grated aged cheddar cheese
⅛ teaspoon dried dill or rosemary
1 large avocado

Cook onion slowly in butter until soft but not browned. Blend in flour and salt. Slowly stir in cream and milk; continue cooking and stirring until mixture boils and thickens. Blend in wine, chicken, mushrooms, about half the cheese, and dill or rosemary. Turn mixture into a shallow baking dish or individual bakers. Cut avocado into slices and arrange over creamed chicken, topping with remaining cheese. Bake in a slow oven, 300 degrees, until cheese melts — about 5 to 10 minutes. Serves 4.

Mrs. Leonard Green, Jr. (June)

CHICKEN-BROCCOLI CASSEROLE

8 chicken breasts or 2 small chickens
Salt and pepper to taste
3 packages frozen broccoli
3 cans cream of chicken soup
1 teaspoon curry
1½ cups mayonnaise
1 tablespoon lemon juice
1½ cups grated cheese
1 cup Ritz cracker crumbs, buttered crumbs, crushed potato chips, or crackers

Boil chicken until tender with salt and pepper to taste. In a bowl, add mayonnaise, curry, lemon juice, and soup. Defrost broccoli and remove excess moisture. Heavily butter or spray with Pam, 2 large baking dishes. Spread drained broccoli on bottom of dishes. Add layer of chicken. Pour soup over chicken. Add layer of cheese and top with crumbs. Bake at 350 degrees in preheated oven, for 20 minutes — or until bubbly all through.

Add a salad and light dessert and you have a complete meal.

One dish may be served upon completion and the other might be frozen and heated later.

Mrs. John R. Clement (Martha)

CHICKEN BROCCOLI

- 6 chicken breasts
- 2 packages frozen chopped broccoli
- 1 10¾-ounce can cream of mushroom soup
- 1 10¾-ounce can cream of chicken soup
- 1 4-ounce can mushroom pieces
- Juice of one lemon
- 1 cup grated cheese

Boil chicken in water with salt and pepper to taste. Remove chicken from broth and put broccoli in broth and cook until a little tender. Debone chicken and place in large baking dish with drained broccoli. Combine soups, mushrooms and lemon juice and pour over chicken and broccoli. Cover with grated cheese and bake at 350 degrees for 45 minutes. Serves 8-10.

Mrs. J. W. Allen (Lois)

CHICKEN CASSEROLE I

- 1 hen or large fryer
- 1 medium onion
- 2 ribs celery
- 1 2-ounce can pimiento
- Salt and pepper
- 1 10-ounce can tomatoes
- 1 8½-ounce can peas
- 1 2½-ounce can mushrooms (pieces)
- 1 4-ounce package noodles (large cut)

Cook chicken until it comes loose from the bone. Remove chicken bones and skins. Remove all chicken from broth. Add noodles to broth. Cook until tender. Add salt and pepper to taste. Onion and celery are chopped up and cooked with the chicken. Last, add all other ingredients and simmer until seasoning is thoroughly cooked through. Put into casserole dish and bake until brown at 350 degrees. Portions left can be frozen for later use.

Mrs. W. S. Bynum (Curla)

CHICKEN CASSEROLE II

- 6 single chicken breasts
- 3 10-ounce boxes frozen broccoli
- 2 10¾-ounce cans cream of chicken soup
- 2 ribs celery
- 1 cup bread crumbs
- Salt and pepper to taste
- ½ tablespoon lemon juice
- 2 green onions (shallots)
- 1 cup mayonnaise
- 1 block sharp cheddar cheese (grated)
- ½ stick margarine

Boil chicken with celery, green onions, salt and pepper until tender. Drain and set aside to cool. Cook broccoli according to directions on box. Drain and set aside. Mix chicken soup and mayonnaise with lemon juice. Grease a 9x12-inch pan. Debone chicken and cut into bite size pieces. Place a layer of chicken, grated cheese, broccoli and ⅓ cup soup-mayonnaise mixture over this. Repeat layers and top with bread crumbs which have been sautéed in margarine. Wrap pan with foil, place in freezer 24 hours. Allow to thaw naturally, place in cold oven. Bake 45 minutes at 350 degrees. Remove foil and bake until crumbs are brown and casserole is bubbling.

Mrs. Lois Mambourg

CHICKEN CASSEROLE III

- 1 chicken cut in serving pieces
- 1 stick butter
- 1 4-ounce can mushrooms
- 1 tablespoon flour
- 2 tablespoons Worcestershire sauce
- 1 bay leaf
- Lemon juice
- 1 can beef bouillon

Melt butter in skillet. Salt and pepper chicken and brown well in melted butter. Take out and put in large casserole dish. Brown mushrooms in some butter, and take out and place with chicken. Add the flour to the butter and mix well. Add Worcestershire sauce, bay leaf, lemon juice and beef bouillon. Pour over chicken and mushrooms and cook for one hour in oven. The chicken and mushrooms get brown and gravy thickens.

This may be prepared a day in advance. Next day, cook in oven until hot and bubbly. Serves 4 people.

Mrs. Jean K. Rice

MOLDED CHICKEN

1 tablespoons unflavored gelatin
2 cups hot stock
1 cooked hen (deboned and skinned, chopped fine)
1 tablespoon Worcestershire sauce
1 2-ounce jar pimiento (cut fine)
Juice of 1 lemon
1 cup celery (chopped)
1 cup nuts (chopped)
1 cup sliced stuffed olives
3 hard boiled eggs
¾ cup mayonnaise

Dissolve gelatin in the cold water. Add the hot stock. Mix well and add other ingredients. Pour into molds and put in refrigerator to set. Unmold and serve on lettuce leaf.

Mrs. Clyde Garner

CHICKEN CACCIATORE

1 medium onion (chopped)
1 medium green pepper (chopped)
3 tablespoons salad oil or olive oil
1 3-pound fryer (cut into serving pieces)
1 teaspoon salt
⅛ teaspoon black pepper
1 clove garlic
1 16-ounce can tomatoes
1 4-ounce can mushrooms (whole)
1 tablespoon wine vinegar
½ teaspoon rosemary
½ teaspoon sugar
½ cup cooking wine (optional)

Sauté onion and green pepper in 1 tablespoon of the oil about 5 minutes. Use a large frying pan. Remove onion and pepper from pan. Sprinkle chicken with salt and black pepper; brown until golden color in same frying pan, using the remaining oil and the garlic. Return onions and green pepper to pan; add tomatoes, mushrooms and liquid, vinegar, rosemary, sugar, and the cooking wine. Cover tightly and simmer 40 minutes or until chicken is tender when pierced with a fork. Serves 4.

Miss Jo Lodestro

CHICKEN TETRAZZINI I

Large hen — cook in plenty of water and let stand in broth overnight.

1 9-ounce package spaghetti
½ pound American cheese
½ pound Old English cheese
1 4-ounce can mushrooms, undrained
1 onion, finely chopped
1 green pepper, finely chopped

White Sauce:
¼ pound butter
¾ cup flour
1 quart milk
Salt and pepper, moderately

Make white sauce as usual.

Chop chicken, mix with spaghetti, add other ingredients. Add cream sauce last and mix all thoroughly. Bake 40 minutes at 350 degrees. Serves 8-10.

Mrs. Margaret Copeland

CHICKEN TETRAZZINI II

2 tablespoons onion (chopped)
1 tablespoon butter or oleo
1 10¾-ounce can cream of mushroom soup
½ cup water
1 cup shredded sharp process cheese
2 tablespoons pimiento (chopped)
1 tablespoon sherry wine (if desired)
6 ounces spaghetti (cooked and drained)
1 cup cooked chicken, turkey, or ham (chopped)
1 tablespoon parsley (chopped)

Place butter or oleo in saucepan, add the onion and cook until tender. Blend in soup, water, cheese and sherry. Cook over heat until cheese is melted. Stir often. Add cooked, drained spaghetti, chicken, pimiento and parsley and heat well. Serves 4.

Mrs. W. A. Doyle (Frances)

JEAN'S CHICKEN TETRAZZINI III

5-6 pound hen
1 8-ounce package egg noodles
½ pound butter or margarine
¾ cup flour
1 quart milk
½ pound Old English cheddar cheese
Salt and pepper to taste
1 3-ounce can grated Parmesan cheese
1 8-ounce can of sliced mushrooms
1 medium onion (chopped)
1 large green pepper (chopped)

Cook hen in salted water until tender. Allow to stand in broth overnight. Debone chicken and cut into bite size pieces. Cook noodles in chicken broth. Melt butter, stir in flour and make a paste. Gradually add milk and stir. Cook until it makes thick smooth sauce. Add both cheese, allowing to melt. Mix chicken pieces, noodles, and the cheese sauce. Add remaining ingredients. Bake 45 minutes to 1 hour at 350 degrees until casserole is bubbling. Great dish for freezing.
Mrs. E. M. Stevens (Jean)

Part of the secret of success in life is to eat what you like and let the food fight it out inside!

Mark Twain

CHICKEN SPAGHETTI I

1 chicken, boiled; de-boned
2 8-ounce cans tomato sauce
Salt to taste
½ tablespoon brown sugar
¼ teaspoon garlic
½ cup onion, chopped fine
½ teaspoon oregano
Pepper to taste
1 whole bay leaf
½ package spaghetti

Boil chicken and remove bones. In a skillet combine all ingredients except for the spaghetti and simmer for about 30 to 45 minutes. Remove bay leaf and pour over the cooked spaghetti. Serves 3 to 4. (Rice may be substituted for the spaghetti.)
Mrs. Kenneth Braswell (Debbie)

CHICKEN SPAGHETTI II

- 1 fryer and 4 chicken breasts
- 3 stalks celery
- 1 large green pepper
- 2 onions
- 1 10-ounce package spaghetti
- 1 pound Velveeta cheese, grated
- 2 pods garlic
- 1 4-ounce can mushrooms
- Parmesan cheese
- 1 can mushroom soup
- 1 can tomatoes
- Salt
- Pepper
- Paprika
- Worcestershire sauce

Cook chicken, debone. In 1 quart of the chicken broth put in celery, pepper, onions, garlic, and cook about 10 minutes or longer. Add spaghetti to broth and cook. Add mushroom soup and tomatoes. Add grated cheese and deboned chicken. Add salt, pepper, Worcestershire sauce, and paprika. Add all of these to your own taste. Put in 9x13-inch Pyrex dish, cover with Parmesan cheese and bake at 350 degrees for 30-45 minutes — until bubbly. Will freeze well. Take out of freezer and let thaw one day in bottom refrigerator. Bake about 1 hour or until hot through and through.

Mrs. Clara Cummins, Bossier City, Louisiana

CHICKEN SPAGHETTI III

- 1 stewing chicken
- 1 stick oleo
- 1 cup bell pepper, chopped
- 1 cup celery, chopped
- 1 cup onion, chopped
- 1 pound Velveeta cheese
- 1 10¾-ounce can mushroom soup
- 1 4-ounce can mushroom pieces
- 1 4-ounce jar pimiento, chopped
- ¾ cup chicken broth
- 1 pound package spaghetti

Boil chicken in enough salted water to cover. Debone chicken and dice. Melt oleo; add pepper, celery, onion, and cook about 30 minutes. Add mushroom soup, ¾ cup broth, pimiento, and mushroom pieces and cook 15 minutes. Add chicken; stir. Add cheese which has been cut in small pieces and cook until melted.

Cook spaghetti in remaining broth. When done, drain and add to chicken mixture.

Mrs. Louis R. Jaudon (Betty)

CHICKEN SPAGHETTI IV

1 chicken (or chicken breasts), boiled and boned
2 cups celery, chopped
1 cup onions, chopped
1 bell pepper, chopped
1 stick oleo
1 16-ounce can stewed tomatoes
1 button garlic, chopped
1 10¾-ounce can cream of celery soup
1 2½-ounce can mushrooms, chopped
1 teaspoon oregano
1 teaspoon paprika
1 teaspoon Worcestershire sauce
½ package spaghetti (cooked with salt and pepper to taste)
½ to 1 cup grated cheddar cheese

Sauté garlic, onions, pepper and celery in oleo. Add seasonings, stewed tomatoes and soup. Simmer about thirty (30) minutes, add mushrooms, chopped chicken and spaghetti. (Cook spaghetti in chicken broth or if mixture seems dry, add cream of chicken soup.) Put in greased baking dish, cover with grated cheese and bake in oven about thirty (30) minutes at 350 degrees.

Mrs. H. Russell Maddox (Tommie Lue)

CHICKEN SPAGHETTI V

1 3 to 5-pound hen, steamed until it falls from bones
1 2-pound package thin spaghetti cooked in chicken stock
1 cup chopped onion
1½ cups chopped celery
1 9-ounce can chopped mushrooms
1 6-ounce can tomato paste
1 teaspoon poultry seasoning
½ teaspoon chili powder
3 minced garlic buttons
1 small bell pepper, chopped
1 14-ounce can tomatoes
1 4-ounce can chopped ripe olives
1 4-ounce can water chestnuts, coarsely chopped

Sauté onion, celery, garlic and bell pepper in bacon fat until soft and golden.

Make browned roux of bacon fat, flour and salt and pepper, using chicken stock for liquid. Add tomatoes, tomato paste, mushrooms, poultry seasoning, ripe olives, water chestnuts and chili powder. Cook slowly until thick. Cut up chicken with scissors and add chicken and spaghetti to sauce in deep kettle. Cook slowly until flavors are well blended. 8 to 10 generous servings.

Bernice W. Stephenson

CHICKEN AND SPAGHETTI VI

2 large fryers
2 cups celery
1 large bell pepper
1 large onion
1 large button garlic (finely chopped)
1 dash chili powder
1 pound package spaghetti

Boil chicken in sufficient amount of water until tender. Remove chicken and chop up. Mix chicken and vegetables and add sufficient amount of broth and cook until tender. Use remaining broth and cook 1 pound package of spaghetti until tender. Mix all ingredients together and season with chili powder. Start with 2 tablespoons and make brick red. If not enough, slowly add more.
Mrs. Jo Whittaker

CHICKEN SPAGHETTI FOR 12 VII

1 5 pound hen
3 1 pound packages spaghetti
1 16-ounce can tomatoes (drained)
1 large onion
1 4-ounce can mushrooms (chopped)
1 tablespoon Worcestershire sauce
1 small bunch celery (chopped)
1 small bunch carrots (diced)
1 bell pepper (chopped)
Salt and pepper to taste
1 teaspoon chili powder
2 tablespoons barbecue sauce

Boil hen and debone. Cut in bite size pieces. Cook all raw vegetables until tender. In deep pot add the chicken, mushrooms, tomatoes, vegetables, salt and pepper. Cover with chicken broth. Simmer on low heat about 10 minutes. Just before serving this over the cooked spaghetti add chili powder, Worcestershire sauce, barbecue sauce and mix well.
Mrs. F. A. Kihneman (Tora)

ROAST WILD DUCK

2 frozen wild ducks
1 cup red wine
1 cup water
1 tablespoon powdered ginger
1 teaspoon whole cloves
2 medium onions

Take frozen ducks and marinate in red wine and water overnight. Next day salt and pepper inside and out. Rub with powdered ginger. Stick whole cloves in onion and put inside duck. Put ducks in roasting pan and bake at 250 to 300 degrees for three to four hours until browned.
R. Ellis Douglass

DUCK GUMBO

Small wild ducks
Roux
Salt and pepper
Quartered onions
Celery stalks and leaves
Bay leaves
Spice Islands Chicken Seasoned Base
Chopped bell pepper
Chopped onion
Chopped celery
Chicken broth
Garlic powder
Tabasco sauce
Oregano
Chopped fresh or frozen okra
Gumbo filé
Rice

I offer no amounts for the above ingredients, as it depends on the number of ducks being used. Judge the amounts accordingly.

Put ducks that have been cleaned (and pin feathers removed as much as possible) in a large pot. Cover well with water. Season this with salt, pepper, quartered onions, celery stalks and leaves, and a couple of bay leaves. Cook covered until ducks are tender. Remove ducks from water and skin them. Skinning them solves the problem of PIN FEATHERS!

While ducks are cooking chop onion, celery and bell pepper. Prepare some chicken broth from Spice Islands Chicken Seasoned Stock Base which is very rich, or use left over chicken stock or canned Swanson's chicken stock.

Make a roux: Put ½ cup oil in heavy iron skillet; add ½ cup flour and mix thoroughly. Cook this over a moderate heat and stir constantly, until the mixture is light brown in color. Add chopped onions, celery and bell pepper and cook until onion is transparent. Keep the chicken stock warm while the roux is being made. Add the stock slowly to the roux and vegetables and stir all the time. It may be necessary to remove the roux and vegetables from the fire before adding liquid — this is important, as you do not want it to brown too fast. Return to low heat and continue to add the liquid until you have the desired consistency. Add to this mixture the chopped duck meat, garlic powder, a little Tabasco to suit your taste, a little oregano, and chopped fresh or frozen okra. Canned okra may be used, but the other is much better. Okra does not have to cook a long time and should be added last. The okra should make the gumbo a thicker substance. Simmer for approximately two hours on a low fire.

You want to have plenty of liquid since it will be served over rice, but you also want it to have body. If the okra doesn't give it the desired thickness, use some powdered gumbo filé, but use it *very* sparingly, as it thickens very fast and can become stringy. Gumbo filé is found in food stores in the spice area.

If you do not have enough duck, chopped cooked chicken would be a good addition.

Mrs. Art Ogletree, Jr. (Ann)

Vegetables

In 1901 oil was discovered near Jennings and White Castle, Louisiana, and at Spindletop near Beaumont, Texas. This set a few Shreveporters to wondering about the gas seeps in Caddo Parish, for the Caddo Indians had found oil long before the white men came to this area.

Chances are that Captain Henry Miller Shreve wondered at the dark greasy scum that floated on the water about his snagboat on some of the bayous and asked the Caddoans about it. No doubt they told him of the oil springs and pools where they bathed to drive away rheumatic pains. He probably saw them apply this same oil as an ointment to cuts, burns and sores or drink it for medicine.

Other white men in other sections of the country saw Indians doing the same thing and began using it for medicine themselves, which led to bottling and selling the oil at $2.00 a gallon. This set the stage for the great American petroleum industry, for it was a bottle of this oil that excited the interest of George H. Bissell and led to the drilling of the first well by Edwin Drake near Titusville, Pennsylvania, in 1859.

Three adventurous spirits, Judge S. C. Fullilove, D. C. Richardson, and Ira G. Hendrick, leased land in Caddo Parish in 1904 for the purpose of looking for oil. This land was located near the two rail stops of Surry and Ananias, which later became Oil City. They induced J. S. Savage and W. A. Savage into coming to Caddo Parish and drilling for oil.

Peter Youree, leading banker in Shreveport then, told prospective investors that "digging for oil is a lot of foolishness and I would not advise anyone to put money in such."

The first oil was seen at 1,400 feet and five barrels of oil were bailed on March 28, 1905. By 1908 even the more cautious citizens of Shreveport and oil producers were convinced that a great oil and gas area was being developed. Oil City came into being as a boom city of shacks and tents. It is said that even the hotel was a tent, but it did have a reputation for good food.

The first marine drilling in the United States got under way on Caddo Lake in 1911. Shreveport was one of the first cities in the south to use natural gas.

With the discovery of oil and gas in Caddo Parish, Shreveport's population figures jumped from 16,013 in 1900 to 28,015 in 1910.

ASPARAGUS CASSEROLE I

1 cup bread crumbs
¾ cup melted butter
2 No. 2 cans cut asparagus
3 hard boiled eggs, sliced
1 small package almonds
Dash cayenne pepper
3 tablespoons flour
1½ cups sweet milk
1 small glass sharp process cheese
1 dash of oregano

Combine crumbs and ½ cup butter. Line casserole with half the crumbs, cover with asparagus and add eggs and almonds. Blend flour into butter in saucepan, stir in milk and stir constantly until thickened. Add cheese and cook until cheese is melted. Pour over asparagus and top with remaining crumbs. Sprinkle with oregano and cayenne pepper. Bake in 450 degree oven for 12 minutes.

Mrs. C. Don Attaway (Frances), Blanchard, Louisiana

ASPARAGUS CASSEROLE II

1 No. 2 can cut asparagus
3 hard-boiled eggs
1 cup grated cheese
Crushed bread crumbs

Medium White Sauce:

1 stick butter
3 tablespoons flour
1 cup light cream

Place layer of asparagus on bottom of baking dish. Cover with layer of hard-boiled eggs, slivered. Make medium white sauce by melting butter, add flour gradually; blend until smooth. Add light cream gradually, stirring constantly; cook over low heat until thickened. Add the grated cheese to sauce; blend until it melts in sauce. Pour sauce over asparagus and eggs. Sprinkle some more grated cheese over this. Add layer of crushed bread crumbs on top. Bake in moderate oven, 350 degrees, until heated thoroughly.

Mrs. John E. Ewing (Helen)

VEGETABLE CASSEROLE

1 16-ounce can green beans (drained)
1 medium size onion, sliced
1 17-ounce can LeSeur English peas
1 10¾-ounce can cream of mushroom soup
½ cup grated cheese
Cracker crumbs for topping

Place in casserole in layers as ingredients are listed above. Bake in 350 degree oven until casserole bubbles real good all over.

Mrs. John L. Hoppe (Jo)

ARTICHOKE AND GREEN BEAN CASSEROLE

1 or 2 14-ounce cans artichoke hearts
2 to 4 cans French style green beans
1 cup seasoned bread crumbs
½ cup olive oil
½ cup grated Romano cheese

Reserve some cheese and bread crumbs to be sprinkled on top of casserole. Drain artichoke hearts and cut up. Combine artichoke hearts with green beans, olive oil, some of the bread crumbs and some of the cheese. Place in baking dish, sprinkle cheese and bread crumbs on top, and bake at 425 degrees, covered, for 25 minutes.

NOTE: I use 2 cans of beans for every can of artichoke hearts.

Mrs. James S. Richardson (Kay), Baton Rouge, Louisiana

HARVARD BEETS

1 bunch fresh beets or 1 can whole or sliced beets
1 tablespoon cornstarch
½ cup sugar
¼ cup water
½ cup lemon juice or vinegar

Cook beets until tender or use canned beets. Make a sauce by cooking one tablespoon cornstarch, sugar, water and lemon juice or vinegar together for five minutes. Pour over beets and allow to stand a few minutes before serving.

Mrs. C. D. Attaway (Margie)

BEETS TORA STYLE

3 16-ounce cans sliced beets
1 cup sugar
2 tablespoons cornstarch
1 cup vinegar
½ teaspoon cloves
3 tablespoons catsup
3 tablespoons oleo
⅛ teaspoon salt
1 teaspoon vanilla
1½ cups beet juice

Mix sugar, cornstarch, vinegar, cloves, catsup, oleo, salt, beet juice, and vanilla and cook over medium flame for 5 minutes or until it thickens. Remove from flame and add your beets. Keeps well and is very tasty.

Mrs. F. A. Kihneman (Tora)

BROCCOLI AU GRATIN

4 tablespoons butter
4 tablespoons flour
1 teaspoon salt
⅛ teaspoon dry mustard
1½ cups milk
½ cup processed cheese
3 cups broccoli
Parmesan cheese
Paprika

Cook broccoli until just underdone. Melt butter, add flour, salt, mustard. Cook over low heat until bubbly. Add milk and cook until thick and smooth. Add cheese and stir until melted. Add broccoli. Pour into buttered casserole, sprinkle with grated Parmesan cheese and paprika. Bake at 350 degrees for 30 minutes until bubbly.
Mrs. Ronny Goodman (Janice)

BROCCOLI CASSEROLE I

2 10-ounce boxes frozen broccoli
1 10¾-ounce can mushroom soup
½ stick butter
1 roll garlic cheese
1 large onion, chopped
Cracker crumbs

Sauté chopped onion in butter. Add frozen uncooked chopped broccoli and cook until tender (about 30 minutes with top on). Put layer of broccoli and onion in casserole, 6 slices of the garlic cheese, pour over half the mushroom soup and repeat the layers. Top with cracker crumbs. Bake in 350 degree oven for about 45 minutes. Serves 8.
Mrs. Velma Dodd, Rodessa, Louisiana

BROCCOLI CASSEROLE II

1 large onion, chopped
½ stick butter
3 10-ounce packages chopped frozen broccoli
2 10¾-ounce cans cream of mushroom soup
1½ packages garlic cheese
1 teaspoon monosodium glutamate
1 2½-ounce can mushrooms
½ cup chopped almonds
½ cup bread crumbs

Sauté onions in butter. Add thawed broccoli and cook until tender. Add soup, cheese (chopped), monosodium glutamate, mushrooms and ¼ cup almonds. Pour in large casserole, sprinkle remaining almonds and bread crumbs on top. Bake at 300 degrees until bubbly. Yield: 8 to 10 servings.
Mrs. Leonard Green, Jr. (June)

BROCCOLI CASSEROLE III

2 10-ounce packages broccoli (chopped or pieces)
2 8-ounce cans water chestnuts (drained)
1 10¾-ounce can mushroom soup
1 2½-ounce can mushrooms (bits and pieces)
1 tablespoon margarine
⅔ cup cream or milk
1 5-ounce package onion rings (Mrs. Paul's frozen)
1 cup cheddar cheese (shredded)
½ cup peanuts(chopped)

Use sauce pan and cook broccoli with margarine until tender and drain. Make sauce with soup, milk, mushrooms, and cheese. In casserole dish chop chestnuts, add onion rings, peanuts if desired, and drained broccoli. Pour the sauce over this and mix gently. Bake uncovered 45 minutes in 375 degree oven. Allow to sit a few minutes before serving. May be prepared in advance and baked later. Optional additions: strips of ham, chopped chicken, or hard-boiled eggs (sliced). Very good.
Mrs. Lewis H. Hendelman (Anice), Fairfax, Virginia

BROCCOLI CASSEROLE IV

2 10-ounce packages frozen chopped broccoli (cooked)
2 eggs, slightly beaten
1½ cups grated cheddar cheese
½ cup chopped onion
½ cup mayonnaise
1 10¾-ounce can cream of celery soup

Mix all of above ingredients in 9x13x2-inch baking dish and bake at 350 degrees for one hour or until golden brown on top.
Mrs. A. H. Otto (Marjorie)

BROCCOLI CASSEROLE V

3 cups frozen chopped broccoli (bag)
3 tablespoons chopped onion
1 4-ounce can sliced mushrooms drained
¾ cup Pepperidge Farm dressing mix
1 stick oleo
¾ cup chopped celery
1 10¾-ounce can mushroom soup
1 roll Kraft nippy cheese
1 can Durkee fried onion rings

Sauté broccoli, mushrooms, onions and celery until broccoli is thawed. Make sauce of cheese and mushroom soup. Add to sautéed mixture. Add dressing mix, onion rings and top with cheese. Bake at 350 degrees until cheese bubbles.
Mrs. Jo Whittaker

BROCCOLI-RICE CASSEROLE

- 2 10-ounce packages frozen chopped broccoli
- 1 cup onion, chopped
- 1 cup celery, chopped
- 8 ounces fresh mushrooms, sliced
- 6 tablespoons butter or margarine
- 1 cup uncooked rice (not instant)
- 1 10½-ounce can cream of mushroom soup
- 1 10½-ounce can cream of chicken soup
- 1 8-ounce jar Cheez Whiz
- 1 teaspoon seasoned salt
- ½ teaspoon pepper
- ¼ teaspoon garlic powder
- 1 4-ounce can water chestnuts, diced

Place frozen broccoli in colander and allow to thaw and drain thoroughly. If time does not allow this, cook broccoli according to package directions until tender and drain. Sauté onion, celery and mushrooms in butter. Cook rice according to package directions. Add soups and Cheeze Whiz to sautéed vegetables. In large bowl mix the cooked rice, soup mixture, drained broccoli, seasonings and diced water chestnuts. Butter a 4-quart casserole for contents. Bake in 350 degree oven for 25 to 35 minutes, until it is heated thoroughly. Yield: 12 to 15 servings (approximately).

Mrs. Art Ogletree, Jr. (Ann)

BROCCOLI AND BROWN RICE CASSEROLE

- 2 cups cooked brown rice
- 2 pounds fresh chopped broccoli
- 1 cup grated cheddar cheese
- 4 eggs, beaten
- 2 tablespoons chopped parsley
- 2 tablespoons dill weed
- 1 teaspoon salt
- 1 tablespoon oil
- 4 tablespoons wheat germ

Steam the chopped broccoli until it is just slightly cooked. Combine cooked rice and cheese. Add eggs, parsley, dill weed and salt. Stir in the broccoli. Pour into an oiled casserole and top with the wheat germ which has been mixed with the oil. Bake in preheated 350 degree oven for 40 minutes. Serves 6 to 8.

Mrs. George Gekakis (Carol) (submitted by Rhonda Berry)

BAKED BEANS I

1 pound navy beans
6 cups water
½ teaspoon salt
½ teaspoon soda
½ pound salt meat cut into ½-inch pieces
½ teaspoon pepper
1 medium onion, chopped
1 cup syrup
¼ cup sugar
1 teaspoon dried mustard

Wash and clean beans and put into large pot. Cover with water and cook for ten minutes. Pour off water and reserve. Put the 6 cups of water, meat, salt, onions, beans, syrup, mustard, sugar, soda, and pepper into 2-quart casserole and cover. Bake in 300 degree oven for two hours. If while cooking it gets dry add a little of the reserved water all along.
Mrs. F. A. Kihneman (Tora)

BAKED BEANS II

10 slices of bacon
3 large onions, sliced
2 large green peppers, chopped
3 28-ounce cans of Campbell's pork and beans
1 8-ounce can tomato sauce
½ cup catsup
1 cup Texas barbecue sauce
⅓ cup prepared mustard
½ cup molasses
½ cup brown sugar

Cut bacon in half-inch pieces and fry on medium heat until partially done. Add onions and peppers. Sauté five minutes. Combine with remaining ingredients. Bake in large oblong pan in 325 degree oven for 1 hour. Reduce heat to 300 degrees and bake an additional hour. Serves 16 to 20.
Mrs. Agnes Saddler

RED BEANS

2 pounds red beans
Ham hock
Salt, black and red pepper to taste
2 onions, chopped fine
4 stalks celery, chopped fine
Dash Tabasco

Simmer ham hocks in 4 quarts water for approximately two hours. Pull meat off of bone and discard bone and skin. Save water and strain it.

Soak beans overnight after washing them several times. In small amount of oil or shortening, sauté onions, celery until soft. Add beans and water to cover. Simmer uncovered for one to two hours until beans are soft, not mushy. Season well with black and red pepper, dash Tabasco, and salt. Just before serving over rice add chopped green onion.
Mrs. Margaret Copeland

HONEY BEANS ROYALE

3 pounds white navy beans
1 14-ounce bottle catsup
2 tablespoons prepared mustard
1 pound bacon
1 pound honey
3 tablespoons brown sugar
6 8-ounce cans tomato sauce

Parboil beans until half cooked, about 40 minutes. Drain. Mix honey, catsup, mustard and tomato sauce. Pour a layer of sauce on bottom of large heavy iron pot. Put in layer of beans, about 2 inches. Cover beans with layer of bacon. Then pour another layer of sauce, a layer of beans and a layer of bacon, and repeat until all is used. Cover last layer with layer of bacon, spread brown sugar over top and cover pot. Cook in oven for 12 hours at 300 degrees. Serves 20.
Mrs. A. R. Snider (Frances)

RED BEANS 'N RICE

1 pound ground lean beef
¼ cup Mazola oil
¼ cup chopped bell pepper
1 large onion, chopped
1 can (303 size) tomatoes
1 cup water
2 teaspoons salt
1 tablespoon chili powder
Dash of black pepper
1½ cups raw rice
1 15-ounce can kidney beans (without chili)

Sauté meat in oil until slightly browned, stirring to keep from sticking. Add bell pepper and onions. Cook until transparent (just a few minutes), stirring all the while. Add tomatoes, water, salt, chili powder and black pepper. Simmer for 10 minutes. Remove from fire. Add raw rice and kidney beans. Pour in buttered, shallow baking pan. Cover well with foil if pan has no lid. Bake at 350 degrees for 1 hour. Stir once lightly. Cover again and bake one half hour longer.
Mrs. Leonard Green, Jr. (June)

ORIENTAL GREEN BEAN CASSEROLE

2 16-ounce cans French cut green beans
1 16-ounce can mixed Chinese vegetables
1 4-ounce can sliced mushrooms
1 10¾-ounce can mushroom soup
1 2-ounce package sliced almonds
3 tablespoons soy sauce
Dash of black pepper
1 can French fried onions

Drain the green beans, vegetables and mushrooms. Combine with mushroom soup, almonds, soy sauce and pepper. Mix well. Heat in buttered 2-quart baking dish for 30 minutes at 350 degrees.

NOTE: Add onions last 10 minutes of baking time.

Mrs. Ellis M. Bush (Juanita)

GREEN BEAN CASSEROLE

3 16-ounce cans Blue Lake whole green beans
3 to 4 teaspoons bacon drippings
1 medium onion, chopped
Salt and pepper to taste
2 10¾-ounce cans cream of mushroom soup
1 package slivered or sliced almonds
1 teaspoon margarine
1 8-ounce can mushrooms, chopped
3 cups (or more) sharp shredded cheese or 1 can fried onion rings

Drain most of liquid off beans. Put approximately 3 to 4 teaspoons bacon drippings in roasting pan. Add beans and chopped onion, salt and pepper. Cover and cook over low heat about 20 minutes. If very much liquid accumulates during cooking, drain it, but keep in reserve; this shouldn't have too much liquid because the soup is added at this point. While beans are cooking toast the almonds by putting in shallow pan, dot with margarine. Put in moderate oven and watch them closely. Takes approximately 10-12 minutes to toast them. (They burn easily.) Add almonds to beans. Butter a large baking dish or pan and add the mixture. Top with grated cheese or can of onion rings. I prefer the cheese. Cook in 325 degree oven 25 to 30 minutes or until it bubbles.

Variation: Sliced water chestnuts may be substituted for almonds. Very good.

This is a large recipe and will serve 12 to 15 people along with other foods.

Mrs. Art Ogletree, Jr. (Ann)

GREEN BEAN CASSEROLE WITH WATER CHESTNUTS

5 strips bacon cooked crisp and crumbled
1 large onion, chopped
1 tablespoon flour
½ teaspoon salt
2 16-ounce cans whole Blue Lake green beans
¾ cup bean liquid
¼ cup vinegar
3 tablespoons sugar
¼ teaspoon pepper
1 can water chestnuts, sliced thinly

Mix dry ingredients and set aside. Sauté onion in bacon drippings left from the 5 strips of bacon. Stir in dry ingredients and brown slightly. Combine the bean liquid and vinegar; add to mixture and boil five minutes. Separately mix the beans and water chestnuts. Put in 2-quart baking dish and pour the warm mixture over beans and water chestnuts. Sprinkle crumbled bacon over top and bake uncovered at 300 degrees until thoroughly heated. Delicious sweet and sour dish!
Mrs. Marco Bayliss

EASY GREEN BEAN CASSEROLE

1 No. 2 can green beans
1 10¾-ounce can cream of mushroom soup
1-2 cups grated cheddar cheese
1 can French fried onion rings

Drain can of green beans and save 2-3 tablespoons of juice. Combine green beans, cream of mushroom soup in sauce pan over heat. Stir in onion rings. Pour into casserole dish and top with cheese. Heat in preheated oven at 350 degrees until cheese is melted and is bubbling. For variety: use Chinese noodles instead of or with cheese.
Mrs. H. Russell Maddox (Tommie Lue)

MARINATED BEANS

1 No. 2 can Blue Lake French style green beans
1 No.2 can cut waxed beans (yellow)
1 No. 3 can kidney beans
½ bell pepper, chopped
1 large red onion, chopped
⅔ cup vinegar
¾ cup sugar
⅓ cup Wesson oil
1 teaspoon salt
1 teaspoon black pepper

Drain the green beans, waxed beans, and kidney beans. Combine all vegetables. Combine vinegar, sugar, oil, salt and pepper; heat. Pour over the vegetables and chill overnight. Keeps well.
Mrs. J. Kent Colvin (Yvonne)

CHOUX GLORIEUX
(Glorified Cabbage)

1 medium head cabbage
¾ stick butter
1 finely chopped onion
1 10¾-ounce can cream of mushroom soup
½ pound Velveeta Cheese
Bread crumbs
Salt and red pepper

Chop cabbage finely and boil until very tender in salted water. Wilt onion in butter. When wilted, add cheese in hunks and allow to melt over low heat. When cheese has melted, add mushroom soup. Still over low heat, blend in soup with cheese mixture. When blended, add boiled cabbage and mix well. Add bread crumbs until of proper casserole consistency, about ¾ to 1 cup. Season to taste. Put in a 1½ to 2-quart casserole, sprinkle bread crumbs on top and bake at 350 degrees about 20 to 30 minutes or until bubbly and hot.
Mrs. Leonard Green, Jr. (June)

MARINATED CARROTS

2 pounds fresh carrots
1 medium onion, chopped
½ bell pepper, chopped

Marinade:
1 can tomato soup
½ cup Wesson oil
½ to ¾ cup white vinegar
¾ to 1 cup sugar
2 tablespoons prepared mustard
Salt and black pepper to taste
Dash of Worcestershire sauce

Cube or slice carrots and cook until done. Combine carrots, onion and pepper. Pour marinade over the combined vegetables and let stand several hours or overnight in refrigerator. This is especially good with meats and will keep well when refrigerated.
Mrs. Doris A. Fisher

CHEESE AND CABBAGE ROLLS

1½ cups cooked rice
¾ cup grated cheese
1 tablespoon butter
6 large cabbage leaves
Salt, pepper, paprika to taste

Wilt cabbage leaves slightly in hot water. Remove and fill with the rice cheese mixture, seasoned to taste. Roll up and place in a buttered baking dish, cover, and bake in a slow oven until tender (about 30 minutes).
Mrs. Leonard Green, Jr. (June)

CREOLE CORN PUDDING

3 tablespoons butter
1 onion, chopped finely
½ bell pepper, chopped
2 cups whole kernel corn (canned or fresh)
1 tablespoon sugar
1 teaspoon salt
1 teaspoon pepper
3 eggs, well beaten
½ cup grated cheddar cheese

Melt butter in skillet. Sauté onion and bell pepper. Add corn, sugar, salt and pepper. Cool and add cheese and well beaten eggs. Pour into buttered 2-quart casserole and set in pan of hot water. Bake 35 minutes in a 350 degree oven. Serve at once.

NOTE: This may be made up ahead of time except for beaten eggs. Add those just before cooking and cook as above. Serves 6.
Mrs. Leonard Green, Jr. (June)

HERBED CORN SCALLOP

2 eggs
2 16½-ounce cans cream style corn
½ cup milk
½ stick butter or margarine, melted
2 tablespoons instant minced onion
½ teaspoon salt
¼ teaspoon pepper
2 cups ready-mix herb-seasoned stuffing (from 8-ounce package)

Beat eggs slightly in a medium size bowl; stir in corn, milk, butter or margarine, onion, salt and pepper. Spoon half of corn mixture into a greased 8-cup baking dish; sprinkle stuffing in an even layer over top; spoon remaining corn mixture over stuffing. Let stand 15 minutes. Bake until center is almost set but still slightly soft — 325 degrees for one hour. Yield: 8 servings.
Mrs. W. D. Sandifer, Jr. (Evelyn)

ACADIAN CUSHAW

1 medium cushaw
1 pound sugar
1 pound butter
1 teaspoon allspice
Brown sugar

Peel and seed cushaw. Cut into small pieces. Cook in ½ cup water until tender. Add sugar and butter; cook, stirring constantly, until a rich color (it will stick quickly). When cooked, add allspice and pour into greased baking dish. Sprinkle top with brown sugar, bake at 400 degrees until hot.
Mrs. Leonard Green, Jr. (June)

CANDIED CUSHAW

2 or 3 pounds cushaw
2 cups sugar
6 tablespoons melted butter

Peel cushaw and cut into small cubes. Cover with hot water, add a pinch of salt and cook until tender enough to pierce with a straw. Drain off water. Put a layer of cushaw in a 9-inch pan or casserole. Cover with 1 cup of sugar and 3 tablespoons melted butter. Add another layer of cushaw and a layer of 1 cup sugar and 3 tablespoons melted butter. Bake at 375 degrees for 20 minutes.
Mrs. A. R. Snider (Frances)

BAKED EGGPLANT

1 pound of eggplant (peeled and cubed)
1 cup dried bread crumbs
1 5.33 ounce can evaporated milk
¼ cup whole milk
¼ cup onion (chopped)
¼ cup green pepper (chopped)
¼ cup celery (chopped)
½ stick margarine
1 teaspoon pimiento (chopped)
Salt and pepper to taste
2 eggs (slightly beaten)
Dash of sage
2 ounces of sharp cheddar cheese (grated)

Soak eggplant in salt water for 6 hours. Soak bread crumbs in the milk. Sauté onion, celery, green pepper in the butter for 15 minutes. Place the eggplant in boiling water, cover and cook until done. Mix bread mixture and eggplant together. Add eggs, pimiento and other seasonings. Blend well and pour in greased casserole dish. Top with cheese and bake at 350 degrees until golden brown.
Mrs. W. A. Doyle (Frances)

EGGPLANT CASSEROLE

1 large eggplant
1 cup raw rice
2 tablespoons Worcestershire sauce
1 small bell pepper, chopped
1 medium onion, chopped
2 ribs celery, chopped
2 drops Tabasco sauce
***1 can shrimp, drained**
2 cups hot water
3 beef bouillon cubes
½ teaspoon salt

Peel eggplant and cut up in pieces. Cook, covered in a small amount of water until tender. It doesn't take long — drain. Sauté onion, bell pepper and celery in bacon drippings until transparent. Remove from fire, add cooked eggplant and all other ingredients. (Melt bouillon cubes in the hot water before adding).

Grease a 2-quart casserole with oleo. Pour mixture in, cover tightly, and bake at 375 degrees for 1 hour and 15 minutes.

*If you prefer, use ½-pound ground beef or ½-pound chopped chicken livers instead of the shrimp. Be sure to sauté the meat or livers in the bacon drippings a few minutes before frying onions, etc.

Mrs. Leonard Green, Jr. (June)

GOLDEN HOMINY CASSEROLE

2 No. 2 cans golden hominy, drained
1 10-ounce can Rotel tomatoes
6 strips bacon, fried and crumbled
1 large onion, chopped and sautéed in bacon fat
8 slices American cheese
1 cup fine browned bread crumbs

Combine hominy, Rotel, bacon crumbs, chopped onion and bread crumbs. Place in a 3-quart soufflé dish, top with cheese slices and bake at 300 degrees until cheese melts and blends, about 15 minutes.

Mrs. Ted Joy (Linda)

HOMINY CASSEROLE

3 No. 1 cans hominy
1 cup green peppers
¼ cup chopped parsley
6 tablespoons oleo
1 12-ounce can whole tomatoes
1 teaspoon onion juice
½ teaspoon salt
1 tablespoon plus 1 teaspoon chili powder

Sauté peppers, parsley in oleo. Add onion juice, salt and chili powder. Combine with hominy and cook until hot through. Place in casserole dish and bake at 350 degrees for 20 minutes. Serve.

Mrs. A. H. Otto (Marjorie)

DINNER MUSHROOMS

2 pounds fresh mushrooms
½ cup honey wine
1 tablespoon Worcestershire sauce
2 tablespoons soy sauce
1 stick butter
1 tablespoon oil
Dash salt and pepper

Wash mushrooms and pat dry with paper towel. Combine all ingredients and place in Dutch oven and simmer covered for about 30 to 45 minutes. Place into individual small bowls with juice to serve. Serves 6 to 8.
Mrs. George Gekakis (Carol), (submitted by Rhonda Berry)

NOODLES ROMANOFF

8 ounces narrow noodles
Boiling, salted water
2 cups cream-style cottage cheese
1 cup dairy sour cream
½ cup buttered crumbs
3 tablespoons melted butter
4 green onions (including tops) chopped
1 clove garlic, minced
½ teaspoon salt

Cook noodles in boiling, salted water until just tender. Drain noodles and combine with cottage cheese, sour cream, butter, onions, garlic, and salt. Place in 1½-quart buttered casserole. Top with buttered crumbs. Bake in a 350 degree oven for 20 to 25 minutes or until piping hot. Makes 8 servings.
Mrs. Marvin Kines (Ora)

CURRY 'N ONIONS

1 pound small white onions
1 10¾-ounce can cream of mushroom soup
⅓ cup milk
½ teaspoon curry powder

Peel the onions and cook in boiling, salted water for 20 minutes or until tender; then drain. Stir in mushroom soup, milk and curry powder. Heat slowly, stirring constantly, until bubbly, hot and cream smooth. Serve at once. Serves 6.
Mrs. Leonard Green, Jr. (June)

ONION PIE

- 1½ cups sifted flour
- ¾ teaspoon salt
- 1½ teaspoons caraway seeds
- ½ cup shortening
- 2 to 3 tablespoons water
- 3 cups peeled onions, thinly sliced
- 3 tablespoons melted butter or oleo
- ½ cup milk
- 1½ cups sour cream
- 1 teaspoon salt
- 2 eggs, well beaten
- 3 tablespoons flour
- Bacon slices, cooked crisp

To make pastry, combine 1½ cups flour, ¾ teaspoon salt and caraway seeds. Add shortening; cut into flour until mixture resembles coarse cornmeal. Stir water in lightly with fork; stir until mixture adheres and follows fork around bowl. Turn onto floured board; roll to ⅛-inch thickness. Fit into 10-inch pie pan, flute edges. Bake in hot oven, 425 degrees, 10 minutes or until lightly browned. Meanwhile, make filling. Sauté onions in butter until lightly browned. Spoon into pastry shell. Add milk, 1¼ cups sour cream, and salt to eggs. Blend 3 tablespoons flour with remaining ¼ cup sour cream. Combine with egg mixture; pour over onions. Bake in slow oven, 325 degrees, for 30 minutes or until firm in center. Garnish with crisp bacon.

Mrs. Leonard Green, Jr. (June)

POTATO CASSEROLE

- 1 large package frozen hash browned potatoes
- 1 10¾-ounce can cream of chicken soup
- 2 8-ounce cartons sour cream or 1 pint carton
- 1 stick butter or oleo
- 1 pound sharp cheese, grated (save ¼ of cheese for top)
- 2 bunches green onions, chopped (use some of tops)

Allow time for potatoes to thaw thoroughly, so take them out of freezer well in advance. Melt butter. Mix all ingredients, but save ¼ of cheese for topping. Butter large oblong baking dish or pan and cook for one hour at 350 degrees. Bake covered with foil until last 15 minutes of baking time. Uncover and put remaining cheese on top for the last 15 minutes. Chives are good in this.

Mrs. Burl L. Eastepp, Jr. (Ann)

POTATOES ROMANOFF

4 medium white potatoes
1 cup sour cream
4 green onions, sliced thin
1¼ cups shredded sharp cheddar cheese
1 teaspoon salt
⅛ to ¼ teaspoon pepper
Paprika

Cook potatoes in jackets until tender. Peel and shred. Combine shredded potatoes with sour cream, onions, ¾ cup cheese, salt and pepper. Turn mixture into buttered 1½-quart casserole. Sprinkle with remaining cheese and paprika. Bake uncovered 30 to 40 minutes at 350 degrees.

This may be made ahead and refrigerated until ready to bake and serve.

Mrs. S. C. Stolzenthaler, Jr. (Betty), Baton Rouge, Louisiana

POTATO-TOMATO SCALLOP

½ cup chopped onion
2 tablespoons butter
2 tablespoons flour
1 teaspoon paprika
½ teaspoon salt
1 cup water
1 pint tomatoes
2 chicken bouillon cubes
5 cups thinly sliced potatoes
⅛ teaspoon pepper

Cook onion in butter until tender. Blend in flour, salt, paprika and pepper. Add water, tomatoes and bouillon cubes. Cook and stir over medium heat until mixture thickens and boils. Place potatoes in greased 2-quart casserole, add sauce, cover and bake at 400 degrees for 1 to 1¼ hours or until potatoes are done.

Mrs. Edward W. Robinson, Keithville, Louisiana

SWEET POTATO BALLS

4 medium sweet potatoes
1 egg
1 tablespoon butter
Marshmallows (large)
Nutmeg to taste
¼ cup sugar
⅓ cup flour
Corn flake meal

Boil potatoes until well done. Drain well. Cream egg, butter, sugar and flour. Mix with potatoes. If potatoes are soft, add a little more flour and cream well. Place in refrigerator until chilled. Spoon into small balls, using ½ marshmallows for the center. Roll in corn flake meal. Fry in deep fat until brown. Makes about 15 medium size balls.

Mrs. Leonard Green, Jr. (June)

CARAMELIZED SWEET POTATOES

1 30-ounce can of sweet potatoes
1/3 cup brown sugar
1/2 teaspoon salt
1/4 teaspoon cinnamon
1/4 teaspoon cloves
1 tablespoon butter or margarine

Drain potatoes. Boil syrup from potatoes with the sugar for 10 minutes. Add seasonings and margarine. Place potatoes in casserole. Pour hot syrup over potatoes and bake in moderate oven (350 degrees) about an hour or until brown, basting occasionally. Serves five.

Mrs. C. D. Attaway (Margie)

SWEET POTATO CASSEROLE

3 medium sweet potatoes
1/2 teaspoon salt
1 stick oleo
1 cup sugar
1 8-ounce can crushed pineapple
1 teaspoon vanilla
2 eggs, beaten
14 large marshmallows

Peel and chop potatoes. Boil with 1/2 teaspoon salt. Drain and mash. Add other ingredients. Mix well. Pour into buttered 2-quart casserole. Bake at 400 degrees for 45 minutes or until set.

Mrs. Ronny Goodman (Janice)

SWEET POTATOES MARMALADE

3 cans (No. 303) sweet potatoes, drained
1/2 stick butter or margarine
1/2 cup brown sugar
1 teaspoon salt
3 tablespoons orange marmalade
2 tablespoons grated orange rind

Combine butter, orange marmalade, brown sugar, orange rind and salt in saucepan and simmer about five minutes, stirring frequently. Add drained potatoes and cook for 15-20 minutes until potatoes are well glazed. Serves 8.

Mrs. Leonard Green, Jr. (June)

SWEET POTATO PONE

(over 100 years old)

2 large Louisiana yams
1 egg
¾ cup brown sugar
1 large lump butter
Vanilla or cinnamon to taste

Peel and grate yams. Stir in whole egg, sugar, butter and flavoring. Place in well buttered baking dish and bake in slow oven for 45 minutes.
Mrs. Leonard Green, Jr. (June)

ALMOND RICE

1 stick oleo
3½ cups water
6 to 8 tablespoons soy sauce
2 cups Uncle Ben's converted rice
Juice of ½ fresh lemon
4 chicken bouillon cubes
½ to ¾ cups slivered almonds
7 to 10 green onions chopped tops and bottoms

In electric skillet melt oleo, add water, bouillon cubes, lemon juice and rice. Cover and simmer for 25 minutes or until water is cooked out. Unplug skillet, add almonds, soy sauce and onions.
BE SURE TO USE UNCLE BEN'S CONVERTED RICE
Mrs. Walter Holder

BAKED RICE

1 stick oleo
1 cup chopped onion (fine)
2 2½-ounce cans mushrooms with juice
1 cup rice
1 cup chopped celery (fine)
1 cup chopped bell pepper (fine)
2 cans beef bouillon, consommé, or onion soup

Sauté celery, onions, peppers. Put mushrooms and soup of your choice in casserole. Stir in rice for 5 minutes, add other ingredients and cook in covered casserole for 45 minutes at 350 degrees. If desired a little garlic salt plus a little plain salt may be added.
Mrs. Billie Ford

BRAZILIAN RICE

4½ cups cooked rice (regular)
6 eggs, beaten
1½ cups milk
1½ tablespoons Worcestershire sauce
1½ tablespoons chopped onion
3 teaspoons salt
½ cup butter or oleo
1¼ pounds grated cheddar cheese
1 10-ounce package frozen chopped spinach (cooked and drained)
½ teaspoon each marjoram, thyme, and rosemary

Melt the butter. Add the eggs, cheese, milk, cooked spinach, onion, Worcestershire sauce, salt and herbs. Mix the sauce well then stir in the cooked rice. Pour into two 1½-quart size baking dishes and bake in a pan of water in 350 degree oven for 35 minutes. Serves 12 to 14.
Mrs. Robert Snead (Shirley)

GENOA STYLE BAKED RICE

½ cup wild rice
¼ cup butter
½ pound smoked Italian sweet sausage
1 2½-ounce can mushroom slices and pieces
4 tablespoons warm water
4 tablespoons Parmesan cheese
1 can sliced artichokes (optional)
½ cup white rice
½ cup chopped onion
1 cup frozen peas
2 tablespoons meat extract or 3 or 4 beef bouillon cubes
½ cup beef stock

Melt butter, add onion and sausage, brown gently, add peas and mushrooms, brown little longer. Add meat extract, stock and water, and artichokes (if desired). In another pan, boil rice 5 minutes (both together). Drain and rinse well.

Add skillet mixture to rice and mix well. Put in casserole and bake at 375 degrees for 30 minutes or until rice is done. Serves 6 to 8 people.
Mrs. Eileen LaBarbera

GOURMET RICE

1 cup rice
1 10¾-ounce can onion soup
½ can water
1 4-ounce can mushrooms, drained
1 stick butter
½ jar (8-ounces) Cheez Whiz

Mix all ingredients and bake in casserole dish for 1 hour at 400 degrees.
Mrs. Fran Lorant Moore

GREEN RICE

2 cups raw rice
⅔ cup chopped bell pepper
1 cup green onions and tops, chopped
⅓ cup minced parsley
¼ cup Mazola oil
1½ tablespoons Worcestershire sauce
1 teaspoon salt
¼ teaspoon red pepper
4 cups beef or chicken bouillon made from 6 cubes and 4 cups hot water or
4 cups chicken stock

Combine all ingredients. Bake without stirring in a greased 2-quart casserole with tight fitting cover for 45 minutes in 350 degree oven. Remove cover and toss, as seasoning stays on top. Serve hot.

This dish needs no gravy. Serve with any meat, fish or fowl. Freeze any green rice that is left over. Just reheat by steaming in top of double boiler.

Mrs. Leonard Green, Jr. (June)

SEASONED RICE

2 cups uncooked rice
4 cups chicken broth
1 small onion, chopped
4 ribs celery, chopped
½ teaspoon thyme
2 tablespoons parsley flakes
1 10¾-ounce can cream of chicken soup
Salt and white pepper to taste

Mix rice, broth, onion and celery in saucepan. Cover and cook for 25 minutes over low heat. Combine soup, parsley flakes and thyme until smooth; toss with rice when done. Add salt and pepper to taste. Transfer mixture to buttered large baking dish and heat in moderate oven until hot and bubbly.

Yield: 12 to 15 servings.

Mrs. Ralph Garrett (Dottie)

WILD RICE

1 cup wild rice
2 tablespoons chopped onion
1 cup chopped celery
1 tablespoon minced parsley
½ cup minced chives
½ cup butter
½ teaspoon poultry seasoning

Soak rice overnight. Drain, cover with salted water and bring to boil. Cook without stirring for about 20 minutes. Brown onion, celery, parsley, chives in butter. Add to cooked rice then add poultry seasoning. Serve.

Mrs. A. H. Otto (Marjorie)

RIZOGALO

(Greek Rice Pudding)

8 cups milk
1 cup rice
1½ cups sugar
2 egg yolks
1 lemon rind
1 tablespoon cinnamon
1 teaspoon cornstarch

Put milk on to boil. Wash rice and add to milk. When it comes to a boil again, reduce heat and simmer for about half an hour, stirring occasionally. Add sugar, lemon rind, and simmer 8-10 minutes longer. Add 2 egg yolks, mixed with cold milk and 1 teaspoon cornstarch and simmer a few minutes longer. Pour into dessert plates. Sprinkle with cinnamon. Refrigerate. Serve.

My children love this one.

Mrs. Fran Lorant Moore

RICE CASSEROLE

1 stick oleo, melted
1 cup raw rice
⅓ cup young onions, chopped
⅓ cup bell pepper, chopped
⅓ cup celery, chopped
1 4-ounce can sliced mushrooms (and juice)
1 bay leaf
1 can beef bouillon
1 can water

Mix all ingredients in a bowl, then pour into buttered casserole. Bake 1½ hours covered. Remove cover and bake 15 minutes longer.

Mrs. W. M. Plaster (Lucile)

SPINACH AND ARTICHOKES

½ cup chopped green onions with tops or ½ cup chopped onion
1 stick oleo
2 10-ounce packages frozen chopped spinach
1 14-ounce can artichoke hearts
½ pint sour cream
½ cup Parmesan cheese

Sauté onion in oleo. Add cooked, drained spinach. Add drained artichoke hearts and sour cream. Sprinkle with Parmesan cheese and bake at 350 degrees for 20 to 30 minutes. Even people who don't like spinach would like this uniquely flavored dish.

Mrs. W. Glen Mangham (Betty)

SPINACH
(for children who do not like spinach)

2 10-ounce packages frozen chopped spinach
½ envelope dry onion soup mix
1 3-ounce package cream cheese
¼ stick butter or margarine
Fritos for topping

Melt margarine or butter in frying pan. Place frozen spinach in pan, cover and cook until spinach is thawed. Add cream cheese and onion soup mix. Simmer about 15-20 minutes. After adding all ingredients this may be placed in a greased casserole dish, topped with crushed Fritos and baked at 300 degrees for 15-20 minutes.

NOTE: This casserole is good for those who do not like spinach. Also, if you like more seasoning, use the whole envelope of onion soup mix.

Mrs. Dale Ward (Renee)

SPINACH-CREAM CHEESE BAKE

2 10-ounce packages frozen chopped spinach
2 3-ounce packages cream cheese, softened
Progresso seasoned bread crumbs

Cook spinach according to directions on package. Drain well. Put back in pan with cream cheese and mix well. Season with salt and pepper. Cover with bread crumbs and dot with butter. Bake at 350 degrees for 15 minutes.

NOTE: This may be made ahead of time and refrigerated. Increase baking time to heat through. Serves 4-6.

Mrs. Leonard Green, Jr. (June)

SPINACH CASSEROLE

2 10-ounce packages frozen chopped spinach
1 15-ounce can artichoke hearts
1 stick oleo
1 3-ounce package cream cheese
Bread crumbs

Cook spinach and drain well. Drain artichoke hearts, cut up and place on bottom of greased casserole. Combine spinach, oleo and cream cheese and place on top of artichokes. Sprinkle bread crumbs on top. Bake 20 to 30 minutes in 350 degree oven.

Mrs. Bruce Baker (Stacy), Baton Rouge, Louisiana

HERBED SQUASH CASSEROLE

2 to 3 pounds squash, sliced
½ cup butter, melted
2 medium onions, finely chopped
1 5-ounce can water chestnuts, drained and sliced
1 8-ounce package herb seasoned stuffing mix
4 slices bacon, fried crisp and crumbled
⅛ teaspoon crushed rosemary
Salt and pepper
1 cup sour cream
1 10¾-ounce can cream of chicken soup
1 2-ounce jar pimientos drained and chopped

Cook squash in boiling water until tender. Drain well reserving 1½ cups liquid. Mash the well drained squash and season to taste with salt and pepper. Combine the reserved liquid, bacon and all other ingredients except ½ cup of stuffing mix. Stir in squash. Pour into a 2½-quart casserole. Top with remaining stuffing mix and bake at 350 degrees for 30-35 minutes. About 16 servings.
Mrs. A. R. Snider (Frances)

YELLOW SQUASH CASSEROLE

2 pounds squash
1 tablespoon sugar
1 teaspoon salt
1 medium onion, grated
4 hard boiled eggs
4 cups Ritz crackers, rolled fine
2 sticks oleo
2 teaspoons butter
2 teaspoons flour
4 cups milk
½ teaspoon salt
¼ teaspoon pepper

Cook squash with sugar and salt until tender. Drain and mash. Make white sauce by melting 2 teaspoons butter and adding flour; gradually add milk and cook until thick. Combine sauce, eggs, onions, and squash.

Melt 2 sticks oleo and add to 4 cups of Ritz crackers that have been rolled fine. Place ⅔ cracker mixture in bottom of casserole dish. Next pour in squash mixture and top with remaining cracker mixture. Bake in 350 degree oven for 25-30 minutes. This dish may be frozen before baking. When frozen, you should double the baking time.
Mrs. Naomi C. Dugan

SQUASH DELIGHT

2 pounds yellow squash
½ stick margarine
½ cup chopped onion
½ cup chopped bell pepper
½ cup sliced water chestnuts
½ cup mayonnaise
1 teaspoon sugar
½ teaspoon red pepper
1 large or 2 small eggs, beaten
Salt and pepper to taste
½ cup grated cheese
½ cup bread crumbs

Cook squash in lightly salted water until barely tender. Drain. Mix squash and all ingredients together except cheese and bread crumbs. Top with grated cheese and bread crumbs. Bake 20 to 30 minutes at 350 degrees. Can be made ahead and frozen in 2 or more small casserole dishes. Thaw in the morning and bake in the evening.

Mrs. James R. Alexander (Betty Lou)

NUTTY SQUASH CASSEROLE

1 pound yellow squash
½ cup grated onion
½ cup green pepper, chopped
½ cup pecans, chopped
1 egg
½ cup mayonnaise
¼ cup pimiento
1 stick oleo
Bread crumbs

Slice squash. Cook squash, onion and green pepper together until tender. Drain. Add pecans, egg, mayonnaise, pimiento and oleo. Cook in 2-quart baking dish. Cover with bread crumbs. Bake at 350 degrees for 40 minutes.

Mrs. Ellis M. Bush (Juanita)

SQUASH SUPREME

2 No. 2 cans or 2 cups fresh cooked squash, undrained
2 medium carrots, grated
2 tablespoons grated onion
1 2-ounce jar pimiento, chopped
1 8-ounce package sour cream
1 10¾-ounce can cream of chicken soup
1 small package herb dressing stuffing (Pepperidge Farm)
½ cup butter

Mix squash, carrots, onion, pimiento, sour cream and soup. Melt butter and pour over stuffing mix. Line casserole with half the stuffing mix, pour in squash mixture and top with the remaining half of stuffing mix. Bake at 375 degrees for 35 minutes.

Mrs. Jo Whittaker

FRESH CURRIED VEGETABLES

1 large yellow onion, chopped
2 tablespoons oil
1 medium-sized head cauliflower, broken into flowerets
1 medium-sized eggplant, cut into cubes
2 green peppers, cut into ¼ inch strips
2 banana peppers, chopped
4 carrots, sliced into rings
1 pound green beans, broken in half
5½ teaspoons curry powder
3 bay leaves
¾ cup boiling water
1 cup tomato sauce

Sauté onion in oil until yellow. Add all the vegetables, curry powder and bay leaf. Cook about 5 minutes. Add boiling water and simmer 15 minutes. Add tomato sauce and cook until vegetables are slightly tender, being sure not to overcook them. Remove bay leaf and serve. Serves 8 to 10.
Mrs. George Gekakis (Carol) (submitted by Rhonda Berry)

OVEN BAKED FROZEN VEGETABLES

2 packages (10-ounces) frozen vegetables
½ cup powdered Coffeemate
2 tablespoons butter
3 tablespoons flour
1 teaspoon salt
1 cup hot water

Preheat oven to 350 degrees. Place frozen vegetables in a 1½-quart casserole; break apart or separate vegetables with a fork. Sprinkle with Coffeemate, flour and salt. Dot with butter. Pour hot water over mixture. Bake 45 minutes or until tender, stirring once during the baking. Stir again before serving. Makes 6 servings. Top with paprika.

Variation: Try broccoli and brussels sprouts,
brussels sprouts and cauliflower,
broccoli and cauliflower,
peas and cauliflower

Mrs. Fran Lorant Moore

INTERESTING FACTS ABOUT SHREVEPORT

Personalities in the national and international news during the 1950's were many. Major William Whisner won the Bendix Transcontinental Air Race with speed a little over 603 miles an hour.

Tommy Bolt, who learned to play golf in Shreveport, won the National Open Golf Championship at Tulsa in 1958.

Van Cliburn, a native of Shreveport, won the Tchaikovsky International Piano Competition in Moscow in 1958.

In August of 1958 Miss Eurlyne Howell of Bossier City was named "Miss U.S.A." and went on to finish in the first five for the title of "Miss Universe".

Dr. Clarence H. Webb, pediatrician and archaeologist, made important Indian history and archaeology contributions with his explorations at the Belcher Mound and Poverty Point.

Other famous people who either claimed Shreveport as their home or received their start here are: Elvis Presley, Tommy Sands and Johnny Horton who got their start on the Columbia Broadcasting System's LOUISIANA HAYRIDE over radio station KWKH.

Other natives in the musical and entertainment world were Gene Austin and Jan Garber.

Sports greats who came from Shreveport are many. Joe Ferguson and Terry Bradshaw played high school football at Woodlawn in Shreveport. Joe plays for the Buffalo Bills and Terry plays for the Pittsburgh Steelers. Pat Tilley, who plays for the Cardinals, went to Fair Park High; Roland Harper, from Captain Shreve High, plays for the Chicago Bears. Bo Harris, also from Captain Shreve, plays for the Cincinnati Bengals and from across the river and Airline High comes Gary "Bighands" Johnson who plays for San Diego.

Others of fame are Farron Young, Howard K. Smith, Perry Como, Geoffery Beene, Tom Jerral, and Karen Black.

Crockpot

The old Peg-Leg Railroad from Bradford to Gillmor. Built, 1877. Abandoned, 1880.

Railroad development began in this area with the chartering of the Vicksburg, Shreveport and Texas Railway and the Texas Western Railway in 1852.

The Texas Western Railway built a line from Marshall, Texas, to Swanson's Landing on Caddo Lake where frieght and passengers were then transferred to river steamboats. All the railroad materials, equipment and even laborers were brought up Red River by steamer. When the first locomotive arrived, settlers for miles around gathered at the landing to see the queer new "contraption." It was called the LOUISIANA, and the little steamer, ALIDA, excited much interest as it chugged through the bayous to Swanson's Landing tugging the locomotive on an old bull-nosed barge.

Bossier City

The railroads also aided in the development of Bossier Parish. Building of the Vicksburg, Shreveport and Pacific railroad bridge over Red River made the area more accessible. Up until then it could be reached only by ferry. With the increase in traffic the little settlement of Cane's Landing or Cane City began to grow. In 1907 it was incorporated and named Bossier City for the famous Creole General Pierre Everiste John Baptiste Bossier, who was Congressman from this district when Bossier Parish was formed in 1843.

CHICKEN BREASTS

- 8 small chicken breasts
- Salt
- Pepper
- 1 10¾-ounce can cream of mushroom soup
- ¼ cup cooking sherry
- 1 pound fresh mushrooms, sliced
- Butter or margarine
- 1 cup sour cream

Place first 5 ingredients in crockpot and cook at LOW for 4 to 6 hours. Sauté mushrooms in butter or margarine and stir into crockpot. Turn off pot to cool. Add the sour cream after the mixture has cooled for about 30 minutes. Serve with rice or as a main dish.

Mrs. Bill Woodall (Iris), Fort Worth, Texas

CHICKEN CACCIATORE

- 2½ to 3 pounds chicken parts
- 1 clove garlic, crushed
- ¼ cup olive oil
- 1¼ teaspoons salt
- Pepper
- 1 teaspoon paprika
- 2 teaspoons oregano
- ½ teaspoon basil
- ½ teaspoon rosemary
- 1 medium onion, minced
- 1 16-ounce can stewed tomatoes
- ¼ to ½ cup sauterne wine

Brown chicken parts in garlic and olive oil. Place in crockpot and add other ingredients. Cook on LOW for 4 to 6 hours. Serve with spaghetti.

Mrs. Court Crow (Jeanne)

CROCKPOT BARBECUE CHICKEN

- 4 boneless chicken breasts
- ¾ cup lemon juice
- ½ cup onion, chopped fine
- 16 ounces barbecue sauce

Place chicken breasts in shallow pan and pour the lemon juice over them. Place in refrigerator and let sit for about 30 minutes. Remove breasts from lemon juice and place in the bottom of the crockpot. Cover with the onion and then pour on the barbecue sauce (undiluted). Let cook on low for 8-10 hours or on high for 4-5 hours. Serves 4.

Mrs. Kenneth Braswell (Debbie)

CHICKEN TETRAZZINI

¾ cups cooked chicken, diced
2 cups chicken broth
¼ cup dry white wine
1 cup half-and-half
1 10¾-ounce can cream of mushroom soup
½ pound fresh mushrooms, sliced

Spaghetti, cooked and buttered
¾ cup Parmesan cheese

Place first 6 ingredients in crockpot and cook at LOW for 4 to 6 hours. Place cooked spaghetti in greased baking dish and pour crockpot mixture over spaghetti. Top with Parmesan cheese and place under broiler until Parmesan cheese browns.
Mrs. Michael J. Lewis (Rhonda)

ROASTED RABBIT

1 or 2 rabbits, cut up
Flour
Salt
Pepper
Oil

Dredge rabbits in flour, salt, pepper and brown in oil. Place in crockpot and cook on LOW all day.
Mrs. Roger Smithson (Karla)

GASLIGHT GOO

1 pound ground beef
½ cup chopped onion
1 15½-ounce can chili (with or without beans)
1 10¾-ounce can cream of chicken soup, undiluted
1 29-ounce can yellow hominy, drained
1 small can black olives, minced
Cheddar cheese, sliced if used in crockpot; shredded if casserole
¼ cup water (for crockpot)

Sauté beef and onions until onions are clear. Add chili, soup, hominy and olives.

For Crockpot: Set temperature on low; add about ¼ cup warm water, pour contents into pot and let simmer about 2 hours. About 10 minutes before serving, put sliced cheese into mixture — about one dozen 1-inch wide pieces.

For Casserole: Spoon mixture into greased, shallow 2-quart casserole. Cover and bake at 350 degrees about 25 minutes. Sprinkle with ½ cup shredded cheese and bake another 5 minutes.
Mrs. Howard Chapman (Stella)

MEATLOAF

- 2½ to 3 pounds lean ground beef or chuck
- ½ pound sausage, browned and drained
- 2 envelopes (any size) onion soup mix
- 6 whole small baking potatoes, peeled
- 1 13-ounce can evaporated milk
- 1 egg
- 1 medium onion, chopped

Mix meat ingredients and form into a loaf. Place in crockpot with potatoes on top. Do not add any liquid. Cook on LOW all day.
Mrs. Court Crow (Jeanne)

CHILI
(For Crockpot)

- 2 pounds ground beef
- 2 to 3 cans kidney beans, drained
- 3 tablespoons chili powder
- Salt and pepper
- 1 32-ounce can tomato juice
- 1 package dry onion soup mix
- 2 cloves garlic

Cook beef until lightly browned, drain. Combine all ingredients in slow cooker. Cover and cook 10 to 12 hours.
Mrs. A. H. Otto (Marjorie)

CHILI WITH BEANS

- 2 large (16-ounce) cans kidney beans, drained
- 2 pounds stew meat, diced (or chuck steak coarsely ground, browned and drained)
- 2 16-ounce cans stewed tomatoes
- 1 6-ounce can tomato paste
- 2 cloves garlic, minced
- 1 medium bell pepper, chopped
- 2 onions, chopped
- 3 tablespoons chili powder
- ½ teaspoon cumin or Tabasco

Place all ingredients in crockpot and cook at LOW all day.
Mrs. Onnie B. Cross (Maree)

CROCKPOT BEEF AND ONIONS

3 pounds beef, cubed
1 envelope (any size) onion soup mix
1/4 cup burgundy wine
Lawry's seasoned salt
Pepper
1 medium onion, sliced
2 medium onions, sliced
Oleo
1 can (10 3/4-ounces) cream of mushroom soup

Place first 6 ingredients in crockpot and cook at LOW all day. Drain, keeping liquid. Sauté the 2 onions in the oleo until browned, add soup; then add mixture to drained meat in crockpot. Serve over rice or noodles.
Mrs. Phil Olinghouse (Loree), Little Rock, Arkansas

ORIENTAL BEEF

3 pounds flank steak, sliced into strips
2 teaspoons salt
2 tablespoons soy sauce
1 1/4 cups water
1/4 cup cornstarch mixed with cold water
3 onions, chopped
2 bell peppers, in chunks
5 tomatoes, in chunks
3 stalks celery, sliced
1 1/2 cups boiling water
1 cup instant rice
1 tablespoon oleo
Onion tops
Nuts

Place first 4 ingredients in crockpot and cook at LOW all day. Add the next 5 ingredients, turn to HIGH and cook for 1 hour or until thick. Bring next 3 ingredients to a boil in a saucepan with a lid. Cook according to directions on the box of rice. Serve meat and vegetables from the crockpot over rice with onion tops and nuts as garnishes.
Mrs. Court Crow (Jeanne)

GREEN BEANS AND BEEF

3 pounds beef, in chunks
1 teaspoon garlic salt
Pepper
1 tablespoon paprika
1 tablespoon Worcestershire sauce
1 16-ounce bag of frozen French cut green beans
1 teaspoon garlic juice
1 3/4 tablespoons soy sauce
1 16-ounce can stewed tomatoes
1 medium onion, sliced

Place all ingredients in crockpot and cook on LOW all day.
Mrs. Michael J. Lewis (Rhonda)

BRASWELL'S BEEF STEW

3 potatoes, cut up
2 pounds cubed beef
2 small cans whole kernel corn
Salt to taste
Pepper to taste
½ cup chopped onion
1 clove garlic, minced
1 bay leaf
1 teaspoon paprika
2 8-ounce cans tomato sauce
1 beef bouillon cube
1 cup water
1 teaspoon Worcestershire sauce
⅓ package uncooked spaghetti

In crockpot place the potatoes, cubed beef, corn, salt, pepper, onion, garlic, bay leaf and paprika. Over this mixture pour the tomato sauce and the bouillon cube which has been dissolved in the cup of water; add Worcestershire sauce. Cook in crockpot for 8 to 10 hours on low. Add the spaghetti for the last hour. This makes a good thick beef stew.
Mrs. Kenneth Braswell (Debbie)

BEEF STEW

4 pounds stew meat
Flour
Paprika
Oil
1 potato, in chunks
2 medium onions, sliced
5 carrots, sliced
½ cup quick cooking tapioca
2 beef bouillon cubes
½ teaspoon seasoned salt
Pepper
½ teaspoon garlic juice
1 bay leaf
1 tablespoon Worcestershire sauce
1 tablespoon soy sauce
¼ cup burgundy wine

Dredge meat in flour and paprika and brown in oil. Place all ingredients in crockpot and cook on LOW all day.
Variation: 1 package frozen boiling onions and 1 package frozen peas (any size packages) may be added to the crockpot 30 minutes before serving.
Mrs. Michael J. Lewis (Rhonda)

CROCKPOT BARBECUE MEATS

Choice of meat to fill crockpot
Garlic salt
Pepper
2 onions, chopped
1 16-ounce bottle of barbecue sauce
⅛ teaspoon liquid smoke

Place all ingredients in crockpot and cook on LOW all day.
Mrs. Court Crow (Jeanne)

PICKLED BEEF

3 pounds beef roast
2 16-ounce cans stewed tomatoes
¼ cup vinegar
1 teaspoon garlic juice
1 bay leaf
5 whole cloves
¼ teaspoon pickling spice
Salt and pepper

Place all ingredients in crockpot and cook on LOW all day.
Mrs. Court Crow (Jeanne)

SMOKED BEEF

Beef brisket
Aluminum foil
1 teaspoon liquid smoke
½ cup barbecue sauce
1 teaspoon garlic salt
Pepper
2 medium onions, sliced

Seal all ingredients in aluminum foil and place in crockpot. Cook on LOW all day.
Mrs. Court Crow (Jeanne)

CROCKPOT BEEF AND BEER

4 pound pot roast
¼ cup oil
Flour
5 onions
2 cloves garlic, minced
1 can of beer
1 tablespoon salt
1 tablespoon vinegar
½ bay leaf or ⅛ teaspoon crushed bay leaves

Dredge roast in flour and brown in oil. Place other ingredients in crockpot with roast and cook on LOW all day.
Mrs. Onnie B. Cross (Maree)

ROAST BEEF AND GRAVY

4 pound roast
Salt
Pepper
1 envelope onion soup mix
1 can (10¾-ounces) cream of mushroom soup

Place ingredients in crockpot and cook at LOW all day.
Variation: 2 or 3 stalks of celery, chopped and 1 can (10¾-ounces) of cream of celery soup may be used in place of the onion and mushroom mixture.
Mrs. Onnie B. Cross (Maree)

CROCKPOT ROAST BEEF

4 potatoes, peeled and cubed
4 carrots, scraped and diced
1 stalk celery, chopped
2 onions, chopped
½ cup red wine
2 teaspoons salt
1 tablespoon Worcestershire sauce
4 pound roast or brisket
1 can bouillon
¾ cup water
2 tablespoons parsley
¼ teaspoon pepper
1 bay leaf

Place vegetables on the bottom of the crockpot and add other ingredients. Cook at LOW all day.
Mrs. Michael J. Lewis (Rhonda)

BEEF STROGANOFF

3 pounds beef cut in strips
Salt
Pepper
Flour
Oil
Salt
Pepper
1 medium onion, chopped
2½ teaspoons tomato paste
1 bay leaf
1 clove garlic, mashed
2 beef bouillon cubes
½ cup sherry
2 cups mushrooms, sliced
Butter
3 tablespoons flour
½ cup sour cream

Dredge beef in salt, pepper, flour and brown in the oil. Place next 8 ingredients in the crockpot with the beef and cook on LOW all day. Sauté mushrooms, butter and flour and stir into crockpot. Add the sour cream to the meat mixture before serving.
Mrs. Fred Collins (Madeline)

RICE WITH AN ORIENTAL TOUCH

2 cups long grain white rice
3 cups canned beef broth or bouillon
Salt
½ cup sliced almonds
Green onion tops, sliced
Pepper
1 small can (8-ounces) crushed pineapple, well drained

Place rice, broth, salt and pepper in crockpot and cook at HIGH for 1¼ hours. Stir occasionally. Stir in pineapple and almonds before serving and garnish with onion tops.
Mrs. Court Crow (Jeanne)

CROCKPOT BAKED POTATOES

About 12 scrubbed and well greased baking potatoes

Put in crockpot. Cover and cook on low for 8 to 10 hours. DO NOT add water.
Mrs. Mary Wells

CROCKPOT HAM AND SCALLOPED POTATOES

6-8 slices of ham
4-5 medium potatoes, peeled and sliced
½ cup onion, chopped fine
Garlic, salt, pepper
1 cup grated cheddar cheese
1 10¾-ounce can cream of mushroom soup
Paprika

In a crockpot place half of the ham and half of the potatoes, sprinkle with half of the onion and season to taste with the garlic, salt and pepper. Sprinkle with half of the cheese. Repeat with the remaining half of the ingredients in the same order as before. Spoon the soup directly from can over the top and sprinkle with paprika. Cover and cook on low for 8-10 hours. Serves 6-8.
Mrs. Kenneth Braswell (Debbie)

CROCKPOT SCALLOPED POTATOES

5-6 potatoes
½ onion, chopped
Salt and pepper to taste
1 10¾-ounce can cream of mushroom soup
Butter
½ pound fresh mushrooms, sliced
½ onion, minced

Place peeled and thinly sliced potatoes, chopped onion, salt, pepper and mushroom soup in crockpot and cook on low all day. Sauté fresh mushrooms and minced onion in butter. Add mushrooms and onion to potatoes just before serving.
Mrs. Bill Alexander (Mary Lynn)

PORK AND SWEET POTATOES

3 pounds pork, in chunks, broiled
1 stalk celery, sliced
1 tablespoon dried parsley
Salt
Pepper
3 medium apples, sliced
1 bay leaf
1 medium onion, chopped
½ cup beef bouillon
2 yams, or sweet potatoes, peeled and sliced

Place ingredients in crockpot and cook on LOW all day.
Mrs. Bill Woodall (Iris), Fort Worth, Texas

PORK CHOPS

6 thick pork chops, fat removed
Flour
Salt
Pepper
Oil
2 cloves garlic, mashed
1 can mushrooms, drained (any size)
1 6-ounce can tomato paste
1 10¾-ounce can cream of mushroom soup
Garlic salt
Pepper

Dredge chops in flour and brown in salt, pepper and oil. Place in crockpot and add other ingredients. Cook on LOW all day. Serve with rice.
Mrs. Phil Olinghouse (Loree), Little Rock, Arkansas

SWEET AND SOUR PORK

3 pounds pork, in chunks, broiled
Salt
Pepper
1 bell pepper, sliced
8 whole boiling onions, peeled
1 16-ounce can pineapple chunks, drained
2 medium tomatoes, chopped
2 tablespoons vinegar
⅓ cup brown sugar, packed
¼ cup soy sauce
½ cup chicken broth or bouillon
¼ cup cornstarch dissolved in water

Mix all ingredients in crockpot and cook on LOW all day.
Mrs. Court Crow (Jeanne)

NEW ORLEANS SECRET CROCKPOT RED BEANS

1 pound dried camelia red beans
1 large onion, chopped in medium pieces
1 pound ham pieces
¼ cup Crisco oil
1 6-inch long smoked sausage (sliced ½-inch thick)
1 teaspoon salt
1 teaspoon pepper
¼ teaspoon garlic powder
¼ teaspoon parsley flakes
¼ teaspoon celery salt

After washing dried beans, put into crockpot; add all dry ingredients. Cover and set on low. Let cook overnight (approximately 9 hours). In morning, cut up onions, sausage and ham and fry approximately 5 minutes in ¼ cup Crisco oil. When onions become a little clear, pour all out of frying pan into beans; stir one time, set on high. The beans should cook on high approximately 35 minutes. Serves 6.
Mrs. Barbara Parnell

CROCKPOT CABBAGE

3 tablespoons bacon grease
1 cup hot water
1½ teaspoons salt
Cabbage, diced, to fill the crockpot
½ teaspoon pepper
1¼ tablespoons sugar
½ cup vinegar

Combine all ingredients and pour over cabbage in crockpot. Cook at LOW all day.
Mrs. Onnie B. Cross (Maree)

APPLESAUCE CAKE SUPREME

1 stick margarine, melted
1 cup sugar
2 tablespoons water
1¾ cup applesauce
2 cups flour
2 teaspoons baking soda
1 teaspoon cinnamon
½ teaspoon cloves
¾ teaspoon allspice
1 cup raisins, or more, to taste

Cream first 3 ingredients together. Add other ingredients. Pour batter into greased, floured coffee can which fits loosely in the crockpot. Fill only ⅔ full. Cover the top of the can with 5 paper towels. DO NOT ADD WATER. Put crockpot lid on slightly off center so excess moisture may escape. Cook on HIGH for 4 hours.
Mrs. Court Crow (Jeanne)

CROCKPOT APPLESAUCE

½ cup water
½ cup brown sugar
½ cup granulated sugar
2½ teaspoons cinnamon
8 to 10 apples, peeled, cored, sliced
2 tablespoons lemon juice
1 teaspoon nutmeg
½ teaspoon cloves, ground
1 tablespoon oleo

Place all ingredients in the crockpot and cook at LOW all day.
Mrs. Court Crow (Jeanne)

APPLE CIDER

8 cups sweet apple cider
¾ cup brown sugar, packed
Dash salt
2 teaspoons cinnamon
1 teaspoon cloves, ground
1 teaspoon allspice
½ teaspoon nutmeg, ground

Place all ingredients in crockpot and cook on LOW heat for 2 hours.
Mrs. Onnie B. Cross (Maree)

CHOCOLATE DRINK FOR A COLD NIGHT

½ cup cocoa
¾ cup sugar
Pinch salt
¼ to ½ teaspoon cinnamon
¼ teaspoon vanilla
¼ stick of butter or margarine
2 tablespoons flour
8 cups milk (whole or skim)
2 cups water

Put ingredients in crockpot and cook on HIGH for 1 hour. Turn on LOW until ready to serve. Serve with whipped cream or marshmallows.
Mrs. Court Crow (Jeanne)

BANANA BREAD

¾ cup melted margarine
1½ cups sugar
1½ cups ripe banana, mashed
2 eggs, beaten
1 teaspoon vanilla
2 cups flour
1 teaspoon baking soda
¾ teaspoon salt
½ cup buttermilk
¾ cup walnuts or pecans, chopped

Pour batter into greased, floured coffee can which fits loosely in the crockpot. Fill only ⅔ full. Cover the top of the can with 5 paper towels. DO NOT ADD WATER. Put lid on crockpot slightly off center so excess moisture can escape. Cook on HIGH for 4 hours.

Mrs. Phil Olinghouse, Jr. (Penny), Little Rock, Arkansas

Microwave

With the coming of the railroad larger livery stables were founded to furnish the passengers of the steamers vehicles and horses for travel to other points. Wagon yards and livery stables were social and news centers for teamsters, coach drivers and interested citizens.

INTERESTING FACTS ABOUT SHREVEPORT

On March 20, 1839, by an act of the State Legislature, Shreve Town was officially incorporated as the town of Shreveport and authorized to function under its own government.

Shreveport's first mayor, John O. Sewall, was killed in a duel by a man named Wilson in Elysian Fields, Texas, in 1840. They met in Texas because it was against the law to duel in Louisiana. Although the mayor had a reputation for being fast with a gun and had dueled before, he had loaned his own gun to someone else and had to borrow a gun. His aim failed and he was shot in the heart.

The first effort at taming the town for the Lord was made by Bishop Leonidas K. Polk from the Episcopal Church.

The first brick house in Caddo Parish was the home of Judge S. J. Whitworth of Greenwood, which was begun in 1839 and finished in 1844. Robert Ripley labeled it "The PWA of the Past!" in his "Believe It Or Not" column since "45 men labored 3 years pressing brick, hewing shingles and making pegs for this homestead."

The marriage of Rolland Polland and Mrs. Elizabeth Williams on April 3, 1838, was the first to be solemnized in Shreveport.

The telephone, invented in 1876, was brought to Shreveport by the Great Southern Telephone Company in 1881.

Cotton production in Louisiana in 1900 was three times higher than it is today, and Shreveport was a leading interior cotton market with only Memphis and Dallas exceeding it in inland port receipts.

SCRAMBLED EGGS

Number of Eggs	Butter or Margarine	Milk	Minutes
1	1 teaspoon	1 tablespoon	1 to 1½
2	2 teaspoons	3 tablespoons	2 to 2½
4	4 teaspoons	4 tablespoons	4½ to 5
6	2 tablespoons	6 tablespoons	4, stir, 2½ to 3½ more

1. Break eggs into soup bowl or glass casserole (1-quart size for 4, 5, or 6). A styrofoam cup can be used.
2. Add milk and beat together with a fork.
3. Add butter and other seasonings to taste.
4. Cover with glass lid or plastic wrap.
5. Microwave on ROAST. Stir once during cooking period.
6. Stir gently with a fork before serving.
7. If cooking scrambled eggs a while before serving, undercook slightly and warm on ROAST when served.
8. Soak cooking dish immediately after emptying for easiest clean-up.

Mrs. Court Crow (Jeanne)

RANCH EGGS

2 tablespoons olive oil
1 small onion, finely chopped
1 small clove garlic, peeled and chopped
½ green pepper, finely chopped
1 cup canned tomatoes with tomato paste
Few drops Tabasco sauce
½ teaspoon dried oregano
¼ teaspoon salt
4 poached eggs

1. In a shallow, 1-quart non-metallic casserole, place olive oil, onion, garlic and green pepper.
2. Heat, uncovered, for 3 or 4 minutes or until vegetables are tender.
3. Add canned tomatoes, Tabasco sauce, oregano and salt. Stir to combine.
4. Heat, uncovered 3 to 4 minutes or until hot.
5. Make 4 wells in tomato mixture. Carefully place one poached egg in each well.
6. Heat, uncovered 1 to 2 minutes depending on desired degree of doneness. Allow to stand 2 to 3 minutes before serving.

NOTE: If canned tomatoes with tomato paste are not available, 1 cup canned tomatoes plus 1 tablespoon tomato paste may be substituted.

Mrs. Court Crow (Jeanne)

FRIED EGGS

Number of Eggs	Minutes
1	45 to 55 seconds
2	1½ to 2 minutes
4	2 to 2½ minutes

1. Preheat microwave browning grill as directed in the browners instruction booklet on HIGH.
2. Melt 1 teaspoon of butter on microwave browning grill.
3. Break egg(s) on browning grill.
4. Microwave on ROAST.

Mrs. Court Crow (Jeanne)

BAKED EGGS

Number of Eggs	Minutes
1	35 to 40 seconds
2	1 to 1¼ minutes
3	2 to 2¼ minutes

1. Break each egg into a buttered custard cup.
2. Cover with plastic wrap.
3. Microwave on ROAST.
4. Let stand, covered, 1 minute before serving.

Mrs. Court Crow (Jeanne)

BACON

COOKING TIMES

Number of Slices	Minutes
2	2 - 2½
4	4 - 4½
6	5 - 6
8	8 - 9

Arrange bacon on the bacon crisper or a paper plate covered with a paper towel. Cover bacon with a couple of paper towels (not napkins, they shred easily). Cook.

Mrs. Court Crow (Jeanne)

BAKED APPLES

Sweet apples
Butter
Red Hots (candies)

1. Core apple but leave the bottom intact.
2. Fill with a small pat of butter and a few Red Hots candies.
3. Place in a custard cup or on a small dish.
4. Cover with plastic wrap, loosely.
5. Bake 2 to 2½ minutes on HIGH.
6. Let stand approximately 2 minutes before serving.

Other fillers:
Brown sugar; sugar and cinnamon; peppermint candy; raisins and nuts. Mix all with butter or margarine.

Mrs. Court Crow (Jeanne)

BAKED GRAPEFRUIT

Grapefruit
Butter or margarine
Brown sugar

1. Remove core and seeds from grapefruit halves; cut edges and between sections.
2. Sprinkle each half with brown sugar; dot with butter or margarine.
3. Microwave on HIGH.
4. If grapefruit is especially juicy, drain some juice as cooking will cause more juice.
   2 halves .... 3 to 3½ minutes
   4 halves .... 4 to 5 minutes

Mrs. Court Crow (Jeanne)

GRILLED CHEESE SANDWICH

1. Place mayonnaise on two slices of bread and place cheese in between bread slices.
2. Preheat browning dish in the oven for 2 minutes on fastest speed.
3. After browning dish is preheated, immediately melt butter on dish.
4. Place sandwich on browning dish, browning both sides.
5. Cook on fastest speed 30 seconds on each side.

NOTE: Do not use PAM as it tends to scorch.

Mrs. Court Crow (Jeanne)

PORK CHOPS AND APPLE SLICES

6 thick pork chops
¼ cup sugar
1 teaspoon salt
½ teaspoon pepper
½ teaspoon cinnamon
¼ teaspoon nutmeg
2 winesap apples, cored
1 large onion

1. Trim excess fat from the chops.
2. Blend sugar, salt, pepper, cinnamon and nutmeg.
3. Coat chops thoroughly. Stand each chop upright in a glass loaf pan.
4. Cut apples into 7 slices and the onion into 5 slices. Place one of each between the chops, and the extra apple slices at each end. Cover tightly with plastic wrap. Microwave for 14 to 16 minutes. Rest 5 minutes before serving.

Makes 6 servings.
Mrs. Court Crow (Jeanne)

SHRIMP CASSEROLE

1 (10¾-ounce) can cream of mushroom soup
2 tablespoons chopped onion
1 tablespoon lemon juice
2 cups cooked rice
½ teaspoon Worcestershire sauce
Butter
Paprika
½ teaspoon dry mustard
¼ teaspoon pepper
½ pound cleaned, uncooked shrimp
¼ cup bread crumbs

1. Combine soup, green pepper, onion, lemon juice, rice, Worcestershire sauce, mustard, pepper and shrimp.
2. Place in a 1½-quart casserole. Top with bread crumbs. Dot with butter. Sprinkle with paprika.
3. Cover and bake 10 minutes. Turn dish halfway through time. Remove lid for last 2 minutes.

Mrs. Court Crow (Jeanne)

FRENCH FISH

1 pound fish filets
¼ cup French dressing
½ cup cracker crumbs
Paprika

1. Dip filets in dressing. Coat with crumbs. Place filets in greased baking dish. Sprinkle with paprika.
2. Bake in microwave for 6 minutes. Turn halfway through the cooking time.

Mrs. Court Crow (Jeanne)

CHICKEN STEW

2 medium potatoes, cut into 16 pieces
1 cup coarsely sliced celery
2 cups coarsely sliced carrots
1 large onion, cut in eighths
2 teaspoons salt
¼ teaspoon pepper
1 teaspoon ground sage
2½ to 3 pound whole frying chicken cut up
2 cans (10¾ ounces each) condensed cream of chicken soup
Parsley

1. Layer vegetables in 4-quart Dutch oven. Season with salt, pepper and sage. Place chicken, skin down and thick edges toward outside of dish, on top of vegetables. Cover with glass lid or plastic wrap.
2. Cook on HIGH for 15 minutes. Drain and turn chicken over. Pour soup over chicken; recover.
3. Cook on SIMMER for 25 to 30 minutes or until fork tender. Let stand, covered, 5 minutes before serving. Garnish with snipped parsley.

Mrs. Court Crow (Jeanne)

CHILI PIE

1½ pounds lean ground beef chuck
1 medium sized onion, thickly sliced
1 (12-ounce) can, whole kernel corn, drained
1 (16-ounce) can whole peeled tomatoes, undrained
1 (8-ounce) can tomato sauce with cheese
1½ cups coarsely crumbed tortilla chips or corn chips
1 to 2 teaspoons dried chili powder
1 teaspoon salt
¼ teaspoon pepper
⅓ cup sliced stuffed olives
½ cup shredded Cheddar cheese

1. Crumble meat into a deep 1½-quart casserole.
2. Add onions and heat, uncovered, 7 to 9 minutes or until meat is browned and onions are tender.
3. Stir occasionally. Drain off excess fat.
4. Add corn, tomatoes, tomato sauce, chili powder to taste and salt and pepper; stir to combine. Heat, uncovered, 4 to 5½ minutes, stirring occasionally.
5. Arrange olive slices on top of meat mixture and sprinkle with cheese.
6. Heat, uncovered, in microwave 2 to 2½ minutes.
7. Sprinkle with tortilla chips and heat, uncovered, for 1 to 1½ minutes.

Serves 4 to 6.

Mrs. Court Crow (Jeanne)

MEAT LOAF

1 clove garlic
1 pound lean ground beef
1 egg, beaten
7 saltines, crushed
1 small onion, minced
1 tablespoon minced parsley
¾ teaspoon salt
¼ teaspoon pepper
¼ to ½ cup chopped green pepper
¼ cup chopped celery
½ cup tomato sauce
¼ cup catsup

1. Rub a 1¼-quart utility dish with cut clove of garlic or sprinkle the bottom evenly with garlic powder.
2. Toss together remaining ingredients except catsup, mixing lightly but thoroughly.
3. Spoon mixture evenly into the utility dish; do not pack.
4. Cook, uncovered, for 6 minutes, turning once (the dish) during cooking period.
5. Drizzle catsup over top of loaf. Cook 5 minutes longer.
6. If a brown crust is desired, place under broiler unit for a few seconds.

Mrs. Court Crow (Jeanne)

PIZZA WITH HAMBURGER CRUST

In a large bowl mix with a spoon:
1 pound ground beef
½ cup dry bread crumbs
1 teaspoon salt
½ teaspoon oregano

Stir in ½ cup tomato sauce

Spread meat mixture in glass 10-inch pizza plate or on the bottom and side of a 10-inch glass pie plate. Bake 5 minutes on HIGH.
Pour on top ¼ cup tomato sauce
Spread on tomato sauce 1 can (8 ounces) kidney beans, drained
Cut into strips 3 slices Cheddar or Mozzarella cheese
Arrange cheese strips in crisscross design on beans. Bake uncovered for 3 to 5 minutes or until cheese melts.
NOTE: Dry store-bought bread crumbs work best.
Mrs. Court Crow (Jeanne)

CHEESEBURGER AND VEGETABLE DISH

1 pound ground beef
½ cup chopped onion
¼ cup butter or margarine
¼ cup all-purpose flour
1 teaspoon salt
Dash pepper
1½ cups milk
1½ cup shredded sharp American cheese (6 ounces)
1 teaspoon Worcestershire sauce
1 10-ounce package frozen mixed vegetables
¼ cup chopped canned pimiento
Packaged instant potatoes, mashed (enough for 4 servings)

1. In a large bowl, crumble the ground beef. Add the chopped onion. Cook, uncovered, till meat is brown, about 5 minutes.
2. Stir several times to break up meat. Drain off excess fat. In a 4 cup glass measure, melt the butter about 50 seconds.
3. Stir in the flour, salt, and pepper. Gradually stir in the milk. Cook, uncovered, 1 minute, stir. Cook till thickened and bubbly, about 3 minutes more, stirring every 30 seconds. Stir in 1 cup of the cheese and the Worcestershire sauce. Add to the meat mix.
4. Break up frozen vegetables. Stir vegetables and pimiento into meat mixture.
5. Turn into 8x8x2-inch baking dish. Cook, covered 10 minutes. Turn after 5 minutes.
6. Prepare the instant mashed potatoes as directed on package except decrease water by ¼ cup. Spoon the potatoes around edge of casserole. Sprinkle remaining cheese over potatoes. Cook, uncovered, till cheese melts.

Mrs. Court Crow (Jeanne)

HAMBURGER

Ground beef
Salt
Pepper
Cooking spray

1. Preheat browning dish 2 to 2½ minutes for a 4 ounce burger.
2. Brown patty on both sides in browning dish.
3. Cook 30 seconds in oven on HIGH.
4. Turn patty and cook 45 seconds to 1 minute longer.
5. For more hamburgers heat browning dish 4 minutes and brown burgers on both sides. Then cook about 1 minute per patty.

Mrs. Court Crow (Jeanne)

STANDING RIB ROAST

COOKING TIMES

First Setting HIGH	Second Setting ROAST
Thermometer	Time
rare — 125	7- 8 minutes per pound
medium — 145	8- 9 minutes per pound
well — 155	10-11 minutes per pound

1. Place roast, fat side down, on roasting rack or inverted plate placed inside a large casserole. Season but don't salt.
2. Microwave on HIGH for half total baking time. Turn fat side up. Insert probe or microwave thermometer. Be sure it does not touch a bone or a fat pocket. (Never use a regular cooking thermometer.)
3. Microwave on ROAST the other half of the total time or until the thermometer reads correct temperature for the doneness you desire or until automatic oven turns itself off.
4. Cover lightly with foil and let stand approximately 5 to 10 minutes before serving.

Mrs. Court Crow (Jeanne)

BROCCOLI DIP MICROWAVE STYLE

1 10-ounce package frozen chopped broccoli
½ cup chopped celery
1 10¾-ounce can cream of mushroom soup
½ cup butter or margarine
½ cup chopped onion
1 8-ounce package process cheese spread

Cook broccoli on HIGH for 8 minutes. Combine butter, celery and onion in 2 quart casserole dish. Cook on HIGH for 3 minutes. Add soup, cheese (cut into cubes) and broccoli to the onion-celery mix. Cook on ROAST for 4 minutes. Stir until well blended; cook an additional 1 minute or 150 degrees with temperature probe. Makes 3 cups. This can also be used for a broccoli-rice casserole dish by cooking 1½ cups of rice and mixing with the prepared dip.

Mrs. Doris Horne

STUFFED PEPPERS

3 medium green peppers
¾ pounds ground chuck
1 8-ounce can tomato sauce
1 egg
⅓ cup water
1 teaspoon salt
¼ teaspoon pepper
¾ cup Minute Rice

1. Slice peppers in half (lengthwise) and hollow out.
2. Combine ½ of the tomato sauce and the remaining ingredients.
3. Place in a 2-quart oblong baking dish.
4. Pour remaining tomato sauce over the top of the peppers.
5. Cook on the fastest speed for 15 minutes.

Makes 6 servings.
Mrs. Court Crow (Jeanne)

MELT IN YOUR MOUTH STRING BEANS

2 tablespoons butter
2 tablespoons flour
1 teaspoon salt
1 teaspoon pepper
1 cup sour cream
About 1 cup grated processed Swiss cheese
2 cans French style string beans

1. Melt butter, add flour, salt, pepper. Add sour cream and Swiss cheese. Put string beans in a medium sized casserole and pour sauce over the beans. Cook on ROAST for 20 minutes stirring gently once.

Mrs. Court Crow (Jeanne)

PARMESAN TOMATOES

4 large ripe tomatoes
¼ cup butter or margarine
½ cup grated Parmesan cheese
¼ cup finely chopped parsley
1 tablespoon dried oregano leaves

1. Wash tomatoes and pat dry.
2. Place cut-side-up in a shallow baking dish.
3. Dot each tomato half with about ½ tablespoon butter.
4. In a small bowl combine remaining ingredients.
5. Top each tomato half with some of the cheese mixture.
6. Heat, uncovered for 5 to 6 minutes or until tomatoes are soft and topping begins to melt.
7. DO NOT OVERCOOK or they will be mushy.

Mrs. Court Crow (Jeanne)

BEAN COMPOTE (THREE BEAN SALAD)

4 slices bacon
1/3 cup sugar
1 tablespoon cornstarch
1 teaspoon salt
1/8 teaspoon pepper
1/2 cup vinegar
1 medium onion, sliced
1 can (16 ounces) cut green beans, drained
1 can (16 ounces) cut wax beans, drained

1. Arrange bacon slices in single layer in 2-quart glass casserole.
2. Cover with a paper towel.
3. Cook on HIGH for 3 to 4 minutes or until bacon is crisp. Remove paper towel and bacon. Blend sugar, cornstarch, salt and pepper with bacon drippings. Stir in vinegar. Add remaining ingredients. Cover with glass lid or plastic wrap.
4. Cook on ROAST for 7 minutes. Stir and continue cooking on ROAST for 6 to 8 minutes or until slightly thickened. Let stand, covered, 3 minutes before serving.

8 to 10 servings.
Mrs. Court Crow (Jeanne)

BAKED POTATO

Medium sized baking potato

1. Pierce potato.
2. Place on a paper plate.
3. Cook for 4 to 4 1/2 minutes.
4. Test to see if potato is soft. If not, cook for another minute.

Mrs. Court Crow (Jeanne)

CORN ON THE COB

Corn on the cob (fresh or frozen)
Butter or margarine
Salt

1. Clean corn.
2. Rub generously with butter; wrap in waxed paper, twisting at each end.
3. Cook on fastest speed for 2 minutes.

1 ear of corn
Mrs. Court Crow (Jeanne)

ONION PIE WITH CHEESE

9-inch baked pastry shell
2 tablespoons butter or margarine
3 cups thinly sliced sweet onions
1 pound cottage cheese (or Ricotta)
⅓ cup whipping cream
2 egg yolks
½ teaspoon salt
⅛ teaspoon pepper

1. Prepare pie shell.
2. Melt butter in browning skillet in oven for 1 minute. Add onions. Cook in oven for 4 minutes. Stir every minute.
3. Warm cheese, cream, and egg yolk for 1 minute. Season, then pour into pie shell. Arrange onions over filling. Cook 10 minutes. Turn dish half-way through cooking time. Let stand 5 minutes before serving.

NOTE: A store-bought frozen pie shell may be used if removed from the foil pan it comes in and baked in a glass pie plate.

Mrs. Court Crow (Jeanne)

PINEAPPLE IN YAM BOATS

4 medium (7 to 8 ounces) yams or sweet potatoes
2 tablespoons butter or margarine
2 tablespoons brown sugar
2 teaspoons grated lemon rind
¼ teaspoon ground ginger
¼ teaspoon salt
1 cup crushed pineapple

1. Scrub yams and prick several times with a fork. Place on a paper towel in the oven, arranging in a circle. Cook 15 minutes until tender, turning over half way through the cooking time.
2. Cool slightly, cut off a thin slice of the top of each. Carefully scoop out the insides, reserving the shells.
3. Add the seasonings to the yams and mash. Drain pineapple adding two tablespoons of the juice to the yams. Carefully fold in the pineapple.
4. Fill the shells with the mixture and reheat 3 minutes.
5. May be garnished with lemon slices or orange slices.

Mrs. Court Crow (Jeanne)

CARROT AND APPLE CASSEROLE

4 to 5 medium carrots, peeled and diced into strips
1 winesap apple, peeled and diced (You may leave the skin on if so desired.)
2 tablespoons butter
2 tablespoons brown sugar
2 tablespoons water

Mix ingredients and cook on fastest speed for 10 minutes. Makes 4 to 6 servings.
Mrs. Court Crow (Jeanne)

CHEESE LOAF

2½ cups Bisquick
1 cup (4 ounces) shredded, sharp cheddar cheese
2 teaspoons poppy seeds
1 egg, beaten
1 cup milk

1. In mixing bowl, combine Bisquick, cheese and poppy seeds. Blend beaten egg into milk. Add to Bisquick mixture, stirring hard until well combined.
2. Pour into an 8-inch square glass pan. Smooth the top. Cook 7 to 8 minutes, until a toothpick inserted into the center comes out clean. Pop under the broiler until the top is brown. Serve immediately.

Makes 9 large squares. It toasts beautifully as a leftover!!
Mrs. Court Crow (Jeanne)

CORNBREAD

1 cup yellow corn meal
1 cup sifted all-purpose flour
¼ cup sugar
4 teaspoons baking powder
½ teaspoon salt
1 egg
1 cup milk
¼ cup soft shortening
Vegetable spray (not Pam)

1. Sift together corn meal, flour, sugar, baking powder and salt.
2. Stir in egg, milk and shortening. Beat with rotary beater until smooth. Spray inside of 9½-inch browning skillet with spray. Preheat 2 minutes. Pour batter in skillet. Bake in oven 5½ to 6 minutes.
3. Turn halfway through cooking time. Cool 10 minutes. Turn onto platter.

Mrs. Court Crow (Jeanne)

PERPETUAL MUFFINS (BRAN)

4 cups All-Bran cereal
2 cups 100% Bran cereal
2 cups boiling water
1 quart buttermilk
3 cups sugar
4 beaten eggs
1 cup soft shortening or oil
5 cups all-purpose flour
5 teaspoons baking soda
1 teaspoon salt

1. Pour hot water over cereals.
2. Stir in buttermilk, sugar, eggs, shortening, flour, soda and salt, in that order. Stir until just blended. Refrigerate.
3. Remove from refrigerator. Without stirring batter, fill paper baking cups half full. Arrange 6 cups in a circle or use the muffin pans made for microwave ovens. Bake in oven 2½ minutes. Remove muffins immediately from custard cups to cooling rack.

Mixture may be stored in the refrigerator for 3 to 4 weeks.

Mrs. Court Crow (Jeanne)

BANANA BREAD

3½ cups unsifted flour
3 teaspoons baking powder
1 teaspoon baking soda
1 teaspoon salt
2 cups mashed ripe bananas
2 tablespoons lemon juice
¾ cup softened butter or margarine
1½ cups sugar
3 eggs
¾ cup milk
1 cup coarsely broken walnuts

1. Lightly grease 2 8½x4½x2½-inch glass loaf pans and set aside.
2. Sift together flour, baking powder, baking soda and salt; set aside. In a small bowl, combine mashed bananas and lemon juice and set aside.
3. In the large bowl of an electric mixer, cream butter and sugar until light and fluffy. Add eggs, 1 at a time, beating well after each addition.
4. Add milk and dry ingredients alternately, beginning with and ending with dry ingredients.
5. Fold in walnuts and banana mixture. Pour batter into prepared pans and bake each loaf, uncovered, 7 to 9 minutes, turning pan twice during cooking time.
6. Bread is done when a toothpick inserted in it comes out clean. Allow bread to cool 10 minutes before removing from loaf pans.

Mrs. Court Crow (Jeanne)

EASY LEMON BARS

½ cup butter or margarine, melted
1 package (18 ounces) lemon cake mix
3 eggs
1 package (8 ounces) cream cheese, soft
1 package (14 ounces) lemon frosting mix

1. Place margarine in a medium sized glass bowl. Cook 45 seconds to melt.
2. Add cake mix and 1 slightly beaten egg. Mix with a fork.
3. Press into an 8x12-inch glass baking pan or two 8-inch square glass pans. Blend frosting mix into softened cream cheese. Remove and reserve ½ cups.
4. Add eggs to remaining frosting mix. Beat 3 to 5 minutes. Spread over cake mixture. Cook 10 minutes, turning pan several times.
5. When done, the top will be fairly dry and the sides pulled away from the pan.
6. Do not over cook. Cool. Spread with reserved frosting mix. Cut into small squares.

Makes about 40 squares. If you like chocolate use devil's food cake instead.

Mrs. Court Crow (Jeanne)

BROWNIES

2 squares or envelopes unsweetened chocolate
⅓ cup butter or margarine
1 cup sugar
2 eggs
1 cup unsalted all-purpose flour
¼ teaspoon baking powder
¼ teaspoon salt
½ teaspoon vanilla
½ cup chopped nuts

1. Combine chocolate and butter in medium glass mixing bowl.
2. Cook on ROAST for 1½ to 2 minutes or until melted. Stir in sugar; beat in eggs. Stir in remaining ingredients. Spread butter into a 2-quart (8x8-inch) glass dish.
3. Cook on SIMMER for 7 minutes.
4. Cook on HIGH for 3 to 4 minutes or until puffed and dry on top. Cool until set; cut into bars.

Makes 24 bars.

Mrs. Court Crow (Jeanne)

BAKED PASTRY SHELLS

HOMEMADE CRUST

1. Prepare as for a regular oven. Place shell in glass pie plate.
2. Microwave, uncovered, 4 to 5 minutes or until crust has a dry, flaky appearance, rotating plate once or twice. Cool.

STORE-BOUGHT FROZEN CRUST

1. Remove frozen shell from metal pie plate.
2. Place in glass pie plate. Prepare as for regular crust and oven.
3. Cook on ROAST for 5 to 6 minutes or until brown spots just begin to appear in crust. Cool. To enhance crust color mix in 1 to 2 drops of yellow food coloring into water before adding it to the dry ingredients of a homemade crust or brush a store-bought crust with the color.

Mrs. Court Crow (Jeanne)

MY FAVORITE PUMPKIN PIE

2 eggs
1 (1 pound) can pumpkin
¾ cup sugar
½ teaspoon salt
1 teaspoon cinnamon
½ teaspoon ginger
¼ teaspoon cloves
1 cup evaporated milk
Unbaked pie shell

1. Mix all ingredients.
2. Pour into unbaked pie shell. Bake in oven for 20 minutes. Turn every 5 minutes.

NOTE: A store-bought pie shell may be used if transferred from the metal pan to a glass pie plate.

Mrs. Court Crow (Jeanne)

MY CAKE CONES (QUICKIE)

Cake mix
Cones

Prepare as directed on cake mix package. Any batter left over can be stored in refrigerator up to a week for convenience. Cook one cone at a time for 15 to 20 seconds on HIGH.

Mrs. Court Crow (Jeanne)

MICROWAVE CAKE CONES

1 package (9 ounces) cake mix
6 flat bottom ice cream cones

1. Prepare cake mix as directed on package. Spoon about 2 tablespoons batter into each ice cream cone. Place in oven; allow about 1 inch space between each cone.
2. Microwave on SIMMER (or LOW);
   1 cone . . . 45 seconds to 1 minute
   2 cones . . . 1½ to 2 minutes
   4 cones . . . 3 to 3½ minutes
   6 cones . . . 4½ to 4¾ minutes
   8 cones . . . 5 to 5½ minutes

Cake cones are done when toothpick inserted near center of each cake comes out clean. Cake will be slightly soft around edges when cones come from oven. Cool on wire rack. Frost. 8 cake cones.

TIP: Top each cake cone with a scoop of ice cream and use colored gum drops to make face on ice cream "head."

Mrs. Court Crow (Jeanne)

GINGERBREAD COBBLER WITH APPLES

4 medium apples, peeled, cored, and sliced (4 cups)
1 cup water
¼ cup plus 1 tablespoon brown sugar, packed
1 tablespoon lemon juice
¼ teaspoon ground cinnamon
1 tablespoon cold water
2 teaspoons cornstarch
1 14-ounce package gingerbread mix
Whipped cream

1. In a 1½ quart casserole, combine apples, 1 cup water, brown sugar, lemon juice, and cinnamon. Cook, covered, till apples are tender, about 6½ to 7 minutes, stirring once.
2. Blend 1 tablespoon cold water into cornstarch; stir into apple mixture. Cook, uncovered, till thickened and bubbly, 1½ minutes, stirring twice. Turn into 12x7½x2-inch baking dish.
3. Prepare gingerbread mix following package directions. Pour 1 cup of the batter evenly over apple mixture. Cook, uncovered, till wooden pick comes out clean, about 5 minutes.
4. Serve warm with whipped cream.

To bake remaining batter, fill paper baking cups half full and bake in custard cups or made-for-microwave muffin pans.

Mrs. Court Crow (Jeanne)

PEANUT AND BUTTERSCOTCH FUDGE

2 6-ounce packages (2 cups) butterscotch pieces
1 14-ounce can sweetened condensed milk
½ cup creamy peanut butter
1 teaspoon vanilla
Dash salt

1. In mixing bowl, cook butterscotch pieces, at HIGH for 2½ to 3 minutes, till melted, stirring once. Blend in milk, peanut butter, vanilla, and salt.
2. Cook, uncovered, at HIGH for 1½ to 2 minutes. Just till bubbly.
3. Turn into buttered 8x8x2-inch baking dish. Chill till firm.
4. Cut into squares. Keep refrigerated.

Makes 2 pounds.
Mrs. Court Crow (Jeanne)

EASY RICH FUDGE

½ cup butter or margarine
2 3- or 3¼-ounce packages regular vanilla pudding mix
½ cup milk
½ teaspoon vanilla
1 16-ounce package sifted powdered sugar (about 4¾ cups)
⅓ cup nuts or candied cherries, chopped

1. In 1-quart glass bowl, melt the butter about 1 minute. Stir in dry mix and milk.
2. Cook, uncovered, till boiling, about 3 minutes; stir occasionally.
3. Cook 1 minute more, stirring every 15 minutes.
4. Add vanilla. Beat in sugar; stir in nuts or cherries. Pour into buttered 10x6x2-inch baking dish. Top with nut halves, if desired. Chill, cut in 1-inch squares. Store in refrigerator.

Makes 2 pounds.
Mrs. Court Crow (Jeanne)

MICROWAVE PEANUT BRITTLE

1½ cups raw peanuts
½ cup white corn syrup
1 teaspoon butter or margarine
1 teaspoon baking soda
1 cup sugar
⅛ teaspoon salt
1 teaspoon vanilla

Stir together peanuts, sugar, syrup and salt in 1½-quart casserole. Place in microwave oven and cook on HIGH for 7 to 8 minutes, stirring well after 4 minutes. Add butter and vanilla to syrup, blending well. Return to oven and cook 1 to 2 minutes more. Peanuts will be lightly browned and syrup very hot. Add baking soda and gently stir until light and foamy. Pour mixture onto lightly greased pizza pan; let cool ½ to 1 hour. When cool, break into small pieces and store in airtight container. Makes about 1 pound. If you use salted peanuts, omit the salt and add peanuts after first 4 minutes of cooking.
Mrs. Doris Horne

Breads

Progress in public education was slow in Louisiana due to the old contempt for public schools as "charity" institutions. The first recorded school in the parish was Caddo Academy, which was incorporated in 1838.

The first high school was established in 1892 in the old YMCA building which was located on the corner of Milam and Edwards Street. It was housed in the Soady building until provisions were finally made for it on the third floor of the Hope Street School. Principal was C.E. Byrd.

Because the people of the city and parish were dependent on private subscription for the acquisition and maintenance of school buildings prior to the state constitution of 1898, H. H. Hargrove proposed a voluntary tax for that purpose in 1895. A citizens' committee canvassed property owners and secured pledges to pay such a tax, which resulted in the erection of a $60,000 red brick building on the Hope Street grounds.

INTERESTING FACTS ABOUT SHREVEPORT

In May, 1922 Shreveport had its first broadcasting station, and on September 25, 1925, radio station KWKH went on the air. W. K. Henderson was one of radio's most colorful pioneers and was remembered by his sign-on "Hello, World, Doggone Ya!" That the world did listen to him during the next seven years was evident by the many thousands of letters he received daily from all over the United States and the 50 to 75 letters a day from Europe.

When Henderson bought the station in 1925 the call letters were WGAQ. He changed the call letters to Kennonwood William Kennon Henderson (KWKH) and moved the station to Kennonwood.

Henderson was the first to use radio as a means of direct sales. His "Hello World" coffee and a picture of himself sold for $1.00. In 1930 Henderson was awarded RADIO DIGEST'S prize for operating the most popular station in the south.

KSLA-TV, channel 12, was a precedent setter for the industry, giving Shreveport and the area television 22 months before a construction permit was granted by the Federal Communications Commission.

KTBS-TV, channel 3, went on the air September 3, 1955.

The 20-story Beck building was the worlds *first* colored aluminum office building. Built with panels of turquoise blue, it was dedicated in 1956.

RAPCON, one of the first radar approach control units in the Air Force, was installed at Barksdale in June of 1956.

Centenary College celebrated its 70 years in Shreveport in 1978.

ICEBOX POTATO ROLLS

2 cakes yeast
¾ cup Crisco shortening
1 cup boiled, mashed Irish potatoes
½ cup sugar
1 cup warm sweet milk
1 tablespoon salt
2 eggs
4½ to 5 cups flour

Scald milk and cool to lukewarm. Dissolve yeast in ¼ cup warm water, add to milk. Add mashed potatoes, shortening, sugar and eggs. Add flour and mix well. Dough will be stiff. Spread a little oil (1 teaspoon) on top of dough to prevent drying. Cover and place in refrigerator overnight. Take out amount of dough needed and shape into rolls desired (3 balls size of walnut will make cloverleaf rolls if placed in greased muffin tins). Let rise for two hours. Bake in 400 degree oven about 15 to 20 minutes, depending on size. Dough may be kept in refrigerator four or five days and used as needed.
Mrs. Leonard Green, Jr. (June)

CHERRY CORDIAL ROLLS

1 small recipe any sweet roll dough
12 maraschino cherries, chopped and drained

Mixture:
½ cup flour
½ cup brown sugar (packed)
¼ cup butter

Add maraschino cherries to sweet roll dough. After dough rises roll out on lightly floured board into a rectangle 18x9-inches. Mix mixture together and spread on dough. Roll up tightly beginning at the wide side. Seal well and cut into 18 slices. Put into a greased muffin pan . . . cut side up. Cover and let rise in a warm place until double (35 to 40 minutes). Heat oven to 375 degrees and bake 20 to 25 minutes. Frost edges with thick confectioners' sugar icing.
Mrs. Court Crow (Jeanne)

ROLLS

1 yeast cake
2 cups lukewarm water
1/3 cup sugar
1 tablespoon salt or to taste
1/2 cup Crisco
1 egg
5 1/2 cups flour

Dissolve yeast in warm water, add sugar, salt and 3 cups of flour. Beat well, add shortening and egg. Beat well. Add remainder of flour and beat again. Let rise. Push down and roll out and cut with biscuit cutter. Let rise. Can be made the night before and put in refrigerator. This dough will keep for several days. Pinch off amount needed each time.

Mrs. Lois Mambourg

MUFFIN TIN ROLLS

1 cup lukewarm water
1 cake yeast
1 teaspoon sugar
4 cups flour
1 teaspoon salt
1/4 cup sugar
2 sticks butter
2 eggs

Mix and set aside the lukewarm water, cake of yeast and teaspoon of sugar. In a bowl mix the flour, salt and 1/4 cup sugar. Cut in the butter; then add eggs and the yeast mixture. Stir until well blended. Cover and place in refrigerator overnight. One and one-half hours before serving make into your favorite shapes. It makes 24 muffin tin rolls. Let rise until double in bulk. Bake at 350 degrees for 12 to 15 minutes, until light brown.

Mrs. Hubert L. Joyner (Virginia)

ICE BOX ROLLS

2 cups sweet milk
1/2 cup sugar
1/2 cup shortening
1 package yeast
1 tablespoon sugar
4 cups flour
1/2 teaspoon salt
1/2 teaspoon soda
1 teaspoon baking powder

Combine sweet milk, sugar, and shortening in a pan and bring to a boil. Then let this mixture cool to lukewarm. Add yeast, one tablespoon sugar, 1/4 cup warm water to the milk mixture. Put 2 cups flour in a large bowl and slowly add milk mixture. Let rise 2 hours then add salt, soda, baking powder, and left over flour. Beat mixture well and put in icebox and use as needed. When making rolls let rise until double in size. Bake in 350 degree oven for 10 minutes till brown.

Mrs. R. C. Wheat

HOT ROLLS

1 yeast cake
1 cup lukewarm water
1 quart sweet milk
4 or more cups flour
⅔ cup sugar
1 cup shortening
1 heaping teaspoon salt
3 teaspoons baking powder
1 teaspoon soda

Soak yeast cake in lukewarm water. Put the quart of sweet milk, the sugar and shortening in a sauce pan and heat to boiling. Let cool to lukewarm and mix with the yeast and use enough flour to make batter stiff like cake batter (approximately 2 or more cups). Cover and let rise for 2 hours. Sift the salt, baking powder and soda with the remaining flour which may be a little more than the 2 cups left. Add to the first mixture and mix. Add extra flour until mixture is same as biscuit dough. Make into rolls and let rise for 2 hours before baking in 400 degree oven. This recipe makes a large amount of rolls. Dough may be kept in refrigerator for several days and made into rolls each day as you need them, or share them with a friend!
Mrs. John L. Hoppe (Jo)

EASY COFFEE ROLLS

1 can biscuits (5 or 10 count)
Cinnamon
Butter or oleo

Cut each biscuit in a spiral strip. Roll each one in pinwheel fashion, putting cinnamon and butter over the strip before rolling. Bake in oven at 350 degrees until brown or butter is melted.
Eugene F. Stewart

WHOLE WHEAT YEAST ROLLS

1 teaspoon salt
¼ cup sugar
6 tablespoons shortening
1 cup hot water
3½ cups flour (½ plain / ½ whole wheat)
1 egg, beaten
1 package dry yeast

Combine salt, sugar, shortening and water. Heat until shortening melts. Cool. Sprinkle yeast in 2 tablespoons lukewarm water. Add beaten eggs and cooled mixture to yeast. Beat in 2 cups combined flour and beat until smooth. Add remaining flours and enough to make dough easy to handle. Store in refrigerator. Roll out ½-inch thick, cut, fold in half. Place on greased cookie sheet and let rise until double, several hours. Bake in 400 degree oven 10-12 minutes.
Mrs. Court Crow (Jeanne)

BANANA BREAD I

1 cup butter (melt and cool)
4 eggs (beaten)
2 cups sugar
6 medium bananas (mashed)
3 cups sifted flour
2 teaspoons soda
1 teaspoon salt (fold in)
1 cup nuts (optional)

Mix all ingredients, and pour into two greased loaf pans or one large Bundt pan. Let stand for 20 minutes before baking in preheated 350 degree oven for one hour. For banana nut bread, you can add 1 cup of your favorite chopped nuts.
Mrs. Louis R. Jaudon (Betty)

BANANA BREAD II

2 sticks oleo
1 cup sugar
2 eggs
2 cups flour
1 teaspoon baking powder
Dash of salt
1 teaspoon vanilla
Juice of ½ lemon
3 bananas
Nuts (½-1 cup)

Put oleo, sugar, eggs, flour, baking powder and salt in mixer and start beating. Mash bananas and add to mixture. Add vanilla, lemon juice and nuts. Put in medium size loaf pan and bake at 350 degrees about 1 hour.
Mrs. James Beasley (Carol)

SOUR CREAM BANANA BREAD

3 teaspoons margarine
1 cup sugar
1 egg, beaten
½ cup sour cream
1 teaspoon salt
1 tablespoon lemon juice
2 cups sifted flour
2 tablespoons baking powder
1 teaspoon soda (heaping)
1 cup bananas (mashed)

Cream margarine and sugar together. Add beaten egg and sour cream. Mix thoroughly. Add the sifted dry ingredients alternately with mashed bananas. Add lemon juice. Pour into greased loaf pan. Bake at 375 degrees for 50 minutes. Cool before cutting.
Mrs. Lois Mambourg

OLD FASHIONED RAISIN BREAD

1 cup white or dark raisins
3 packages dry yeast
1 tablespoon sugar
1 tablespoon coarse salt
2 tablespoons soft margarine
3 eggs
½ cup dark Karo
3 cups white flour
2 cups whole wheat flour

Plump raisins in water for 10-15 minutes. Proof yeast in 1 cup lukewarm water in large bowl. Add sugar, salt, softened butter, eggs and Karo. Add whole wheat flour and 2 cups white flour. Drain raisins and add. Beat thoroughly, then turn out onto lightly floured board. Knead well, adding one more cup white flour. Place dough in large buttered bowl. Cover and let rise in warm draft-free place until doubled in bulk. Turn dough out onto lightly floured board. Punch down with fist and divide into two loaves. Grease two 9x5x3-inch loaf pans and put in loaves. Cover and let rise again until doubled in bulk. Brush tops with one egg yolk and two tablespoons cream. Bake in preheated 400 degree oven for 10 minutes, then lower temperature to 350 degrees for 25-30 minutes until loaves sound hollow when tapped on bottom.
Mrs. A. H. Otto (Marjorie)

PUMPKIN BREAD

3 cups sugar
4 eggs
1 cup salad oil
2 cups pumpkin (canned)
⅔ cup water
3½ cups flour
1 teaspoon salt
2 teaspoons soda
1½ teaspoons cinnamon
½ teaspoon cloves
1 cup pecans (chopped)
1 cup raisins or dates

Mix sugar and oil. Add eggs and beat well. Add pumpkin and water. Sift flour with spices, salt and soda. Add pumpkin mixture and blend well. Then add raisins and nuts. You can use one half cup raisins and one half cup chopped dates instead of a full cup of either. Grease 4 one pound coffee cans. Fill cans ½ full and bake in a 350 degree oven for one hour or until an inserted straw comes out clean. Let cool in cans for about 15 or 20 minutes and bread will pop right out. Wrap in waxed paper or foil when cool and store in refrigerator or can be frozen.
Mrs. C. D. Attaway (Margie)

APRICOT WALNUT BREAD

2 cups biscuit mix
1 cup oats (quick cooking)
¾ cup sugar
1 teaspoon baking powder
¼ teaspoon salt
½ cup snipped dried apricots
1 cup chopped walnuts
1 egg, well beaten
1¼ cup milk

Stir together first five ingredients. Mix in apricots and walnuts. Combine egg and milk and add to dry ingredients. Beat hard 30 seconds. Pour into greased 9x5x3-inch loaf pan. For a plumper loaf, let stand for 20 minutes. Bake at 350 degrees for about 60 minutes. Let cool in pan for 10 minutes.
Mrs. R. W. Fletcher (Sue)

CRANBERRY FRUIT NUT BREAD

2 cups flour, sifted
1 cup sugar
½ teaspoon soda
1½ teaspoons baking powder
1 teaspoon salt
¼ cup shortening
1 teaspoon grated orange peel
¾ cup orange juice
1 egg, well beaten
1 cup fresh cranberries (coarsely chopped)
½ cup chopped nuts
½ cup candied red and green cherries

Sift together flour, sugar, soda, baking powder, salt; cut in shortening, combine peel, juice and egg. Add to dry ingredients, mixing just to moisten. Fold in cranberries, nuts and cherries. Turn into greased loaf pan and bake for one (1) hour at 350 degrees. Cool and wrap and store overnight.
Mrs. H. Russell Maddox (Tommie Lue)

STRAWBERRY BREAD

3 cups flour
2 cups sugar
3 teaspoons cinnamon
1 teaspoon soda
1 teaspoon salt
1¼ cups salad oil
4 eggs
2 10-ounce packages frozen strawberries
1¼ cups chopped nuts

Combine all ingredients in large mixing bowl and mix well. Pour into two greased and floured loaf pans. Bake at 350 degrees for 1 hour and 15 minutes. Makes two loaves.
Mrs. Hal Johnson, Jr. (Shirley)

ANGEL BISCUITS

1 package dry yeast
1/4 cup lukewarm water
5 cups flour
1 teaspoon soda
3 tablespoons baking powder
4 tablespoons sugar
1 1/2 teaspoons salt
2/3 cup cooking oil
2 cups buttermilk

Dissolve yeast in lukewarm water and set aside. Sift flour, soda, baking powder, sugar, and salt together; add oil, milk, and yeast mixture. Mix well. Turn out on floured board and knead a few minutes. Divide into 30-40 biscuits and bake on greased pans 10-12 minutes in a 400 degree oven.

Dough may be kept in air-tight container in the refrigerator about a week. Biscuits can be made about 30 minutes ahead of time, or can be baked at once.

Number of biscuits made will depend upon the size and thickness desired.

Mrs. John R. Clement (Martha)

YEAST BISCUITS

1 package dry yeast
1/4 cup warm water
2 teaspoons baking powder
1 tablespoon sugar
1 teaspoon salt
2 cups flour
1 cup buttermilk
3 teaspoons shortening

Dissolve yeast in warm water. Mix dry ingredients with flour, adding yeast mixture and milk. Knead for 1 or 2 minutes. Roll on floured board, 2/3 inch thick and cut into biscuits. Place in greased pan. (I melt oleo and dip biscuits in this.) Let rise until doubled in bulk. Bake at 425 degrees or until brown.

Mrs. Onnie B. Cross (Maree)

WHOLE WHEAT BISCUITS

2 cups whole wheat flour
1/2 teaspoon salt
2 teaspoons baking powder
2 tablespoons shortening
1 cup milk, scant

Mix together the flour, salt and baking soda. Cut in shortening and add milk. Turn onto a well floured board and knead well. Roll and cut. Bake at 425 degrees until brown.

Mrs. Court Crow (Jeanne)

OLD TIME BUTTERMILK BISCUITS

2 cups sifted flour
½ teaspoon salt
3 teaspoons baking powder
¼ teaspoon soda
5 tablespoons shortening
1 cup buttermilk

Sift flour, salt, baking powder and soda into bowl. Add shortening and cut in with pastry blender, or two knives until mixture resembles coarse meal. Add buttermilk, all at once, and stir until dough follows fork around bowl. Turn out on lightly floured surface; knead half a minute. Roll out ⅜ inch thick, brush with melted fat; fold over and cut with biscuit cutter. Bake on ungreased baking sheet in 450 degree oven for 12-15 minutes. Makes 14-16 biscuits.
Mrs. Edward W. Robinson, Keithville, Louisiana

BUTTERMILK BISCUITS

5 cups self-rising flour
1 cup Crisco
2 cups buttermilk
1 tablespoon sugar
¼ cup warm water
Oleo
1 teaspoon soda
1 package yeast

Dissolve yeast in water and set aside. Sift flour but save 1 cup. Cut Crisco into flour; add sugar and soda to buttermilk and add yeast mixture to flour. Turn out on board covered with saved cup flour and knead. Roll out to ½-inch and cut. Put in pan and dab oleo on each one. Bake at 350 degrees until done. Takes about 30 minutes.
Mrs. A. H. Otto (Marjorie)

QUICK BISCUITS

2 cups plain flour
2 teaspoons salt
1 cup milk
4 teaspoons baking powder
4 tablespoons mayonnaise

Sift flour, baking powder and salt. Mix mayonnaise and milk, add sifted ingredients; mix well. Drop by spoon on greased cookie sheet. Press with floured fork. Bake in preheated oven at 400 degrees until lightly brown.
Mrs. Joseph LaBarbera (Billie)

SOUR DOUGH BISCUITS I

1 cup water (warm)
2 packages dry yeast
¼ cup sugar
½ cup cooking oil
2 cups buttermilk
6 cups self-rising flour

Mix water and yeast; set aside. Mix sugar, cooking oil, and buttermilk. Add water and yeast mixture. Mix in flour to form soft dough. Cover and place in refrigerator. It will keep a week or longer.

To make biscuits rub hands together with flour and pinch off a small amount of dough. Turn over in greased pan. Let set 30 minutes or place in cold oven and set at 400 degrees. Cook until brown.

Mrs. H. H. Hand (Henry Ella)
Mrs. Jo Whittaker

SOUR DOUGH BISCUITS II

1 package yeast
1 cup warm water
¼ cup sugar
2 cups buttermilk
¾ cup Wesson oil
3 cups flour
4 teaspoons baking powder
2 scant teaspoons salt
¼ teaspoon soda

Dissolve yeast in warm water. Add sugar, buttermilk, oil, flour, baking powder, salt and soda. Add more flour to make batter. Pour on pastry cloth and knead until consistency of thin biscuit dough. Make out biscuits and put in pan. Bake in oven at 400-450 degrees until brown.

Mrs. Floyd Hughes (Maxine Dennis)

MAYONNAISE BISCUITS

1 cup self-rising flour
½ cup milk
¼ cup mayonnaise

Mix flour and milk well. Beat in the mayonnaise. Spoon into greased muffin tins and bake at 400 degrees until lightly browned. Makes six large or nine small muffins.

Mrs. Bill Nolan (Pearl)

CORNBREAD I

1 cup corn meal
1 cup flour
3 teaspoons baking powder
½ teaspoon salt
1 egg
1 cup milk
¼ cup melted shortening or salad oil or bacon drippings

Mix corn meal, flour, baking powder and salt. Beat egg, add milk and shortening. Add to dry ingredients, stirring just enough to moisten. Pour into greased iron skillet, bake in hot oven (400 degrees) for 30 minutes.
Mrs. Louis R. Jaudon (Betty)

CORNBREAD II

¾ cup flour, sifted
1 teaspoon salt
3 teaspoons baking powder
3 tablespoons sugar, optional
1½ cups yellow corn meal
2 eggs, beaten
1½ cups milk
¼ cup shortening, melted

Sift flour, salt, baking powder and sugar, if used, and add corn meal. Combine eggs with milk and shortening and use to moisten dry ingredients. Turn into a shallow well-greased pan and bake at 400 degrees about half an hour. Serves 6
Mrs. Jean Rice

BUTTERMILK CORNBREAD

1 cup corn meal
2 tablespoons flour
¼ teaspoon sugar
2 level teaspoons baking powder
1 teaspoon salt
¼ teaspoon soda
1 cup buttermilk
2 tablespoons bacon drippings or cooking oil
1 or 2 eggs

Sift meal, flour, sugar, salt, and baking powder together. Dissolve soda in buttermilk and add to dry ingredients, then add beaten eggs. Pour hot drippings into mixture. Pour into hot greased skillet. Bake at 425 degrees until golden brown. Let cool for about ten minutes before removing from pan.
Mrs. C. D. Attaway (Margie)

MEXICAN CORNBREAD I

1½ cups yellow meal
1 cup sweet milk
2 eggs
1 teaspoon salt
½ teaspoon soda
1 cup yellow cream corn
½ cup grated sharp cheese
¼ cup bacon drippings
1 large onion, chopped
Garlic salt to taste
4 jalapeno peppers, cut up

Mix all together and pour in greased muffin pan. Bake 1 hour in 350 degree oven. Makes 24 muffins.
Mrs. Clara Cummins, Bossier City, Louisiana

MEXICAN CORNBREAD II

1 cup corn meal mix
1 onion, chopped
3 hot peppers, cut up
2 eggs
1 can cream style corn (16 ounces)
Cheese or meat optional as center filling

Mix corn meal mix with eggs; add chopped onions and cream corn. Mix in chopped peppers. Grease iron skillet. Pour ½ of batter in skillet. Put layer of cheese or meat, and pour rest of batter over cheese or meat. Bake in oven 350 degrees 40 to 45 minutes.

Left-over meats are good for this cornbread.
Mrs. Mary E. Jenkins

CORN SPOON BREAD

2 slightly beaten eggs
1 8½-ounce package corn muffin mix
1 8-ounce can cream style corn
1 8-ounce can whole kernel corn, drained
1 cup dairy sour cream
½ cup butter or margarine
1 cup shredded cheese

Combine eggs, muffin mix, cream style and whole kernel corn, sour cream and butter. Spread in greased 11x7x1¾-inch baking dish. Bake in 350 degree oven for 35 minutes. Sprinkle cheese atop; bake 10 to 15 minutes more or until knife comes out clean. Yield: 8 servings.
Mrs. Art Ogletree, Jr. (Ann)

TORTILLAS

1 cup flour
½ cup corn meal
¼ teaspoon salt
1 egg
1½ cups cold water

Filling:
2 cups grated sharp cheddar cheese
1 cup minced onion
½ teaspoon salt

Measure flour by dip-level method. Combine in bowl. Beat with rotary beater until smooth. Spoon 3 tablespoons batter onto a moderately hot ungreased griddle to make a very thin 6-inch pancake. Turn tortillas when edges begin to look dry . . . not brown! Bake other side. Keep warm in covered pan. Makes 12.

Mix filling well and cover. Fold or serve flat.

Mrs. Court Crow (Jeanne)

JALAPENO CORNBREAD

3 cups cornbread mix
2½ cups milk
½ cup salad oil
3 eggs, beaten
1 large onion, grated
2 tablespoons sugar
1 cup cream style corn
½ cup fresh or canned jalapeno peppers (chopped very fine)
1½ cups sharp cheese, grated
¼ pound bacon, cooked and crumbled
¼ cup pimientos, chopped
½ clove garlic, crushed (optional)

Put cornbread mix in large bowl; add milk and stir. Add other ingredients in order given. Bake in three greased 8x8x2-inch pans at 400 degrees about 35 minutes or until done. Yield: 12 to 16 servings.

This freezes well and is excellent served with vegetables or as base for chili shortcake.

Mrs. Leonard Green, Jr. (June)

CORN MEAL PUFFS

½ cup flour
1 tablespoon sugar
½ teaspoon salt
¾ cup sweet milk
2 teaspoons baking powder
1½ cups corn meal
1 egg
Oil for frying

Mix ingredients together. Drop from spoon into oil for deep fat frying. Cook until golden brown.

Mrs. C. D. Attaway (Margie)

HUSH PUPPIES I

2 cups corn meal
2¼ teaspoons baking powder
1 teaspoon salt
Oil for frying
1 large finely chopped onion
1 cup sweet milk
¼ cup warm water

Sift corn meal, baking powder and salt into bowl containing the onion. Add milk and water and mold into small pones or golf ball size. Drop in deep hot fat and fry until golden brown. These are perfect served with hot fried fish.
Mrs. C. D. Attaway (Margie)

HUSH PUPPIES II

3 cups corn meal
1 cup flour
4 teaspoons baking powder
1 teaspoon salt
1 medium onion (chopped fine)
2 medium eggs
1¾ cups milk

Combine above ingredients and drop by spoonfuls into deep, hot fat. Cook until they float. Remove and drain.
Mrs. Edward W. Robinson, Keithville, Louisiana

SURPRISE CORN MUFFINS

1 cup yellow corn meal
1 cup unsifted flour
3 tablespoons sugar
4 teaspoons baking powder
1 teaspoon salt
1 cup milk
½ cup mayonnaise (not salad dressing)

Grease 12 muffin cups. Mix corn meal, flour, sugar, baking powder and salt. Stir milk into mayonnaise and stir into flour mixture until moistened. Batter will be lumpy. Fill each cup ⅔ full. Bake at 400 degrees for 20 minutes or until browned.
Mrs. A. R. Snider (Frances)

SCOTTISH SHORTBREAD

2 sticks butter or margarine
½ cup sugar
2¼ cups flour
Sugar for topping

Cream together the butter and sugar. Gradually add the flour. Beat until all dissolved and smooth. Pat out on a cookie tray. Keep hands floured. Refrigerate (over night is best). Bake at 325 degrees until golden brown, about 15 or 20 minutes. Turn oven off; leave shortbread in the oven 10 minutes longer. Sprinkle with sugar. Cut into small squares while hot.
Mrs. Louis R. Jaudon (Betty)

CORNBREAD DRESSING

2 packages Gladiola Cornbread Mix
6 slices of bread, crumbed
Broth
1 large onion, chopped
1½ cups celery, finely chopped
Chopped giblets or chicken

Prepare and bake cornbread mix according to instructions. Crumble cornbread and add bread crumbs. Pour broth over bread to make soft consistency. Add onion, celery, and giblets or chicken. Bake at 350 degrees approximately 30 minutes until brown.
Ms. Dianne Crook, Longview, Texas

SWEET POTATO BREAD

3 cups sugar
1 cup Wesson oil
2 cups mashed cooked sweet potato
4 eggs
1 teaspoon soda
1 teaspoon nutmeg
1 teaspoon cinnamon
1½ teaspoons salt
3½ cups flour
⅔ cups orange juice
1 cup chopped dates (8 ounces)
1 cup raisins
1 cup candied cherries
2 cups pecans

Mix sugar, Wesson oil, mashed potatoes and well-beaten eggs with 2½ cups of flour. Add spices. Save 1 cup flour to dredge dates, raisins, pecans and cherries. Add these to mixture. Grease and flour 4 1-pound coffee cans. Fill each can about ¾ full. Bake 1 hour 15 minutes at 350 degrees. Can be stored in cans in freezer.
Mrs. H. H. Hand (Henry Ella)

HOMEMADE LIGHT BREAD

1½ cakes yeast
1 cup warm water
1 cup shortening
½ cup sugar
1 tablespoon salt
1 cup boiling water
2 beaten eggs
7 cups flour, sifted

Dissolve yeast in 1 cup warm water. Cream together the shortening, sugar and salt. Add 1 cup boiling water. Let mixture cool slightly and add yeast mixture. Add beaten eggs and flour. Work and knead on floured board until not sticky. Put in greased bowl. Let rise. Knead on floured board; put in greased bowl and let rise again. Knead again on floured board. Put into greased loaf pans. Let rise again. Brush melted butter on top. Bake 45 minutes in preheated oven at 350 degrees. Makes two loaves. This makes the best thick breakfast toast ever!
Mrs. Frederick F. Webb III (Adrienne)

HOMEMADE BREAD

1 cup hot milk
2 teaspoons salt
2 tablespoons margarine
2 tablespoons sugar
1¼ cup warm water
Butter
1 cup stone ground corn meal
1 cup stone ground whole wheat flour
4 to 5 cups white all-purpose bleached flour
1 package dry yeast

Add margarine, sugar, water, salt, corn meal, whole wheat flour, to hot milk. Add yeast to flour. Add flour/yeast mixture to above mixture. Let rise to double in bulk after kneading. Knead a short time and shape into two loaves. Cook 30 minutes in 375 degree oven. Open oven and butter top generously and return to oven for 10 minutes.
Mrs. R. Ellis Douglass

QUICK CHEESE BREAD

2 5½-ounce packages Bix-Mix or Bis-Kits
2 eggs
¾ cup water
1½ cups grated cheddar cheese
2 teaspoons dry mustard
2-3 teaspoons butter or margarine

Mix first three ingredients together. Stir in 1 cup grated cheese and the dry mustard. Pour batter into a loaf pan, which has been sprayed with Pam. Spread evenly, top with the remaining ½ cup of grated cheese and dot with the butter or margarine. Bake at 350 degrees for about 40 minutes or until a toothpick comes out clean. Serve warm with soft butter.
Mrs. Dale Ward (Renee)

FRENCH BREAD

2 cups warm water (105-110 degrees)
1 package active dry yeast
1 tablespoon salt
6 to 6½ cups all-purpose flour
Sprinkling of corn meal

Measure water into large bowl. Sprinkle in yeast. Stir to dissolve. Beat in salt and 4 cups flour until smooth. Add enough flour to make a stiff dough, mixing with your hands, if necessary. Turn dough out onto floured board, Knead about 5 minutes or until smooth and elastic. Place dough in large bowl with fairly vertical sides rather than slanted ones — it helps the rising. Cover with a heavy towel folded in half. Set in a warm place (75-80 degrees), on a towel or board. Let the dough rise about 2½ hours or until tripled in bulk. Punch dough down and let rise 30 to 45 minutes or until more than double. Punch down again. Loosen from sides of bowl with a rubber spatula. Turn out onto floured board. Cut into 3 or 4 equal pieces and roll each back and forth with your palms, sliding hands gradually toward ends as dough lengthens. Roll it to a length to fit your cookie sheet. Sprinkle cookie sheet with corn meal and place bread on cookie sheet. With a razor blade or very sharp knife make 3 or 4 long lengthwise slashes in each loaf ¼ to ½-inch deep. Let dough rise, uncovered, in warm place about 2 hours or until doubled in bulk. While dough rises heat oven to 400 degrees. Put a shallow pan of boiling water on bottom shelf to create steam. Brush loaves with cold water, using a soft brush. Bake 20 minutes. Brush again. Bake 20 minutes. Transfer loaves to wire racks and cool.
Mrs. L. A. McKinley (Elizabeth), Magnolia Springs, Alabama

SHORT-ORDER CHEESE BREAD

3¾ cups packaged buttermilk biscuit mix
1¼ cups shredded natural sharp cheddar cheese
1 egg, beaten
1¼ cups milk
½ teaspoon dry mustard
Sesame seeds

Preheat the oven to 325 degrees. Grease or spray with Pam, a glass baking dish (1½-quart). In a large mixing bowl, mix all ingredients just to blend, then beat vigorously for one minute. Pour into prepared pan. Sprinkle top with sesame seeds. Bake for 55 to 60 minutes, then cool slightly before slicing.
Mrs. Marvin Kines (Ora)

TOASTY GARLIC SLICES

⅓ cup butter or margarine
1 or 2 cloves garlic
6 1-inch slices French bread

Melt butter in 11x7x1½-inch baking dish. Add 1 or 2 cloves garlic, minced. Add six slices French bread, turning quickly to butter both sides. Let stand ten minutes. Heat in 350 degree oven about 20 minutes.
Mrs. Art Ogletree, Jr. (Ann)

CRAZY CRUST

1 cup flour
2 tablespoons sugar
1 teaspoon baking powder
½ teaspoon salt
¾ cup water
¾ cup Crisco
1 egg

Use small bowl of the electric mixer. Combine all ingredients and beat 2 minutes at medium speed. Spread into 2 9-inch greased pie pans. Fresh fruit can be used in making your filling or you can use any canned fruit. Mix your filling as you would for any fruit pie. This crust is easy and very good.
Mrs. F. A. Kihneman (Tora)

CREAM CHEESE PASTRY

1 3-ounce package cream cheese
½ cup butter or oleo
1 cup sifted flour

Allow cheese and oleo to soften at room temperature. Blend in flour. Chill for one hour.

Shape into 2 dozen one-inch balls and shape small shells in tiny ungreased 1¾-inch muffin tins. (Large shells can be made in medium muffin tins.) Bake at 325 degrees for 25 minutes or until golden brown. Do not overcook.
Mrs. Art Ogletree, Jr. (Ann)

NEVER FAIL DUMPLINGS

1½ cups flour
3 tablespoons shortening (Crisco)
1 egg
1½ teaspoons salt
5 tablespoons cold water

Beat egg, add other ingredients and mix well, roll very thin and cut into 1-inch strips about 2 or 3 inches long. Let stand for about 20 minutes and then drop into hot broth and simmer until done.
Mrs. John Hoppe (Jo)

APPLE MUFFINS

1 egg
1½ cups flour
1½ cups sugar
½ cup milk
1 cup grated raw apple
2 teaspoons baking powder
¼ teaspoon salt
½ teaspoon cinnamon
¼ cup melted shortening or salad oil

Beat egg slightly. Add milk, grated apple, shortening and mix. Sift together and add the rest of the ingredients to the liquid mixture. Stir only slightly. Bake at 400 degrees about 15 minutes.
Mrs. Court Crow (Jeanne)

MAGNIFICENT MUFFINS

2 cups sifted flour
¼ cup sugar
3 teaspoons double acting baking powder
3 tablespoons melted shortening
1 teaspoon salt
1 cup milk
1 egg, slightly beaten

Mix flour, sugar, baking powder and salt in a bowl. Combine milk with egg. Stir in melted shortening. Mix liquid and dry ingredients together lightly until just moistened. Fill greased muffin cup ⅔ full. Bake at 400 degrees for 20 to 25 minutes.
Author unknown — submitted by Mrs. Court Crow (Jeanne)

BANANA MUFFINS

2 cups flour
1 teaspoon soda
¼ teaspoon salt
¾ cup sugar
2 tablespoons vinegar
1 egg, beaten
1 cup mashed bananas
½ cup melted shortening
6 tablespoons milk

Sift together flour, soda, salt and sugar. Add egg, bananas, shortening, vinegar, and milk. Stir lightly and quickly with a fork until just mixed. Fill greased muffin pans ⅔ full. Bake at 400 degrees about 20 minutes.
Mrs. Court Crow (Jeanne)

ORANGE MUFFINS

1 cup sugar
½ cup oleo
2 eggs
2 cups flour
1 teaspoon soda
½ teaspoon salt
1 cup buttermilk
1 orange
1 cup raisins
½ cup chopped pecans
⅓ cup sugar

Mix in regular way. Grind orange rind and raisins. Add chopped nuts, mix and bake at 350 degrees until done.
Reserve juice of orange and mix with ⅓ cup of sugar. Pour over muffins while hot.
Mrs. Court Crow (Jeanne)

WHOLE WHEAT/BUCKWHEAT MUFFINS

1 cup whole wheat flour
3 tablespoons self-rising flour
2 teaspoons baking powder
1 egg
1 tablespoon sugar
¼ teaspoon salt
¾ cup milk
1 tablespoon oil

Mix flours, baking powder, salt, sugar. Add milk, egg, oil, and beat. Fill greased tins ⅔ full. Bake at 375 degrees for 15-20 minutes.
Mrs. Court Crow (Jeanne)

APPLE, CINNAMON GRANOLA

5 cups oats, uncooked
1 cup flaked shredded coconut
½ cup cashews, finely chopped
½ cup wheat germ
1 teaspoon ground cinnamon
1 teaspoon firmly packed brown sugar
½ cup honey
⅓ cup vegetable oil
1 teaspoon pure vanilla extract
1½ cups chopped dried apples

1. Preheat oven to 350 degrees. Spread oats in ungreased 13x9-inch pan and heat 10 minutes.
2. Combine coconut, cashews, wheat germ and cinnamon in a large bowl. Stir in honey, oil and vanilla thoroughly with large cooking spoon until dry ingredients are well coated.
3. Spoon into baking pan with oats and bake 30-35 minutes stirring often to brown evenly.
4. Cool. Toss apples in brown sugar, stir into granola until crumbly.
5. Store in tightly covered container in refrigerator.

One cup raisins or chopped apricots may be added.
Mrs. Fain Ney

WHOLE WHEAT MIX
(for waffles, pancakes and biscuits)

8 cups white flour
2 cups whole wheat flour
1 cup nonfat powdered milk
2 cups shortening
⅓ cup baking powder
1 tablespoon salt
¼ cup sugar

Mix all ingredients in large container. Will keep many weeks on kitchen shelf. FOR PANCAKES/WAFFLES: Use 2 cups mix, 1 egg and 1 cup water. FOR BISCUITS: Use 1½ cups mix and ⅓ cup water.
Mrs. David L. Richardson (Nancy), Baton Rouge, Louisiana

WAFFLES

1½ cups milk
2 eggs, separated
2 teaspoons salt
2 teaspoons baking powder
2 cups flour
¼ cup melted shortening

Mix dry ingredients, sift once. Add to dry ingredients the beaten egg yolk, milk and melted shortening. Stir until mixed, fold in beaten egg whites and bake in a waffle iron until brown.
Mrs. Court Crow (Jeanne)

CHOCOLATE WAFFLES

½ cup butter or margarine
2 eggs, beaten
1 teaspoon vanilla
¾ cup sugar
½ cup sweet milk
1¼ cups flour
6 tablespoons cocoa
½ teaspoon salt
1 tablespoon baking powder

Cream together butter, eggs, vanilla and sugar. Mix flour, cocoa, salt and baking powder, mixing alternately with the milk. Heat waffle iron . . . not as hot as for breakfast waffles. Serve with vanilla ice cream.
Author unknown — submitted by Mrs. Court Crow (Jeanne)

WAFFLE RECIPE

1 egg
1 cup milk
1 cup cream (half & half)
2 cups flour
⅛ teaspoon salt
¾ ounce (1½ tablespoons) baking powder
1 cup sugar
2 tablespoons margarine (room temperature)

Mix all ingredients. For best results, let batter sit over night (in refrigerator if warm, on counter top if cool). This makes 8 double waffles.
Mrs. Louis R. Jaudon (Betty)

OATMEAL PANCAKES

1 cup biscuit mix
1 cup rolled oats
1 egg
1⅔ cups sweet milk

Mix all ingredients and beat with rotary beater until well mixed. Cook as you would any pancake mix.
Mrs. F. A. Kihneman (Tora)

PUFFY FRENCH TOAST

1 cup flour
1½ teaspoons baking powder
½ teaspoon salt
⅛ teaspoon ground cloves
1 egg, beaten
Fat for deep frying
1½ teaspoons sugar
1 teaspoon ground cinnamon
¼ teaspoon ground nutmeg
1 cup milk
12 slices bread

Stir together dry ingredients. Blend milk and egg; add to flour mixture and beat until smooth. Lightly dip bread into batter, coating both sides evenly. Fry in preheated 375 degrée deep fat until golden brown — about 2 minutes on each side. Drain on paper towels and serve hot with butter and syrup.
Mrs. John H. Lenard, Jr. (Carol), Lenexa, Kansas

Cakes · Pies

Louisiana produced 1,000,000,000 board feet of lumber in 1900, and Shreveport was known for its yellow pine and several varieties of hardwood. Railroads were responsible for the growth of the lumber industry, as prior to 1890 Louisiana virgin timber was virtually untouched due to the scarcity of labor and capital, lack of transportation facilities, a limited market and little technical know-how.

Northern lumbermen came to Louisiana behind the railroads and acquired large tracts of timber and land for as little as 25 cents an acre. Sawmills were erected and log-roads were constructed through the forests to connect the mills to markets.

One of Shreveport's pioneers in this field was John R. Jones, owner of Caddo Mills, located on Cross Bayou and Red River. Quick to perceive the uses of lumber in connection with the construction of railroads, Jones enlarged Caddo Mills, organized the firm of Jones, Cowan and Knowlton for bridge and railroad construction and opened branch mills in Pleasant Hill and Victoria, Louisiana; Abilene, Texas, and Ballinger Indian Territory. As a result, these mills furnished the bulk of lumber for ties and bridge work to the railroads in Louisiana, as well as in Texas and westward.

Other outstanding lumbermen and financiers were L. C. Allen, S. H. Bolinger, E. A. Frost, and Hiram J. Allen.

Some of the lumber companies organized during this time and still in operation today are the Bolinger Lumber and Supply Co., Inc., the Victoria Sash and Door Company, Longleaf Lumber, Inc., and Allen Mill Work.

INTERESTING FACTS ABOUT SHREVEPORT

Miss Nell Querbes, daughter of Mr. and Mrs. Justin R. Querbes, struck the blow that sent the U.S.S.SHREVEPORT down the ways at the Walter Butler Shipbuilding Company in Superior, Wisconsin, on July 15, 1943. It was commissioned by the Navy and served in convoy guard duty and in weather patrol duty.

General Eisenhower spoke at a rally at the Greater Shreveport Municipal Airport during his campaign in 1952.

An All America City Award for outstanding citizen action was conferred on Shreveport in 1953 by the National Municipal League and LOOK Magazine.

OATMEAL DATE CAKE

1 cup dates, chopped
1 cup quick Quaker oats
1½ cups boiling water
1 stick oleo
1 cup brown sugar
1 cup white sugar
2 eggs
1⅓ cups flour
1 teaspoon baking soda
1 teaspoon cinnamon
½ teaspoon nutmeg

Mix in small bowl dates, oats and boiling water. Let stand 20 minutes; then mix in large bowl oleo, brown sugar, white sugar and eggs. Sift flour, baking soda, cinnamon and nutmeg. Add to other ingredients and beat with a spoon; then add oats and water mixture. This is quite thick — all the water is absorbed. Bake at 350 degrees for 35 to 45 minutes in two 8-inch layer pans which have been greased and floured.

Icing:
½ stick oleo
¼ cup brown sugar
¼ cup cream or condensed milk
1 cup coconut

Mix oleo, sugar and condensed milk and boil for two minutes. Add coconut. Flavoring is optional. Also, grated orange peel or lemon peel is good and may be used. Nuts can be used in cake and icing if desired. This cake is very moist and can be kept for many days.
Mrs. William Perry (Mattie), Haughton, Louisiana

PRUNE CAKE

2 cups sugar
3 eggs
1 cup finely chopped pecans
1 teaspoon cinnamon
½ teaspoon nutmeg
1 teaspoon soda
1 cup buttermilk
1 cup Wesson oil
1 cup cooked mashed prunes
2 cups flour
1 teaspoon cloves
1 teaspoon salt
½ teaspoon baking powder

Beat eggs, sugar, and oil. Mix all dry ingredients. Add dry ingredients alternately with buttermilk to eggs, sugar and oil mixture. Add pecans and prunes. Bake 1 hour at 325 degrees. Makes 4 small loaves (7½x3½x2½-inches) or oven large Bundt pan. Grease and flour small loaf pans (either metal or foil). Butter, but do not flour, Bundt pan.
Mrs. Gladys Poore

FRESH APPLE CAKE I

1 cup dates
1½ cups chopped nuts
3 cups flour
2 cups sugar
1½ cups salad oil
3 eggs
2 teaspoons vanilla
1 teaspoon soda
1 tablespoon baking powder
1 teaspoon salt
1 teaspoon cinnamon
1 teaspoon nutmeg
3 cups of grated fresh apples

Mix dates and nuts with one cup flour and set aside. Cream sugar and salad oil well. Add eggs one at a time, beating well as each is added. Sift together the remaining two cups of flour, soda, baking powder, salt, cinnamon and nutmeg. Add to the wet mixture, beating well. Add small amounts at a time. Add grated apples and vanilla. Mix well and add date and nut mixture. Mix the mixture well and bake in a tube pan at 300 degrees for one hour and forty minutes. Allow to cool before removing from pan.

Mrs. Bill Nolan (Pearl)

FRESH APPLE CAKE II

2 cups sugar
1½ cups salad oil
2 teaspoons vanilla
2 well beaten eggs
Juice of ½ lemon
1 teaspoon salt
3 cups sifted flour
1¼ teaspoons soda
3 cups peeled and chopped apples
1½ cups chopped pecans

Combine in a mixing bowl the sugar, oil, vanilla, eggs, lemon juice and salt. Beat well, but not too long. Mix the flour and soda, add to first mixture and beat well. Stir in the apples and nuts. Bake at 325 degrees about 1½ hours in a tube pan which has been greased and floured. (Do not invert pan until completely cool.) This is a moist cake which keeps well indefinitely.

Mrs. Mary Wells

APPLE CAKE

3 large apples (chopped fine)
1 cup granulated sugar
1 cup light brown sugar
½ teaspoon cinnamon
1 cup oil
2 large eggs
3 cups flour
1½ teaspoons soda
½ teaspoon salt
1 cup nuts (if desired)

Sprinkle sugars and cinnamon over apples and let sit 20 minutes to ½ hour. Add oil and eggs to apple-sugar mixture. Sift flour, soda, and salt together and stir into above mixture. Grease and flour tube pan. Cook at 325 degrees for about 1 hour and 10 minutes. For holiday cake, if you wish add the nuts and ¾ cup maraschino cherries.

Mrs. James Carr (Paula)

APPLESAUCE CAKE

1¾ cups sifted flour
1 teaspoon baking powder
½ teaspoon salt
½ teaspoon nutmeg
1½ teaspoons cinnamon
¼ teaspoon cloves
1 cup raisins
1 cup firmly packed brown sugar
½ cup shortening
1 egg
1¼ cups applesauce

Set oven at 350 degrees. Sift flour, baking powder, salt and spices. Beat sugar, shortening and egg until light and fluffy. Mix in dry ingredients alternately with applesauce. Stir in raisins. Pour into 8-inch square pan. Bake about 45 minutes or until toothpick inserted in center comes out clean. Serve warm or cool.

Powdered sugar may be sifted lightly over top. Makes about nine servings.

Mrs. Margaret Copeland

PEACH CAKE

3 eggs
1½ cups sugar
⅔ cup butter or margarine
3 tablespoons buttermilk
1½ teaspoons soda
1½ cups flour
1½ cups peaches (chopped and drained)
1 cup pecans (chopped)
1 teaspoon almond flavoring

Mix in order listed and pour into 2 8-inch cake pans or 1 9x13x2-inch pan. Cook at 350 to 375 degrees for 45 minutes. Let cool a few minutes in the pan and then turn onto rack for further cooling.

Mrs. Peggy Darden, Haynesville, Louisiana

ORANGE SLICE CAKE

2 cups pecans
1 pound orange slices (candied)
1 cup melted butter
1 small can coconut
1 8-ounce package dates
2 cups flour
4 eggs
1 teaspoon soda
½ cup buttermilk
1½ cups sugar

Chop nuts, dates, candy and combine with coconut. Pour melted butter over this and set aside. Beat eggs, add sugar slowly, then add other ingredients. Mix with nut mixture, bake in greased and floured tube pan for 2 hours at 300 degrees.

For glaze combine 1 cup orange juice and 2 cups powdered sugar. Mix well and pour over hot cake just as it comes from the oven. Let stand overnight before removing from pan.

Mrs. Gene Hallman (Stella)

ORANGE GUM DROP CAKE

1 cup butter or margarine
2 cups sugar
½ cup buttermilk
½ teaspoon soda (added to buttermilk)
4 eggs slightly beaten
3½ cups flour
16 ounces orange slice or gum drop candy (cut up)
½ pound dates (cut up)
2 cups pecans (chopped)
2 cups coconut

Reserve ½ cup of flour to toss last four ingredients in to hold them together. Cream butter and sugar. Add soda to buttermilk and add. Beat eggs slightly and add to this mixture. Gradually add flour. After tossing candy, dates, pecans and coconut in the flour add to first mixture. Grease and flour a tube pan or Bundt pan and pour batter in. Cook for 2-2½ hours at 250 degrees, or until done.

Glaze:

2 cups powdered sugar
¼ cup orange juice

Mix thoroughly and spread over cake while warm.

Mrs. W. D. Taylor (Tommy)

ORANGE JUICE CAKE

½ cup shortening
1 cup sugar
2 eggs (unbeaten)
½ cup orange juice
1½ cups flour
1½ teaspoons baking powder
¼ teaspoon salt
1 teaspoon grated orange peel (optional)

Cream together shortening and sugar. Add eggs one at a time. Sift together dry ingredients and add alternately with orange juice and grated orange peel. Cook in 325-350 degree oven until brown. Use 9x12x2-inch pan.
Mrs. H. Russell Maddox (Tommie Lue)

BLUEBERRY CAKE

1 package Duncan Hines butter cake mix
3 eggs
1 8-ounce package cream cheese, softened
½ cup oil
1 15-ounce can blueberries, drained

Cream the cheese, add eggs; beat well, add oil. Blend; add cake mix. Fold in drained blueberries. Grease and flour tube or Bundt cake pan. Bake in 350 degree oven 45 to 50 minutes or until done when toothpick is inserted. This is a very moist cake and is good served while warm.
NOTE: Butter cake mix may be substituted with yellow cake mix and add ½ teaspoon imitation butter flavoring.
Mrs. Ralph Garrett (Dottie)

TWO HUNDRED YEAR OLD RAISIN CAKE

1 cup raisins
2 cups water
½ cup butter
1¾ cups flour
½ teaspoon nutmeg
1 teaspoon soda
½ teaspoon salt
1 cup sugar
½ teaspoon cinnamon
1 cup finely chopped nuts (optional)

Mix all ingredients together well. Pour in greased 9x9-inch pan. Bake in 350 degree oven for 35 minutes. Add nuts last if so desired. Good with hot lemon sauce.
Mrs. F. A. Kihneman (Tora)

STRAWBERRY CAKE I

Cake:

1 16-ounce box white cake mix
1 3-ounce box strawberry gelatin
4 eggs
¾ cup oil
¾ cup fresh or frozen strawberries, crushed

Icing:

1 stick butter
½ cup crushed strawberries
1 box powdered sugar

Combine cake mix and gelatin. Add eggs and oil and blend until smooth. Add berries and mix one minute. Pour into 9-inch greased and dusted cake pans or tube pan. Bake at 350 degrees until cake springs back when touched in center, about 25 or 30 minutes. Allow cake to cool. Combine icing ingredients and ice cake.

Mrs. Ronny Goodman (Janice)
Mrs. H. Russell Maddox (Tommie Lue)

STRAWBERRY CAKE II

1 pound box Duncan Hines yellow or white cake mix
1 3-ounce package strawberry Jello
⅓ cup salad oil
¼ cup water or frozen berry juice
3 eggs
1 cup frozen strawberries (cut up)

Frosting:

1 stick margarine
1 pound box powdered sugar
½ cup frozen strawberries

Empty cake mix into large bowl or mixer bowl. Add Jello and mix thoroughly; then add salad oil, water or berry juice and eggs. Mix well. Stir in frozen strawberries. Pour into 2 9-inch cake pans with waxed paper, greased slightly. Bake in 350 degree oven 30 to 35 minutes or until done. Cool before icing.

Frosting: Cream margarine, add sugar and stir in strawberries. Spread on cake.

Mrs. Lois Mambourg

STRAWBERRY ICE BOX CAKE

- 2 3-ounce packages strawberry Jello
- 2 cups boiling water
- 2 10-ounce packages frozen strawberries (drained)
- 1 pint whipping cream
- 1 10-inch angel food cake (torn in small pieces)

Dissolve Jello in hot water. Chill until slightly thickened and beat until fluffy. Fold in drained berries and whipped cream. Toss cake and gelatin mixture. Pour into angel food cake pan. Chill until firm. Drizzle with ruby glaze.

Mrs. Clyde Garner

BANANA CREAM CAKE

- 1 stick butter
- ½ cup Wesson oil
- 2 cups sugar
- 5 eggs, separated
- ¾ cup buttermilk
- 1 teaspoon baking soda
- 2 cups flour
- 1 teaspoon vanilla
- 1 cup shredded coconut
- ½ cup nuts, chopped
- 2 cups mashed bananas (5 or 6 bananas)

Cream butter, oil and sugar. Add egg yolks one at a time, beating well after each addition. Stir baking soda into buttermilk. Add sifted flour into batter, alternating with buttermilk mixture. Add vanilla, coconut, nuts and mashed bananas. Beat egg whites and fold into mixture. Pour into a greased and floured 9x13-inch cake pan for a sheet cake or three 8-inch or 9-inch layer pans. Bake at 325 degrees for 45 minutes. Cool and ice.

Icing:

- 1 8-ounce package cream cheese, softened
- 1 stick butter, softened
- 1 teaspoon vanilla
- 1 box powdered sugar
- ½ cup nuts, chopped fine

Beat cream cheese and butter. Add vanilla, powdered sugar and nuts. Continue to beat until of spreading consistency.

Mrs. Art Ogletree, Jr. (Ann)

PLUM CAKE

- 2 cups self-rising flour
- 2 cups sugar
- 1 cup Wesson oil
- 3 eggs
- 2 small jars strained baby food plums
- 1 teaspoon cinnamon
- 1 teaspoon cloves
- 1 cup of chopped nuts or raisins

Glaze:

- 1 cup powdered sugar
- Juice of 1 lemon

Mix flour, sugar, cinnamon, cloves; add Wesson oil, and eggs. Add baby food plums, and nuts or raisins. Pour into lightly greased and floured Bundt pan, bake in oven 350 degrees for 1 hour or until springs back to touch.

Heat juice of 1 lemon, add 1 cup powdered sugar, mix well, pour over cake while warm.

Mary E. Jenkins

FRESH CRANBERRY AND APPLE CAKE

- 1½ cups sugar
- 1 cup vegetable oil
- 3 eggs
- 3 cups flour
- 1 teaspoon soda
- 1 teaspoon cinnamon
- ½ teaspoon salt
- 2 cups whole fresh cranberries
- 2 cups peeled and chopped apples
- 1 cup chopped pecans
- 1 teaspoon vanilla
- Confectioners' sugar

Beat oil, sugar and eggs in electric mixer until smooth. Mix dry ingredients together and add to oil mixture, stirring by hand — dough will be stiff. Add cranberries, apples, pecans, and vanilla, stirring well. Bake in greased Bundt pan in preheated oven 325 degrees for sixty (60) minutes, then in 350 degree oven for fifteen (15) to twenty (20) minutes. Remove from oven and cool in pan for fifteen (15) minutes. Turn out and dust with confectioners' powdered sugar.

Mrs. Nell B. Guilliams, Springhill, Louisiana

FRESH CRANBERRY CAKE

2½ cups all-purpose flour
¼ teaspoon salt
1 teaspoon baking powder
¾ cup Wesson oil
1 cup fresh whole cranberries
1 cup finely chopped walnuts
Grated rind of 2 oranges
1 cup granulated sugar
1 teaspoon baking soda
1 cup buttermilk
2 eggs
1 cup diced dates (roll whole dates in flour, dice and reroll in flour)

Syrup:
1 cup *fresh* orange juice (do not use frozen or concentrate)
1 cup granulated sugar

Mix well.

1st step: Prepare and measure fruits, nuts and orange rind. Put in individual containers and set aside.
2nd step: Heavily grease tube pan. Preheat oven to 350 degrees.
3rd step: Sift together in large bowl all dry ingredients.
4th step: Stir in well, fruits, nuts and orange rind.
5th step: Slightly beat eggs in medium size bowl. Stir in and mix well, oil and buttermilk.
6th step: Add eggs, oil and milk to other mixture. Mix well.
7th step: Pour in greased pan. Bake approximately 1 hour.
8th step: Remove pan from oven and cook 'til lukewarm (about 15 minutes). Take silver knife and run around edge and stem of pan to loosen cake. Punch holes all over cake with icepick or small knife. Slowly pour on syrup mixture. When syrup mixture has soaked into cake, set pan in refrigerator for 2 hours to chill (or in refrigerator for 30 minutes and in freezer for 30 minutes). Flip cake out of pan into the palm of your hand and turn right side up on large piece of heavy foil. Wrap foil tightly around cake. Cake must be kept refrigerated and foil tightly closed.

Serve plain or topped with whipped cream.
Mrs. Jo Whittaker

PUMPKIN CAKE

4 eggs
2 cups sugar
1 cup cooking oil
2 cups all purpose flour (sifted)
2 teaspoons soda
2 teaspoons cinnamon
½ teaspoon salt
2 cups pumpkin (canned)

Icing:
1 3-ounce package cream cheese
1 stick margarine
1 teaspoon vanilla
1 pound box powdered sugar
1 cup broken pecans

Beat eggs and sugar until well blended and light. Add oil and continue beating. Sift dry ingredients together. Add flour mixture to egg mixture. Add pumpkin. Bake in greased and floured 9-inch tube pan for 55 minutes. Cool for 10 minutes on rack. Remove cake when cooled. Frost with icing.

Icing: Cream together butter, cheese, and vanilla. Add sugar. Beat until creamy. Stir in pecans. If icing is too thick, add small amount of milk.

Mrs. Lois Mambourg

MEMAW'S FRUIT COCKTAIL-COCONUT CAKE

1½ cups sugar
2 eggs
½ cup oil
2 cups flour
½ teaspoon salt
2 teaspoons soda
1 No. 2 can fruit cocktail
½ can coconut

Icing:
1 stick oleo
¾ cup sugar
½ cup evaporated milk
½ cup pecans
½ can coconut
1 teaspoon vanilla flavoring

Blend together sugar, eggs and oil. Drain fruit cocktail and use juice in dough. Add flour, salt and soda. Fold in fruit cocktail — do not beat — blend well. Pour into pan. Sprinkle coconut on top before putting in oven. Bake at 350 degrees for forty minutes. (Pyrex dish 9x12-inch)

Icing: Boil one minute — pour over cake — cool and serve.

Mrs. Gladys Powell, Jackson, Mississippi

MIRACLE FRUIT CAKE

1 cup Dromedary Dates, sliced
1 cup seedless raisins
⅔ cup butter or substitute
1¼ cups brown sugar, packed
¼ cup dark molasses
1½ cups hot water
2 eggs
1 pound jar Dromedary Fruits and Peels (2 cups)
1 cup chopped nuts
3 cups sifted all-purpose flour
½ teaspoon cinnamon
½ teaspoon nutmeg
1 teaspoon soda
1 teaspoon baking powder
1 teaspooon salt

Combine dates, raisins, butter, brown sugar, molasses and hot water. Boil gently for three minutes. Cool in a large mixing bowl. Beat in eggs. Add fruits and peels and nuts. Sift together flour, cinnamon, nutmeg, soda, baking powder and salt.
Add gradually the flour mixture to fruit mixture, beating well after each addition. Pour into 9-inch tube pan, lined with greased waxed paper. Bake in a very slow oven (275 degrees) for 2½ hours, or until completely baked. Remove cake from pan. Cool thoroughly. Wrap securely in aluminum foil or waxed paper. Store in clean, air-tight container in cool place. Will store well for 6 weeks.
NOTE: Place a pan of water on lower shelf of oven while baking to prevent dryness.
Mrs. Floyd Cunningham (Nell)

CHRISTMAS FRUIT CAKE

1¾ cups sugar
6 eggs
4 cups flour
1 teaspoon baking soda
2 pounds candied pineapple
2 sticks real butter
1 cup bourbon
1 teaspoon salt
2 pounds candied cherries
2 quarts pecans

Cream well sugar and butter; add eggs, one at a time; add bourbon. Beat well. In separate bowl, sift flour, salt, baking soda. Add half of the flour mixture to the batter; add fruit, mixing well. Then add remaining flour to fruit. Add pecans, mix well. Grease pans (usually two tube pans). Start at 200 degrees for 45 minutes, reduce to 120 degrees for 2½ hours. Make before Thanksgiving for Christmas. Wrap in foil and store in cake tins. Check and add more bourbon if desired.
Mrs. Louis R. Jaudon (Betty)

APPLESAUCE FRUIT CAKE

1¼ cups applesauce
½ cup butter (or 1 stick oleo)
1 cup sugar
2 cups flour
2 teaspoons soda
½ teaspoon allspice
½ teaspoon cinnamon
½ teaspoon nutmeg
½ teaspoon ground cloves
½ pound raisins
1 cup pecans

Heat applesauce, stir in butter, sugar, spices and flour. Add the soda which has been dissolved in a little of the hot applesauce. Add nuts and raisins. Pour into loaf cake pan and bake in a slow oven (325 degrees) about 1 hour. Test with toothpick to see if done at 45 minutes. If not, bake another 15 minutes and test again.

Mrs. H. W. Maddox (Charlotte)

FAT PORK CAKE

1 pound fat pork, ground finely
2 teaspoons soda
2 teaspoons cinnamon
2 teaspoons nutmeg
2 teaspoons allspice
2 teaspoons cloves
¾ teaspoon salt
3 eggs
3 cups sugar
2 cups sweet milk
5 cups flour
1 pound pecans
1 pound raisins

Have the pure fat cut off of a fresh loin of any pure white fat that is firm and without lean. Have this ground in sausage or hamburger mill and it will be like lard or butter. Cream fat and sugar well. Sift only four cups of flour, add all dry ingredients and sift again and add eggs, one at a time, to your creamed fat, beating well after each egg is added.

Add your milk alternately with the flour mixture. Sift your other cup of flour into a paper bag. Add the nuts and raisins to this flour and shake well and dump the fruit into batter and fold in well.

Bake at about 325 degrees for one and one-half hours. Check cake after 45 minutes, may need to reduce heat. This makes a very large cake. I always use two stem pans. It is enough to make two nice cakes.

Mrs. Leonard Green, Jr. (June)

PLAIN LAYER CAKE

1 cup butter
2 cups sugar
3 eggs
1 cup milk
3 cups flour
1½ teaspoons baking powder
½ teaspoon lemon extract

Cream butter. Add sugar to butter, creaming until real fluffy. Add egg yolks and cream again. Add milk and flour, alternating small amount at a time. Add baking powder and lemon extract. Beat egg whites and fold in cake batter. Makes 2 large 8-inch layers. Bake at 350 degrees until done. Frost with favorite icing.
Mrs. Christine Waites

PLAIN TWO LAYER CAKE

2 cups flour
3 teaspoons baking powder
½ teaspoon salt
¼ cup shortening
⅔ cup sugar
1 or 2 eggs
¾ cup milk
½ teaspoon vanilla flavoring

Sift together flour, baking powder, and salt. Cream sugar and shortening until light and fluffy. Add beaten eggs, vanilla and mix thoroughly. Add sifted ingredients alternately with milk. Beat well. Bake in two layers about 20 minutes in moderate oven.
Mrs. Ruth V. Glenn

MAGIC WHITE CAKE

2 cups flour
1⅓ cups sugar
½ cup Crisco
½ teaspoon salt
⅔ cup milk
3½ teaspoons baking powder
4 egg whites (unbeaten)

Sift flour and sugar together. Add Crisco, salt, milk and beat for 2 minutes. Add baking powder and egg white unbeaten. Blend batter for 2 minutes or until smooth. Pour into 3 8-inch greased and floured cake pans. Cook in 350 degree oven for 25 minutes. Don't overbake. Use 7 minute icing for topping and between layers.
Mrs. F. A. Kihneman (Tora)

NATCHEZ BUTTERMILK CAKE

1 cup butter or margarine
½ cup shortening
2½ cups sugar
4 eggs
3½ cups flour
1 tablespoon lemon extract
1 tablespoon hot water
1 teaspoon soda
1 cup buttermilk

Cream butter or margarine and shortening; add sugar, then eggs — one at a time, beating well after each addition.
Mix soda with hot water and add to buttermilk. Add lemon extract. Then add milk mixture alternately with flour to creamed mixture. Bake in greased tube pan at 325 degrees for one and one-half hours. (This cake is too large for an average sized Bundt cake pan.) Pour glaze over cake while still hot in pan. Let pan cool before removing from pan.

Glaze:
Juice of one lemon
(3 tablespoons)
½ cup sugar
1 teaspoon water

Mix lemon juice, sugar and water in saucepan. Bring to boil and pour over cake while still hot in pan.
Mrs. Art Ogletree, Jr. (Ann)

CARAMEL NUT POUND CAKE

1 cup (2 sticks) butter
½ cup Crisco
1 box light brown sugar
1 cup white sugar
5 eggs
½ teaspoon baking powder
½ teaspoon salt
3 cups all-purpose flour
1 cup milk
1 teaspoon vanilla
1 teaspoon butter extract
1 cup chopped nuts

Cream butter, shortening and brown sugar until well mixed, then gradually add white sugar and cream well. Add eggs one at a time, beating thoroughly after additions. Combine flour, salt and baking powder. Add alternately with milk to creamed mixture beginning and ending with flour. Add flavoring and nuts. Beat well. Pour into greased and floured tube pan and bake at 325 degrees for about one hour and 15-20 minutes. Turn on plate and drizzle with 2 cups sifted powdered sugar with enough milk to make right consistency.
Mrs. Jo Whittaker

CHOCOLATE POUND CAKE

2 sticks margarine
1 cup Crisco
3 cups sugar
5 eggs
3 cups flour
½ teaspoon baking powder
½ teaspoon salt
½ cup cocoa
1¼ cups sweet milk
1 teaspoon vanilla

Cream margarine and shortening, add sugar gradually. Add eggs one at a time and beat well after each addition. Sift all dry ingredients; add alternately with milk. Grease and flour tube pan and bake at 325 degrees for 1 hour and 20 minutes.
Mrs. A. H. Otto (Marjorie)

CREAM CHEESE POUND CAKE

1 stick butter
2 sticks oleo
1 8-ounce package cream cheese
3 cups sugar
3 cups flour
3 teaspoons vanilla
6 eggs

Cream butter, oleo and cheese. Add sugar, vanilla and eggs. Add flour. Mix well. Bake in a COLD oven (no preheating) 325 degrees for 65 minutes in a tube pan.
Mrs. Jo Whittaker

HOLIDAY POUND CAKE

1 pound (2 cups) butter
1 tablespoon vanilla
9 large eggs
1 cup chopped candied green cherries
1 cup finely chopped pecans
1½ teaspoons salt
2¼ cups sugar
1 tablespoon grated lemon rind
1 cup chopped candied red cherries
4½ cups sifted all-purpose flour

Butter bottom of 10-inch tube pan and line with waxed paper; set aside. Cream butter until soft and fluffy. Add sugar gradually, beating thoroughly. Blend in vanilla and lemon rind. Add eggs one at a time, beating well after each addition. Toss cherries and nuts with 1 cup of the flour. Sift remaining flour with salt and fold into batter, ½ cup at a time, mixing only until smooth. Fold in cherries and nuts. Bake at 325 degrees 1¾ hours. Cool on wire rack at least 10 minutes before turning out onto platter. Cake will keep several weeks if stored in a tightly covered container.
Mrs. A. H. Otto (Marjorie)

MAMA BURN'S POUND CAKE

1½ cups shortening
3 cups sugar
2-3 drops yellow food color
5 eggs
3 cups all-purpose flour
½ teaspoon salt
1 teaspoon baking powder
1 cup sweet milk
1 teaspoon vanilla flavoring

Cream shortening, sugar and food coloring together; add eggs beating well after each egg. Sift together flour, salt, baking powder alternating with milk. Add vanilla. Beat well with wooden spoon (340-400 times). Have well greased and floured tube pan and bake in oven at 350 degrees one hour or more. Cool some before turning out of pan.
Mrs. Iris Burns, Jackson, Mississippi

MOLASSES POUND CAKE

3 sticks margarine (1½ cups) softened
1¼ cups firmly packed brown sugar
6 eggs
5 cups sifted cake flour
1 tablespoon ground cinnamon
½ cup milk
1½ tablespoons ground ginger
1 teaspoon ground nutmeg
½ teaspoon salt
1½ teaspoons soda
2 cups light molasses

Cream butter and sugar until light and fluffy. Add eggs, one at a time, beating well after each addition. Combine flour, spices, and salt. Dissolve soda in molasses. Add dry ingredients to creamed mixture, alternately with molasses and milk. Spoon into greased and floured 10-inch tube pan and bake in 325 degree oven for 1½ to 2 hours or until cake tests done with straw. Cool in pan 5 minutes then turn on cake rack to cool. 1 cup nuts can be used also but optional.
Mrs. A. L. Belluomini (Verda), Kerrville, Texas

SOUR CREAM POUND CAKE I

½ pound butter (real)
3 cups sugar
3 cups flour
¼ teaspoon salt
6 eggs
¼ pint sour cream
1 teaspoon vanilla

Have butter, eggs, sour cream at room temperature. Cream butter and sugar together. Add cream, flavoring, and eggs. Add salt. Add flour last. Beat well. Bake 1½ hours at 275 degrees.
Miss Rhonda Berry

SOUR CREAM POUND CAKE II

1 package Duncan Hines white cake mix
¾ cup Wesson oil
½ pint sour cream
½ cup sugar
4 eggs
½ teaspoon vanilla
½ teaspoon almond extract
½ cup chopped nuts
3 tablespoons brown sugar
2 teaspoons cinnamon

Combine with cake mix the oil, sour cream, sugar and eggs; adding eggs one at a time and beating well after each addition. Pour half of the batter into a greased tube pan. Combine the nuts, brown sugar and cinnamon and sprinkle on top of the batter in pan. Add remaining batter and cook for 1 hour in 325 degree oven. Add glaze to top after removing from pan.

Glaze:
1 cup powdered sugar
1 teaspoon vanilla
3 tablespoons milk

Combine sugar, vanilla and milk. Mix well and drizzle on cake.
Mrs. R. W. Fletcher (Sue)

SOUR CREAM POUND CAKE III

3 cups sugar
3 cups flour
2 sticks butter
¼ teaspoon baking powder
1 teaspoon lemon flavoring
1 teaspoon vanilla flavoring
1 cup sour cream
6 eggs

Cream sugar and butter together. Add eggs — one at a time. Beat each egg one minute before adding another egg. This is very important. Into a separate bowl sift flour as you take it from container. Measure 3 cups into sifter, adding baking powder after first cup. Add dry mixture to other mixture gradually, mixing thoroughly. Add sour cream, vanilla and lemon flavorings. Grease and flour tube pan. Bake at 325 degrees for one hour and fifteen minutes.
Miss Delores Lynn, Atlanta, Georgia

POUND CAKE

3 cups sugar
2 sticks oleo
½ cup Wesson oil
5 eggs (add one at a time)
1 teaspoon vanilla
3 cups flour
½ teaspoon salt
½ teaspoon baking powder
1 cup sweet milk

Cream the first five ingredients. Mix the next three ingredients and add to the creamed mixture. Add one cup sweet milk. Beat 12 minutes at medium speed. Bake in tube pan at 325 degrees for 1½ hours. Start cake in cold oven.
Mrs. Gladys Poore

THRIFTY POUND CAKE

3 cups all purpose flour
½ teaspoon double acting baking powder
1 cup shortening
4 eggs (unbeaten)
1 cup buttermilk
½ teaspoon soda
¾ teaspoon salt
2 cups sugar
1 teaspoon vanilla
1 teaspoon lemon flavoring

Sift together flour, soda, baking powder, and salt. In mixer, mix shortening, sugar, eggs, vanilla, lemon. Beat about 2½ minutes. Add sifted mixture alternately with the buttermilk. Pour in greased and floured loaf pan, bake at 350 degrees for 1 hour and 10 minutes.
Mrs. W. W. Hall, Coatopa, Alabama

OLD TIME GINGERBREAD

1 egg
1 cup syrup
1 cup brown sugar
1 teaspoon soda in 1 cup hot water
½ cup bacon drippings (grease)
1½ cups flour
1 teaspoon cloves
½ teaspoon allspice
1 teaspoon nutmeg
½ teaspoon ginger
½ teaspoon cinnamon

Mix and bake in sheet style pan. Bake at 350 degrees until done. About 25 to 30 minutes.
Mrs. Nancie Sumner

GINGERBREAD

½ cup sugar
⅓ cup margarine, creamed
2 eggs well beaten
½ cup molasses
1 teaspoon soda
½ teaspoon ginger
½ teaspoon cinnamon
½ teaspoon allspice
2 cups flour
½ cup boiling water

Sauce:
1¼ cups sugar
2 tablespoons flour
Water to mix
2 cups milk
1 tablespoon butter
1 teaspoon vanilla
Dash of nutmeg

Mix sugar, margarine, eggs, molasses and ginger, cinnamon, allspice and flour. Add the soda dissolved in the water. Turn mixture into lightly greased pan and bake at 350 degrees until springs back when pressed in the center.

Sauce: Mix sugar, flour, water and milk. Stir until thick. Add butter and vanilla. Sprinkle with nutmeg. Pour over cooled gingerbread.

Mrs. Court Crow (Jeanne)

LEMON BUTTERWHIP ICING

1 stick margarine
½ cup shortening
2 drops butter concentrate
3 tablespoons lemon juice (do not use lemon flavoring)
1 egg
Water
2½ pound bag of powdered sugar

Cream margarine and shortening at high speed until light and creamy. Add butter concentrate, powdered sugar and lemon juice. (If using one of the variations listed below, omit lemon juice and add the desired ingredients at this point.) Blend in 1 egg and add water one tablespoonful at a time until icing reaches the desired consistency. This amount will ice a 3 layer cake or 2 sheet cakes.

Variations

1. *Substitute orange juice instead of lemon juice and add two tablespoons grated orange rind.*
2. *For a spice cake, substitute apple juice and add butter rum flavoring to taste.*
3. *For a mocha icing, use strong instant coffee and a dash of cinnamon.*
4. *Mix 1 tablespoon instant coffee and 3 teaspoons cocoa with the dash of cinnamon for a strong mocha flavor.*

Mrs. James Carr (Paula)

PEANUT BUTTER FUDGE CAKE

2 cups sugar
2 cups flour
1 teaspoon soda
2 sticks margarine
4 tablespoons cocoa
1 cup water
½ cup buttermilk
1 teaspoon vanilla
2 eggs, beaten

Mix sugar, flour and soda. Combine margarine, cocoa, water, buttermilk, vanilla and eggs. (I always add eggs last.) Mix ingredients and bring to boil. Pour boiled mixture over flour mixture and mix well. Pour into a well greased oblong baking pan and bake for 25 minutes at 350 degrees. Let cake cool in pan. When cake has cooled, spread with Peanut Butter Mixture.

Peanut Butter Mixture:
1½ cups nutty or creamy peanut butter
1½ tablespoons oil

Combine peanut butter and oil and mix well; spread over cooled cake. Top with Fudge Frosting.

Fudge Frosting:
1 stick margarine
4 tablespoons cocoa
6 tablespoons buttermilk
1 box powdered sugar
1 teaspoon vanilla

Bring to boil the cocoa, milk and margarine. Pour over sugar; add vanilla. Spread over Peanut Butter Mixture.
Mrs. Ellis M. Bush (Juanita)

FUDGE MUFFINS

4 blocks semi-sweet chocolate
2 sticks oleo, melted
1¾ cups sugar
Pinch of salt
1 cup flour
4 eggs
1 teaspoon vanilla
2 cups pecans, chopped

Melt oleo and chocolate in top of double boiler. Pour into large mixing bowl; add sugar, salt and flour. Beat well. Add eggs, one at a time — stirring in — not beating. Add vanilla and chopped nuts.

Bake in muffin liners in muffin tins at 325 degrees for 25 minutes. Makes 24 delicious muffins. These may also be baked in tiny muffin papers.
Mrs. Olin P. Oden (Ruth)

GERMAN CHOCOLATE CUP CAKES

2 sticks oleo
1 4-ounce package German chocolate
1 cup unsifted flour
1¾ cups sugar
4 eggs
1 teaspoon vanilla
½ teaspoon butter flavoring
1½ cups chopped pecans

In a large heavy fry pan melt and mix oleo and chocolate over low heat. Remove from heat and when slightly cooled, add sugar, flour and eggs all at once. Barely stir, do not beat; add pecans and flavorings; still mix by barely stirring.

Spoon into muffin tins lined with cup cake papers, about one half full. Bake in preheated oven, 325 degrees, for 30 minutes, DELISH!
Mrs. Olin P. Oden (Ruth)

CHOCOLATE SHEET CAKE

Cake:
2 cups sugar
2 cups flour
2 sticks oleo
4 tablespoons cocoa
1 cup water
½ cup buttermilk
2 eggs, slightly beaten
1 teaspoon soda
1 teaspoon cinnamon
1 teaspoon vanilla

Icing:
1 stick oleo
4 tablespoons cocoa
½ cup milk
1 pound box powdered sugar
1 teaspoon vanilla
1 cup chopped pecans

Cake: Sift together the sugar and flour. Mix in saucepan the oleo, cocoa and water. Bring to boil. Pour over flour mixture and stir until mixed well. Add the buttermilk, eggs, soda, cinnamon and vanilla; mix well. Pour into greased 11x16x1½-inch pan. Bake 20 minutes at 400 degrees. Shortly before cake is done, make icing and have ready to pour on hot cake.

Icing: Melt oleo, add cocoa and milk; heat to boiling. Remove from heat and add powdered sugar and vanilla. Beat until smooth. Add chopped pecans. Pour over hot cake.
Mrs. Ralph Garrett (Dottie)

CHOCOLATE-CHERRY CAKE

1 package Devil's Food cake mix
2 eggs, beaten
1 can cherry pie filling
1 teaspoon almond extract

Mix cake mix, eggs, cherry pie filling and almond extract by hand. Spread in 13x9-inch pan which has been greased and dusted with cocoa (or flour — cocoa doesn't show on cake, though). Bake at 350 degrees about 25 to 30 minutes.

Icing:
1 cup sugar
⅓ cup milk
5 tablespoons oleo
1 cup (or small package) Nestle's semi-sweet chocolate bits

Mix sugar, milk and oleo together in saucepan. Boil one minute after it begins to boil. Remove from heat and add chocolate bits.
Mrs. Raymond L. McDaniel (Eugenia)

MISSISSIPPI MUD CAKE I

Cake:
2 cups sugar
1 tablespoon vanilla
1½ cups flour
4 eggs
¼ cup cocoa
1½ cups pecans
1 cup coconut
1 teaspoon vanilla

Topping:
1 7-ounce jar marshmallow cream
½ cup oleo
1 cup chopped pecans
1 box (16 ounces) powdered sugar
¼ cup cocoa
¼ cup Pet milk

Mix sugar, flour, cocoa, add eggs. Mix well, add coconut, pecans and vanilla. Pour into 9x13x2-inch pan and bake in preheated oven at 350 degrees for 35 to 40 minutes or until cake springs back at touch of finger.

Spread marshmallow cream on top of warm cake.

Heat 1 box powdered sugar, ¼ cup cocoa, ½ cup oleo and 1 cup of chopped pecans, adding the Pet milk. Pour mixture over cake and marshmallow cream.
Mrs. D. C. Berry

MISSISSIPPI MUD CAKE II

½ cup cocoa
2 cups sugar
1½ cups flour
Pinch of salt
Small package miniature marshmallows (6¼ ounces)
2 sticks margarine (melted)
4 eggs (beaten)
1 teaspoon vanilla
1 cup nuts (chopped)

Beat eggs 'til thick; add sugar; beat well. Combine melted butter, flour, cocoa, vanilla, and nuts. Mix well; add to egg mixture. Add salt and stir. Pour into greased floured 9x13-inch pan. Bake at 350 degrees for 30 minutes. Remove from oven and immediately cover with miniature marshmallows. Return to oven and lightly brown marshmallows. Top with frosting.

Frosting:
1 stick margarine
1 box powdered sugar
⅓ cup cocoa
⅓ cup evaporated milk
1 teaspoon vanilla
⅔ cup nuts (chopped)

Mix all ingredients except nuts. Beat 'til well blended; spread over browned marshmallows and sprinkle nuts on top.
Mrs. Jack Culpepper, Jr. (Vickie)

HERSHEY CAKE

2 sticks oleo
2 cups sugar
4 eggs
2½ cups flour
2 teaspoons vanilla
1 teaspoon soda
1 cup buttermilk
8 small plain Hershey bars or 1 large 5-ounce bar
2 cups pecans

Cream together oleo and sugar. Melt Hershey bars with buttermilk, set aside to cool. Mix eggs with creamed oleo and sugar. Add flour with soda. Mix with cooled bars. Add nuts and vanilla. Bake in tube pan at 325 degrees for 1 hour and 45 minutes. No icing necessary.
Mrs. R. C. Wheat

SCOTCH CHOCOLATE CAKE

1 stick margarine
4 tablespoons cocoa
2 cups sugar
½ cup buttermilk
1 teaspoon soda
1 teaspoon vanilla
½ cup Crisco
1 cup water
2 cups flour
2 eggs
1 teaspoon cinnamon

Icing:
1 stick margarine
6 tablespoons milk
1 teaspoon vanilla
1 cup angel flake coconut
6 tablespoons cocoa
1 box powdered sugar
1 cup chopped pecans or walnuts

In a heavy pan melt the margarine, Crisco, cocoa and water. Bring to a rapid boil and pour over the sugar and flour. Mix well and add the buttermilk, eggs, soda, cinnamon and vanilla. Mix and pour into a greased and floured sheet cake pan 9x13-inches. Bake at 400 degrees for 25 to 30 minutes. When cake is firm all over, remove from oven. Do not overcook.

Icing: In a saucepan bring to a boil the margarine, cocoa and milk. Add the powdered sugar, vanilla, nuts and coconut. Mix together well and spread carefully on hot cake as soon as you remove the cake from the oven.

Mrs. Evelyn F. Johnson, Bossier City, Louisiana

CHOCOLATE CHIP COOKIE CAKE

2 rolls of chocolate chip cookies
2 8-ounce packages cream cheese
3 eggs
2 cups sugar

Slice 1 roll of cookies into a 9x13-inch pan. Mix cream cheese, eggs, and sugar. Spread on sliced cookies. Slice second roll of cookies and place on top. Bake at 350 degrees for 1 hour.

Mrs. James H. Worley (Wincie)

ITALIAN CREAM CAKE

1 stick margarine
½ cup vegetable shortening
2 cups sugar
5 eggs, separated
2 cups flour
1 teaspoon soda
1 cup buttermilk
1 cup angel flake coconut
1 cup chopped nuts
1 teaspoon vanilla

Frosting:
1 8-ounce package cream cheese
½ stick margarine
1 pound box powdered sugar
1 teaspoon vanilla
chopped nuts

Cream margarine and shortening. Add sugar and beat until smooth. Add egg yolks and beat well. Combine flour, soda, and add to creamed mixture, alternately with buttermilk. (Mother always told me when you use buttermilk and flour, always end up with flour last.) Stir in vanilla. Add coconut and nuts. Fold in stiffly beaten egg whites. Pour batter into three greased and floured 8-inch cake pans. Bake 350 degrees for 25 minutes or until done. This can be baked in a well greased floured Bundt pan for approximately 45 minutes or until a straw comes out clean. Use cream cheese frosting if desired.

Frosting: Beat cream cheese and margarine until smooth; add sugar and mix well. Add vanilla and beat again until smooth. Spread between layers and on top of cake. Garnish with chopped nuts.
Mrs. Jo Whittaker

GOOEY BUTTER CAKE

1 3-ounce package cream cheese
1 box yellow cake mix
1 egg
1 tablespoon cold water
1 stick soft oleo
1 box powdered sugar
1 8-ounce package cream cheese
1 teaspoon vanilla
2 eggs

Mix the 3-ounce package of cream cheese with the yellow cake mix, 1 egg, cold water, and oleo. Spread in a lightly greased and floured 9x13x2-inch pan. Put this aside for later use. It will be slightly stiff.

Mix powdered sugar, 8-ounce package of cream cheese, vanilla, and 2 eggs. After mixing these ingredients spread all of this on top of the first batter already in the pan. Bake at 350 degrees for 40 minutes. Let cool in pan and cut into desired pieces.
Mrs. Marjorie Rodriguez

JIMMY CARTER CAKE

(Peanut Carrot Cake)

2 cups unsifted flour
2¼ teaspoons baking powder
½ teaspoon baking soda
½ teaspoon salt
1 teaspoon ground cinnamon
1 teaspoon ground ginger
½ teaspoon ground cloves
4 eggs, separated
2 cups sugar
1 cup peanut oil or other cooking oil
1½ cups grated raw carrots
1 cup chopped peanuts
¼ cup hot water

Combine flour, baking powder, soda, salt, cinnamon, ginger and cloves; stir to blend well. Set aside. Beat egg whites in small bowl until soft peaks form; set aside.

In large bowl combine sugar and oil; blend well. Add egg yolks, one at a time, beating well after each addition. Mix in carrots and peanuts. Alternately blend in dry ingredients and hot water. Fold in beaten egg whites. Turn batter into a greased and floured 12-cup Bundt cake pan or a 10-inch tube pan, or two small 8-inch Bundt pans. Bake at 350 degrees about 55 minutes, less for the smaller Bundt pans, or until cake tests done.

Cool in pan on wire rack 10 minutes. Frost with Peanut Butter Frosting.

Peanut Butter Frosting:

2 tablespoons butter or margarine
¼ cup peanut butter
3½ cups powdered sugar, sifted
About 6 tablespoons milk

Blend butter and peanut butter. Add sifted powdered sugar and enough milk to make frosting soft enough to spread. Makes enough to cover top and sides of cake. Decorate top of cake with pitted dates (optional).

Mrs. Olin P. Oden (Ruth)

7-UP CAKE

3 sticks butter
3 cups sugar
5 eggs
3 cups flour
2 teaspoons lemon extract
¾ cup 7-Up

Cream butter and sugar together 20 minutes. Add eggs, one at a time, add flour, extract and fold in 7-Up. Pour into well greased Bundt pan. Bake at 325 degrees for 1 to 1¼ hours or until done.

Mrs. Jo Whittaker and Mrs. Mary Jenkins

HUMMINGBIRD CAKE

3 cups flour
1 teaspoon salt
1 teaspoon cinnamon
1½ cups oil
1 cup (8 ounces) crushed pineapple, undrained
1 cup chopped nuts
2 cups chopped bananas
2 cups sugar
1 teaspoon soda
3 eggs, beaten
1½ teaspoons vanilla

Combine and sift dry ingredients. Add eggs and oil; mix. Add pineapple, vanilla, nuts and bananas. Pour batter into three greased and floured cake pans and bake at 350 degrees for 20-30 minutes.

Icing:
2 sticks butter
2 8-ounce packages cream cheese
2 teaspoons vanilla
2 boxes powdered sugar

Mix ingredients thoroughly and spread between layers and on top of cake. Sprinkle nuts on top of cake if desired.
Mrs. Carter Graham (Jackie), Tulsa, Oklahoma

HEAVENLY HASH CAKE

3 eggs, beaten until light
1 cup sugar
2 1-ounce squares chocolate (melted)
1 stick oleo
¾ cup flour (all-purpose)
1 teaspoon baking powder
¼ teaspoon salt
1 teaspoon vanilla
2 cups pecans
2 cups quartered large marshmallows

Icing:
1 box powdered sugar
2 squares chocolate
½ stick margarine
1 teaspoon vanilla
¼ cup milk

Combine ingredients as listed above. Mix baking powder and salt with flour before adding to other ingredients. Beat well. Add vanilla and nuts last. Bake in 13x9-inch pan at 325 degrees for 20 to 30 minutes. Immediately pour 2 cups quartered large marshmallows on hot cake. Wait a short time and ice if desired.

Mix icing ingredients together and use enough milk to spread easily. Blend until creamy and top the cake.
Mrs. Velma Dodd, Rodessa, Louisiana

COCA COLA CAKE

½ cup shortening
1 1-ounce package Redi-Blend chocolate
½ cup buttermilk
2 eggs
2 cups flour, sifted
1 stick oleo
1 cup Coca Cola
1½ cups miniature marshmallows
½ teaspoon soda
2 cups sugar
1 teaspoon vanilla

Icing:
1 stick oleo
6 tablespoons Coca Cola
1 package confectioners' sugar
½ cup chopped nuts (optional)
1 1-ounce package Redi-Blend chocolate
1 teaspoon vanilla

Put shortening, oleo, chocolate and cola in saucepan. Bring to boil. Remove from heat and stir in marshmallows until dissolved. Set aside. Dissolve soda in buttermilk. In large mixing bowl, beat eggs and add sugar gradually. Add flour and buttermilk alternately, mixing well, and then pour in chocolate mixture and mix well. Add vanilla. Pour into either a sheet cake pan or layer pans and bake at 325 degrees for approximately 45 minutes. DO NOT OVERBAKE CAKE.

To make frosting, put oleo, chocolate and coke in saucepan. Bring to a boil. Beat in powdered sugar and vanilla until smooth. Add nuts if desired. Frost the cake while it is still warm.

NOTE: 1 King Size Coca Cola is correct measure – 1 cup for cake, balance for icing.

Mrs. Jo Whittaker

HOT MILK SPONGE CAKE

1 cup sifted flour
1 teaspoon baking powder
¼ teaspoon salt
½ cup milk
2 tablespoons butter or margarine
2 eggs
1 cup sugar
1 teaspoon vanilla

Sift together flour, baking powder, and salt (set aside). Heat milk and butter until melted. Keep hot (do not scorch). Beat eggs until thick and lemon colored, about three minutes on high speed of electric mixer. Gradually add sugar, beat constantly at medium speed for about 4 minutes. Add sifted dry ingredients to egg mixture, stir just till blended. Stir in hot milk mixture and vanilla. Blend well, turn batter into greased and floured 9x9x2-inch pan. Bake at 350 degrees for 25 to 30 minutes. Do not invert, cool in pan. For large group, double recipe and use a sheet pan. This does not do well in loaf pan. TASTES BEST WHEN EATEN WARM. Serve with butter.

Mrs. L. R. Jaudon (Betty)

OKLAHOMA CAKE

2 cups sifted flour
1½ cups sugar
1 teaspoon soda
½ teaspoon salt
2 tablespoons oil
1 egg
1 20-ounce can crushed pineapple

Sift dry ingredients together — flour, soda, salt. Mix oil and sugar; add egg and beat well. Add crushed pineapple and flour mixture, mixing well. Pour into a well greased 13x9x2-inch pan and bake for 35 minutes in 350 degree oven. While still hot cover with the following icing; then place in refrigerator so it will cut better.

Icing:
1 5.33-ounce can evaporated milk
1¼ cups sugar
¾ stick butter
¾ cup chopped nuts (optional)

Mix the milk, sugar and butter. Bring to a boil and boil for seven minutes. Nuts may be added to icing if desired.

I find that one half of this icing is sufficient and keep the other half in refrigerator for another cake, but some of my friends like the whole recipe.

Mrs. Olin P. Oden (Ruth)

DELICIOUS CAKE

1 box Duncan Hines butter recipe cake mix
¾ cup cooking oil
4 eggs
1 11-ounce can mandarin oranges

Frosting:
1 15¼-ounce can crushed pineapple
1 3¾-ounce package vanilla instant pudding
1 9-ounce carton of Cool Whip

Mix cake mix, cooking oil and eggs in large bowl or mixer bowl. Beat well. Add oranges, juice and all. Stir this in with a spoon to keep from tearing orange sections. Grease and flour 3 8-inch cake pans. Bake at 350 degrees for 20 minutes.

Frosting: Mix instant pudding mix and pineapple well. Fold in Cool Whip and frost cake. Delicious!

Mrs. James Kelly (Mercille)

AUNT LILLIAN'S CARAMEL CAKE

Cake Batter:

1½ cups sugar
¾ cup shortening
3 eggs
2¼ cups flour
2¼ teaspoons baking powder
½ teaspoon salt
¾ cup milk
1 teaspoon vanilla flavoring

Icing:

1½ cups sugar
1 cup milk
½ stick oleo
1 teaspoon vanilla flavoring

Mix sugar and shortening together well. Add eggs, one at a time. Sift together dry ingredients alternately with milk. Add vanilla.

Divide batter into three greased and floured pans for 3-layer cake. Bake in oven at 350 degrees until each layer is done.

Icing: In a small black skillet put ½ cup sugar. (Start first mixture heating to the boil stage first.) Brown sugar slowly until it melts. Slowly pour melted brown sugar into boiling milk and sugar pan stirring constantly. Test in ice water until soft ball forms. Remove from heat and add oleo and vanilla. Cool and beat until it reaches spreading consistency. Ice cake in layers.

Miss Lillian Arnold, Jackson, Mississippi

WATERGATE CAKE

1 white cake mix
¾ cup oil
½ cup chopped nuts
1 3-ounce package Pistachio Instant Pudding
3 eggs
1 cup 7-Up
½ cup coconut

Icing:

1 3-ounce package Pistachio Instant Pudding
1½ cups milk
2 packages Dream Whip (2 cups)

Mix cake mix, eggs, oil, 7-Up, nuts, coconut and pudding and turn into a tube pan. Bake at 350 degrees for 50 to 55 minutes. When cake is cool, ice with pudding, milk and Dream Whip mixture which has been beaten until thick.

Mrs. Jo Whittaker

POPPY SEED CAKE

½ cup poppy seed
1 cup milk
1 teaspoon vanilla
¾ cup butter or margarine
1½ cups sugar
2 cups flour
2 teaspoons baking powder
½ teaspoon salt
4 egg whites (stiffly beaten)

Soak poppy seed overnight in the milk and vanilla. Cream margarine and gradually add sugar. Sift flour, baking powder, and salt together. Blend alternately flour and poppy seed mixtures. Cream well. Fold in stiffly beaten egg whites. Pour into 2 8-inch cake pans and bake for about 30 minutes at 350 degrees. Cool five minutes in pan, then turn onto wire rack for further cooling.

Filling (for between layers):
¾ cup sugar
4 egg yolks
2 tablespoons cornstarch
1½ cups milk
¼ teaspoon salt
½ cup nuts (chopped)
1 teaspoon vanilla

Cook in double boiler five minutes, stirring constantly. When thick, cool and add nuts and vanilla.

Icing (for top):
1 13-ounce package cream cheese
1 tablespoon milk
2½ cups sifted powdered sugar

Blend the cream cheese and milk. Add the sugar gradually and blend well, add vanilla.
Mrs. C. E. Clawson (Frances)

NO-CRUST COCONUT PIE

4 eggs
1¾ cups sugar
½ cup self-rising flour
1 stick oleo, melted
2 scant cups milk
1 teaspoon vanilla
1 7-ounce package flaked coconut

Beat eggs well. Add sugar and flour, then add other ingredients. Pour into two well greased pie tins. Bake at 350 degrees for 30-40 minutes.
Mrs. Floyd Cunningham (Nell)

FRENCH COCONUT PIE

1 stick oleo
1½ cups sugar
3 eggs
1 unbaked pie shell
1 teaspoon vinegar
1 teaspoon vanilla
1 small can angel flake coconut

Melt oleo in saucepan. Add sugar, eggs, vinegar, vanilla and coconut. Pour into an unbaked pie crust. Bake in a moderate oven at 325 degrees for one hour.

Mrs. Louis R. Jaudon (Betty)

ICE BOX FRUIT PIE

1 baked pie crust or graham cracker crust
½ cup sugar
1 3-ounce package cream cheese*
Small can crushed pineapple
Large carton (9 ounces) frozen whipped topping (use about ¾ of it)*

Cream sugar with cream cheese. Drain pineapple, add to cheese mixture. Fold in thawed whipped topping (do not use quite all of it). Put mixture in graham cracker crust or cooled baked pie crust — both crusts are good. Chill several hours before serving.

Other fruits may be used in place of pineapple. Use approximately one cup, well drained.

**(If one 8-ounce package of cream cheese and whole nine-ounce carton of whipped topping are used, it will make two 8-inch pies.)*

Mrs. M. J. Hodges (Mary)

CRAZY BLUEBERRY PIE

1 9-inch graham cracker crust
¼ cup cold water
1 14-ounce can Eagle Brand milk
1 envelope Knox unflavored gelatin
⅓ cup lemon juice
1 cup sour cream
2½ cups (1 pound, 5-ounces) can blueberry pie filling

Place water and gelatin in small sauce pan over direct heat. Stir until dissolved and mixture is clear. In a medium bowl combine milk and lemon juice, stir in gelatin mixture. Fold in sour cream. Mix in half the blueberry pie filling; turn into the crust. Refrigerate three hours. Garnish top with remaining pie filling and serve.

Mrs. Richard Schreiner (Lois)

FRESH STRAWBERRY PIE I

1 9-inch pie shell
2 cups 7-Up
1 cup sugar
4 tablespoons cornstarch
1 teaspoon lemon juice
Red food color
1 to 1½ pints strawberries, fresh, whole
1 9-ounce carton Cool Whip or whipped cream

Bake pie shell according to directions. In a saucepan, combine 7-Up, sugar, and cornstarch. Cook over medium heat until clear and firm. Add food color and lemon juice. Set aside to cool completely. Then stir in whole strawberries and turn into completely cooled pie shell. Top with Cool Whip or whipped cream. Garnish with fresh strawberries, if desired.
Mrs. John R. Clement (Martha)

FRESH STRAWBERRY PIE II

2 cups fresh strawberries
1 9-inch baked pie shell
1½ cups water
¾ cup sugar
2 tablespoons cornstarch
1 3-ounce package strawberry gelatin
½ pint heavy cream (whipped)

Wash and dry strawberries. Cut into halves. Place strawberries in baked pie shell. Mix water with sugar and cornstarch. Cook two to five minutes on low heat or until clear and thick. Remove from heat and add strawberry gelatin; stir until dissolved. Pour over strawberries in crust. Chill and top with whipped cream. Yields 8 servings.
Mrs. Mary Ray, Haynesville, Louisiana
Mrs. Lois Mambourg

BETTY'S 3 LEMON ICEBOX PIES

3 eggs
1 cup sugar
1½ cups pineapple juice (12-ounce can)
1 5½-ounce (family size) lemon Jello
1 can (16-ounces) cold Carnation milk
1 16-ounce box vanilla wafers

Mix eggs, sugar, pineapple juice; bring to a boil, add lemon Jello, cool. In mixing bowl, whip the cold Carnation milk until it peaks, add the cooled mixture. Pour this into the prepared pie pans that have been lined with the vanilla wafers. You may crumble the wafers if you prefer. One box of vanilla wafers will line 3 9-inch foil pans. Makes 3 lemon icebox pies.
Mrs. Louis R. Jaudon (Betty)

LEMONADE PIE

1 14-ounce can condensed milk
1 3½-ounce can frozen lemonade
1 9-ounce carton Cool Whip
1 9-inch cookie crumb crust

Blend condensed milk with thawed lemonade. Fold in Cool Whip and pour into crumb crust. Chill until firm.
Mrs. Julius Waits

LEMON MERINGUE PIE

⅓ cup cornstarch
¼ teaspoon salt
4 egg yolks
2 tablespoons grated lemon peel
2 tablespoons butter
1½ cups sugar
1½ cups water
¼ cup lemon juice
1 9-inch baked pie shell

Combine cornstarch, sugar and salt in medium sized heavy bottomed saucepan. Add water and eggs, mixing well. Bring to a boil over medium high heat, stirring constantly. Boil one minute and remove from heat. Add lemon juice, peel and butter. Stir until all ingredients are blended. Pour into pie shell and top with meringue and bake in 375 degree oven for 10 minutes.
Mrs. A. H. Otto (Marjorie)
Mrs. Louis R. Jaudon (Betty)

BLENDER LEMON PIE

1 lemon (seeds out), quartered
1½ cups sugar
1 8-inch unbaked pie shell
1 stick oleo, chopped
3 eggs

Mix all ingredients in blender and blend well. Pour into unbaked pie shell (8-inch) and bake at 350 degrees for 30 minutes.
Mrs. Lawrence A. McKinley, Magnolia Springs, Alabama

BANANA SPLIT PIE

2 cups graham cracker crumbs
1 stick melted butter
2 cups powdered sugar, sifted
2 eggs
2 sticks butter
5 bananas
Lemon juice
1 20-ounce can crushed pineapple
1 large carton Cool Whip
½ cup chopped pecans
¼ cup maraschino cherries, split

Mix graham cracker crumbs and butter and press into 9x13-inch pan. In a bowl, beat powdered sugar, eggs, and butter on medium speed for 15 minutes. Pour over crust. Cut bananas length-wise and dip in lemon juice. Lay the bananas on top of mixture. Drain pineapple thoroughly and pour over bananas. Cover completely with Cool Whip and top with pecans and cherries. Serves 20-24.

Mrs. Joe D. Clement (Paula), Fort Worth, Texas
Mrs. Jo Whittaker
Mrs. Clara Cummins, Bossier City, Louisiana

CONCORD GRAPE PIE

1 quart canned concord grapes
2 cups sugar
4 heaping tablespoons flour
¼ teaspoon salt
Butter or oleo
Pastry for double crust pie

Empty grapes into a large mixing bowl. Sift dry ingredients together and stir into grapes — mix well. Pour grape mixture into crusts — dot with butter. Put on top crust, tuck it under bottom one and flute edges. Make several holes in top crust and bake at 450 degrees for about 40 minutes. It is best to preheat oven to 425 degrees. Put pie on cookie sheet to catch any drippings.

Preparation of Grapes for Pie:
When grapes are in season, usually late August, buy six to eight hand baskets of them — this yields about 7 to 8 quarts when canned. (Probably 1 basket would suffice if all the grapes were good.) Wash each bunch thoroughly. Pick one at a time and into one large container squeeze out the pulp and put hulls in another large container. (This takes about 30 minutes per basket.) When containers are full, cook in their own juice (do not add water) until they boil (pulp will be clear). Stir frequently. Remove back from fire and put pulp through a ricer to remove seeds. Empty pulp juice into the hulls and bring to boil and can as you would any other fruits. Grapes, if properly sealed, will keep 3 or 4 years.

YIELD: One 9½ or 10-inch deep pie or 2 smaller shallow pies
Mrs. Dorothy S. Thomas

PEACHES AND CREAM PIE

¾ cup flour
½ teaspoon salt
1 teaspoon baking powder
3¼-ounce package dry vanilla instant pudding mix
3 tablespoons butter
1 egg
1 29-ounce can sliced peaches
1 8-ounce package cream cheese
½ cup sugar
1 tablespoon sugar
½ teaspoon cinnamon

Combine flour, salt, baking powder, pudding mix, butter, and egg. Beat 2 minutes. Pour into greased 10-inch pie plate. Drain peaches, reserving juice. Pour peaches over batter. Combine cream cheese, 3 tablespoons peach juice, and sugar (½ cup). Pour over peaches. Combine 1 tablespoon sugar and cinnamon. Sprinkle over top. Bake at 350 degrees for 30 minutes or until crust is brown.
Mrs. Billy R. Goodman, Jr., Longview, Texas

I have never met anyone who couldn't tell me something that I hadn't known before.

DELICIOUS PEACH PIE

5 cups sliced fresh peaches
2 tablespoons cornstarch
½ cup honey
½ teaspoon lemon juice
1 teaspoon vanilla
¾ cup whole wheat flour
¾ cup unbleached flour
⅔ cup peanut oil
⅓ cup cold water

Combine peaches, cornstarch, honey, lemon juice and vanilla. Set aside. Mix the two flours and gradually add the peanut oil. Pour in the cold water and mix well. Divide the dough in half. Roll out one half to fit a 9-inch round pie pan. Place in oiled pie pan. Pour in peach mixture. Roll out remaining dough and cut in ½ inch strips and form in a lattice fashion over top of pie. Bake at 425 degrees for 15 minutes, turn down to 325 degrees and bake for 30 minutes.
Mrs. George Gekakis (Carol) (submitted by Rhonda Berry)

PEACH PIE

1 unbaked pie crust
1 layer of table peaches
2 eggs
1 cup sugar
½ stick butter
Pinch of salt
¼ teaspoon almond flavoring
½ teaspoon vanilla flavoring

Line a small pie pan with your favorite crust. Put a layer of table peaches in crust. Beat the eggs, sugar, butter, salt and flavorings. This is better if you beat by hand — do not use a mixer. If you use a mixer it beats the eggs too much and the custard will not stay together. Pour mixture over the peaches and bake as for a custard pie in 325-350 degree oven — depends on your oven.

Mrs. Roy Thigpen, Sr., Mansfield, Louisiana

RAISIN PIE

½ cup margarine
¾ cup sugar
2 eggs
½ teaspoon cinnamon
¼ teaspoon nutmeg
¼ teaspoon salt
1 teaspoon vinegar
½ cup chopped nuts
½ cup raisins
9-inch pastry shell

Combine all ingredients and pour into pastry shell. Bake about 30 minutes at 400 degrees.

Mrs. Christine Waites

HONEY RAISIN PIE

2¼ cups honey
3 eggs
4½ cups raisins
⅔ cup flour
½ teaspoon salt
3 cups water

Cook raisins until swollen. Mix honey, flour and salt. Combine raisins and flour mixture. Pour into pie crust and bake at 450 degrees for 10 minutes, then at 350 degrees for 30 minutes or until crust is lightly browned.

Pie crust can be your own or one from the frozen foods department of your supermarket.

Mrs. Edward W. Robinson, Keithville, Louisiana

OLD TENNESSEE CHESS PIE

1 cup sugar
¾ stick butter or margarine
3 eggs
1 unbaked pie shell
¼ cup flour
¼ cup milk
1 teaspoon vanilla
3 tablespoons sugar

Cream butter and sugar until light. Add egg yolks. Cream well, add flour and milk alternately. Add vanilla. Pour into unbaked pie shell. Bake in moderate oven about 30 minutes. Let cool. Add three tablespoons sugar to egg whites; beat well. Spread mixture with beaten egg whites. Brown meringue in oven.
Mrs. Leonard Green, Jr. (June)

BUTTERMILK PIE

3 egg yolks
1½ cups sugar
1½ cups buttermilk
2 tablespoons flour
1 tablespoon butter
1 unbaked pie shell

Mix all ingredients together and pour into unbaked pie crust. Top with meringue. Bake at 450 degrees for ten minutes; reduce to 300 degrees for forty minutes.
Mrs. Leonard Green, Jr. (June)

OLD SOUTH BUTTERMILK PIE

1 9-inch pastry shell, unbaked and chilled
1½ cups sugar
3 tablespoons flour
2 eggs, well beaten
1 stick butter, melted
1 cup buttermilk
1 tablespoon lemon juice
1 teaspoon vanilla
Nutmeg, freshly grated, if possible

Combine flour and sugar in a large mixing bowl. Add the beaten eggs; stir in the butter and buttermilk, mixing well. Add the lemon juice and vanilla and stir again. Pour into the chilled unbaked shell and grate nutmeg over top. Place pie in center third of preheated 425 degree oven for 10 minutes. Lower heat to 350 degrees and continue to bake for 35 minutes. After first bite, your stomach will say "howdy."
Mrs. W. D. Sandifer, Jr. (Evelyn)

PECAN PIE

½ cup sugar
2 eggs
1 teaspoon vanilla
1 unbaked pie shell
¾ cup light Karo corn syrup
½ stick butter or margarine (melted)
1 cup chopped pecans

Mix sugar, corn syrup, eggs, melted butter, vanilla together, add pecans last. Pour mixture into unbaked pie shell. Place on a cookie sheet. Bake at 350 degrees for 40 minutes or until set.
Mrs. Jerrold Weaver

PINEAPPLE PECAN PIE

2 graham cracker crusts
1 13½-ounce size Cool Whip (thawed)
⅓ cup lemon juice
1 large can (drained) pineapple
1 cup chopped pecans
1 can Eagle Brand milk

Fold milk into Cool Whip; then, fold in lemon juice; add pineapple and pecans; pour into pie crusts and chill. Makes 2 pies.
Mrs. Russell Smith (Liz)

SOUTHERN PECAN PIE

3 eggs
½ cup sugar
¼ cup butter or margarine
1 cup white Karo syrup
½ teaspoon salt
1 cup pecans
1 9-inch unbaked pie crust

Cream butter to soften, add sugar gradually and cream until fluffy. Add syrup and salt, beat well. Add eggs one at a time, beating well after each. Stir in pecans. Pour into pie shell and bake at 350 degrees for approximately one hour.
Mrs. F. A. Kihneman (Tora)

SWEET POTATO PIE

2 cups cooked mashed sweet potatoes
½ cup butter or margarine (room temperature)
2 egg yolks
1 cup brown sugar
¼ teaspoon salt
½ teaspoon cinnamon
½ teaspoon nutmeg
½ teaspoon ginger
½ cup milk
2 egg whites
¼ cup sugar
1 9-inch unbaked pie shell

Mix first eight ingredients while potatoes are still warm. Add milk. Beat egg whites until stiff, gradually adding sugar. Fold into the potato mixture and pour into an unbaked pie shell. Bake at 400 degrees for 10 minutes, then lower heat to 350 degrees and bake until set.
Mrs. C. D. Attaway (Margie)

DAIQUIRI PIE

1 3¾-ounce package Jello lemon pie filling
1 3-ounce package lime Jello
⅓ cup sugar
2½ cups water
2 eggs (slightly beaten)
¼-ounce rum extract or ½ cup of rum
2 cups prepared Dream Whip or Cool Whip
1 9-inch pie shell (baked)

Mix lemon pie filling and lime Jello together. Add sugar and blend in the ½ cup water to make smooth paste of the first 3 ingredients. Add eggs, slightly beaten and the other 2 cups water. Cook on low fire until comes to a full boil. Set aside to cool. When cooled add rum. Chill real well, then fold in whipped topping or Dream Whip. Pour into the baked and cooled pie shell.

Pie Shell:
1 cup presifted flour
¼ cup presifted powdered sugar
½ stick margarine
½ cup chopped pecans

Mix all together with hands until well mixed, then press into pie pan and bake at 375 degrees for 10 to 12 minutes or until slightly brown.
Mrs. Joe East (Leona)

ICE CREAM MERINGUE PIE

For a 10-inch pie:

2 egg whites, beaten stiff
½ cup sugar
½ cup graham cracker crumbs
½ cup nuts (optional)
1 quart ice cream

Add sugar slowly to beaten egg whites. Fold in graham cracker crumbs and nuts, if used. Spoon into well greased 10-inch Pyrex pie plate, shaping well to sides of pie plate. Bake in 350 degree oven for 30 minutes. Cool. Freeze. Fill crust with 1 quart ice cream. For Chocolate Chip Pie spoon on warm chocolate sauce; for Lemon Custard Pie, use lemon custard ice cream, swirl the top and sprinkle on toasted almonds; for Praline Pie, use butter pecan ice cream and sprinkle chopped pecans on top or use bottled caramel sauce spooned over each slice; for Coconut Pie use vanilla ice cream, stirring in 3 ounces of angel flake coconut (save some to sprinkle on top) . . . and you have desserts fit for a King, a Queen — or your Pastor.

Mrs. William J. Box (Doris)

GRASSHOPPER PIE

For Pie Crust:

4 tablespoons butter
24 crushed chocolate wafers

For Filling:

24 large marshmallows
4 tablespoons green Creme de Menthe
1 cup whipped cream
½ cup milk
2 tablespoons white Creme de Cacao
Maraschino cherries for garnish

Melt butter and stir in the 24 crushed chocolate wafers, press into 8-inch pie plate.

Melt the marshmallows in the ½ cup milk, and cool. Stir in Creme de Menthe and Creme de Cacao. Fold in the whipped cream. Pour into pie shell and garnish with the cherries or grated chocolate curls. Freeze. Serve frozen.

Mrs. Joseph LaBarbera (Billie)

BLACK BOTTOM PIE

½ cup sugar
1 tablespoon cornstarch
2 cups milk (scalded)
4 beaten egg yolks
1 teaspoon vanilla
1 6-ounce package semi-sweet chocolate pieces
1 envelope unflavored gelatin
¼ cup cold water
4 egg whites
½ cup sugar
1 baked pie shell

For the first six ingredients listed above you combine sugar and cornstarch, add milk to beaten egg yolks; add to sugar mixture. Cook over hot, not boiling water until it coats a spoon. Remove from heat and add vanilla. To 1 cup of this mixture add semi-sweet chocolate. Stir until chocolate melts. Pour into cooled baked pie shell and chill. Soften gelatin in cold water; add to remaining hot custard. Stir until dissolved. Chill until thick. Beat egg whites to form soft peak. Gradually fold in the last ½ cup sugar and beat until stiff. Fold in gelatin-custard mixture. Pour over chocolate layer and chill until set. Garnish with cherry halves or banana slices and shaved chocolate.
Mrs. James Carr (Paula)

CHOCOLATE FUDGE PIE

1 cup evaporated milk
1 6-ounce package semi-sweet chocolate morsels
1 cup miniature marshmallows
¼ teaspoon salt
Vanilla wafers to line a 9-inch baking dish
1 quart vanilla ice cream
½ cup chopped pecans

In a sauce pan put the evaporated milk, chocolate, marshmallows and salt. Stir over low heat until chocolate and marshmallows are melted and blended. Remove from heat and allow to cool. Line bottom and sides of 9-inch baking dish with the vanilla wafers and spoon half of the ice cream evenly over the wafers. Cover this with half the chocolate mix. Repeat the procedure with remaining ice cream and chocolate mixture and top with pecans. Place in freezer compartment of refrigerator until firm. Serve at once when removed from freezer.
Mrs. Ike Cullick (Barbara)

CHOCOLATE PIE I

1½ cups sugar
3 heaping tablespoons flour
3 heaping tablespoons cocoa
½ teaspoon salt
1 cup water
2 egg yolks
1 small can evaporated milk
¼ stick butter

Mix sugar, flour, cocoa and salt. Add water and mix into paste; blend in slightly beaten egg yolks and milk. Cook the mixture over slow flame, stirring frequently. Add butter and vanilla. Pour into baked pastry shell and top with meringue or whipped cream.
Zelma Long Frazier (First cousin of Gov. Huey P. Long)
Submitted by Mrs. Leonard Green (June)

CHOCOLATE PIE II

1 cup sugar
4 tablespoons flour
3 tablespoons cocoa
½ teaspoon salt
3 egg yolks
1 teaspoon vanilla
2 cups milk
⅓ stick oleo

Meringue:
3 egg whites
3 tablespoons sugar to each egg white
¼ teaspoon cream of tartar

Combine all above ingredients in sauce pan. Cook over medium heat until thick, stirring constantly. Cool. Pour into baked 9-inch cooled pie crust.
Meringue: Mix together above ingredients, beat until stiff. Spread on top of pie and brown in 400 degree oven.
Mrs. Clara Cummins, Bossier City, Louisiana

FRENCH CHOCOLATE PIE

1 baked 9-inch pie shell
½ cup butter
2 eggs
2 cups thawed Cool Whip
¾ cup sugar
2 squares unsweetened chocolate

Melt chocolate over hot water and set aside. Cream butter and sugar. Stir in melted chocolate. Add eggs, one at a time, beating at high speed 5 minutes after each addition. Fold in Cool Whip and pour into pie shell. Chill until firm. About 2 hours, or freeze. Will serve 6-8
Mrs. A. R. Snider (Frances)

BROWNIE PIE

3 egg whites
Dash of salt
¾ cup sugar
½ cup pecans
½ package thin chocolate wafers
½ teaspoon vanilla
½ pint sweetened whipping cream
3 teaspoons sugar

Beat egg whites to soft peak. Gradually add sugar. Beat until stiff. Fold in crushed wafer crumbs, nuts and vanilla. Spread in 8-inch or 9-inch buttered pie plate. Bake in 325 degree oven about 35 minutes. Cool thoroughly. Add 3 teaspoons sugar to whipping cream while beating.

Optional: Sprinkle chocolate crumbs over top.

Mrs. Carroll Morris (Mervin), Tulsa, Oklahoma

SWEET GERMAN CHOCOLATE PIE

1 4-ounce package Baker's Sweet German Chocolate
¼ cup butter
1⅔ cups evaporated milk
1½ cups sugar
⅛ teaspoon salt
3 teaspoons cornstarch
2 eggs
1 teaspoon vanilla
1 9-inch pie shell, uncooked, highly fluted
½ cup chopped pecans
1⅓ cup Baker's Angel Flake Coconut

Melt chocolate and butter over low heat, stirring until blended. Remove from heat; gradually blend in milk. In a separate bowl, mix sugar, cornstarch, and salt thoroughly. Beat in eggs and vanilla. Gradually blend in chocolate mixture. Pour into pie shell. Combine coconut and pecans; sprinkle over filling. Bake at 375 degrees for 45-50 minutes or until puffed and browned. (The filling will be soft, but will set while cooling.) Cool at least 4 hours before cutting.

NOTE: If the top browns too quickly, cover loosely with foil for the last 15 minutes of baking.

Mrs. John R. Clement (Martha)

Cookies · Candies

The years of 1870 and 1871 marked the granting of charters for two horsedrawn street railways in Shreveport. On August 6, 1870, the Shreveport City Railroad Company was permitted to operate "one or more lines of street railways through the streets of the city, within the city limits, the cars to be propelled by horses, mules, steam or other power."

Shreveport was the first city in Louisiana and one of the first in the South to adopt electric street cars. The first car over the line in September 1889 was a momentous occasion. It was recorded that "when the first car went over the line and flashes of electricity flamed from the rails, terror-stricken mothers gathered their children from what they thought was impending danger."

A popular Sunday afternoon amusement was a ride around the belt line on a street car. One-way fare was five cents and gentlemen paid before taking their seats. Ladies, however, sat down and gave their fare to the nearest man, who passed it forward to the coin box or to the conductor.

INTERESTING FACTS ABOUT SHREVEPORT

The year 1939 brought an end to the era of peace with the outbreak of the war in Europe. This, along with the Air Corps expansion bill of that year, more than doubled the personnel strength at Barksdale. Colonel Charles A. Lindbergh visited Barksdale in 1939.

The European war was brought very close to Shreveporters with the announcement that Captain Robert M. Losey, a former Barksdale man, was the first American killed in the fray.

Commanding the 2nd Armored division, which passed through Shreveport in two 70-mile columns of army vehicles on August 13 and 14, and was called "Hell on Wheels" was General George S. Patton, Jr.

Many war heroes were from Shreveport and Bossier or had served at Barksdale Air Force Base. In 1945 Barksdale sent more medium bombardment crews to overseas commands than any other continental station.

A national heroine and Shreveport's most bemedaled woman was Lieutenant Edith Wimberly, nurse, and one of 69 rescued "Angles of Bataan and Corregidor," who cared for civilian internees who were prisoners of the Japanese. For her heroism she received the Bronze Star, Asiatic Theater and American Defense medals, Philippine Defense and Liberation medals and two Presidential Citations.

BROWNIES

1 cup margarine
4 squares (1 ounce each) unsweetened chocolate
1 tablespoon light corn syrup
1½ cups all-purpose flour (sift before measuring)
1 teaspoon salt
1 teaspoon baking powder
4 eggs
2 cups sugar
2 teaspoons vanilla
2 cups pecans (coarsely chopped)

Place margarine and chocolate together in an uncovered sauce pan. Cook on very low heat until blended well. When melted add corn syrup and set aside to cool. Sift the flour, salt, and baking powder together. Pour chocolate mixture into large bowl of electric mixer and mix at medium speed. Add sugar gradually and beat for about 1½ minutes. Add eggs all at one time and continue beating one minute longer. Add dry ingredients and vanilla. Beat again for one minute. Add nuts. Pour in well greased 12x9x2-inch pan. Bake in preheated oven at 350 degrees for 35 to 40 minutes. Let cool and cut into squares. Makes 24 squares.
Mrs. C. D. Attaway (Margie)

DOTTIE'S SPECIAL BROWNIES

1 family size box (1 pound, 10 ounces) Duncan Hines brownie mix
2 tablespoons water
3 eggs
½ cup chopped nuts (if desired)

Following directions on box for "cake like" brownies, empty mix and chocolate flavor packet into medium size mixing bowl. Add water, eggs and nuts. Mix well. Use 13x9-inch metal or glass pan which has been greased. Spread the following topping on batter evenly:

Topping:
½ stick oleo, melted
¾ cup light brown sugar
¾ cup large pecans, broken

Combine melted oleo, brown sugar and pecans. Mix well. Spread on batter.
Bake at 350 degrees for 25 to 30 minutes. Brownies will look gooey, but take them out and let cool before cutting. Do not overcook!
Mrs. Ralph Garrett (Dottie)

CORN FLAKE PECAN COOKIES

¾ cup butter
1 cup sugar
2 eggs, beaten
2 cups sifted flour
1 teaspoon baking powder
½ teaspoon salt
2 cups whole pecans
1 cup chopped dates
2 cups corn flakes
1 teaspoon vanilla

Cream butter and sugar. Stir in eggs and mix well. Sift flour with baking powder and salt, and add. Finally, add pecans, dates, corn flakes and vanilla. Drop by teaspoonfuls on a buttered cookie sheet and bake in a 350 degree oven for 15 minutes or until the cookies are brown. Makes 5 dozen.
Mrs. Leonard Green, Jr. (June)

PECAN DAINTY COOKIES

1 egg white
⅔ cup brown sugar
Pinch of salt
2 cups of pecans
1 teaspoon vanilla

Beat egg whites until stiff. Continue beating as you add sugar by spoonfuls. Add pecans, vanilla and salt. Stir until pecans are thoroughly covered. Drop on well greased cookie sheet. Bake at 300 degrees for 30 minutes. Let cool before removing.
Mrs. H. H. Hand (Henry Ella)

PECAN FINGERS

2 cups flour, sifted
2 cups pecans
½ cup shortening
½ teaspoon vanilla
½ cup butter
2 tablespoons water
½ cup brown sugar

Cream shortening and butter; add sugar, water, vanilla, and pecans. Mix well, add flour and shape into finger size rolls. Chill before cooking at 350 degrees. Cook to a golden brown and roll each in powdered sugar.
Mrs. C. Don Attaway (Frances), Blanchard, Louisiana

CHEWY COCONUT BARS

½ cup brown sugar, finely packed
1¼ cups all-purpose flour
½ cup butter

Topping:

2 eggs
½ cup granulated sugar
½ cup dark corn syrup
1 teaspoon vanilla
1 teaspoon baking powder
1 cup flaked coconut
1 cup chopped walnuts
½ cup raisins
1 tablespoon cornstarch
½ teaspoon salt

Preheat oven to 350 degrees. Mix brown sugar and flour together in medium sized bowl. Work in butter, using a pastry blender, until dough is soft. Pat this mixture into a 9x9x2-inch baking pan. Bake for 15 minutes in preheated oven.

For topping, beat together eggs, sugar, corn syrup, and vanilla in medium sized bowl with electric mixer on medium speed. Stir in coconut, walnuts, raisins, cornstarch, baking powder and salt. Spread evenly on top of pre-baked crust and bake for 25 minutes. Cool, cut into 36 bars. Store in air tight container.

Mrs. Mary Lurline Wilson

CHERRY-COCONUT BARS

Pastry:

1 cup sifted flour
½ cup butter
3 tablespoons confectioners' sugar

Filling:

2 eggs, slightly beaten
1 cup sugar
¼ cup flour
½ teaspoon baking powder
½ cup quartered maraschino cherries
¼ teaspoon salt
1 teaspoon vanilla
¾ cup chopped nuts
½ cup coconut

Preheat oven to 350 degrees. With hands, mix flour, butter, confectioners' sugar until smooth. Spread thin with fingers in 8-inch square pan that is greased and floured. Bake about 25 minutes.

Stir rest of ingredients into eggs. Spread over top of baked pastry (no need to cool). Bake about 25 minutes. Cool. Cut into bars.

Mrs. Odell R. Moore (Mary)

GRAHAM-NUT SQUARES

Graham crackers to layer a 9x12-inch baking pan (whole crackers)
2 sticks Mazola margarine, melted and cooled
1 cup sugar
½ cup evaporated milk
1 egg
1 cup chopped nuts
1 cup coconut
1 cup graham cracker crumbs
Second layer of whole graham crackers

Layer 1 9x12-inch baking pan with whole graham crackers. Combine margarine, sugar, evaporated milk and egg. Mix well and cook over medium heat until thickened; approximately 10 minutes. Remove from heat and add chopped nuts, coconut and graham cracker crumbs. Spread this mixture over graham crackers in pan. Cover with another layer of whole graham crackers. Top this with icing listed below.

Icing:
1 stick Mazola margarine, melted
¼ cup evaporated milk
1 box confectioners' sugar
2 teaspoons vanilla

Combine margarine, milk, sugar and vanilla. Beat until smooth and spread on top. Refrigerate. Cut in small squares, as this is very thin. Keep refrigerated. This is better if prepared a day in advance. It keeps well for days.
Mrs. Ralph Garrett (Dottie)

GRAHAM CRACKER PRALINE COOKIES

1 package of graham crackers (from a 3 package carton)
1 cup light brown sugar
2 sticks margarine
1 cup chopped pecans

Split graham crackers in two (long way), using care or crackers will break easily. Place on a cookie sheet.

Mix brown sugar and margarine together, place on low fire and let come to a boil. Boil one minute. Remove from fire and stir in chopped pecans. Pour this mixture over graham crackers, spreading with spoon or spatula. Bake in a 325 degree oven for eight minutes. This means eight minutes — not seven or nine minutes.

Let cool slightly, then cut in two with a knife, using care.
Mrs. Olin P. Oden (Ruth)

PRALINE COOKIES

1½ cups flour
1½ cups dark brown sugar
1 egg
½ cup butter
1 teaspoon vanilla
1 cup chopped pecans

Cream butter and sugar. Add egg and vanilla, beating well. Add flour, then nuts. If mixture is a bit dry, add enough water to enable you to drop by teaspoons onto greased cookie sheet. Bake at 370 degrees for 12 minutes or until lightly brown.
Mrs. Floyd Cunningham (Nell)

OATMEAL COOKIES

1 cup brown sugar
1½ teaspoons vanilla
2 eggs
2 cups flour
1 teaspoon baking powder
1 cup raisins
¾ cup honey
¾ cup salad oil
2 tablespoons milk
1 teaspoon soda
½ teaspoon salt
2 cups oats (uncooked)

Preheat oven to 350 degrees. Beat sugar and honey, oil, eggs, vanilla and milk until smooth. Sift flour, baking powder, soda, and salt. Add all at once to egg mixture and beat until smooth. Add raisins and oats and mix well. Drop from teaspoon onto greased cookie sheet 2 inches apart. Bake 12 minutes.
Mrs. Edward W. Robinson, Keithville, Louisiana

QUICK OATMEAL COOKIES

1 cup butter or oleo, softened
2 tablespoons cold water
2 teaspoons vanilla
2 teaspoons almond flavoring
1 cup granulated sugar
1 cup brown sugar
2 eggs
2 cups flour
1 teaspoon soda
1 teaspoon baking powder
½ teaspoon salt
3 cups quick oatmeal
½ cup nuts or raisins
1 cup coconut or 2 teaspoons coconut flavoring

Mix together the butter, cold water, vanilla, almond flavoring, granulated sugar, brown sugar and eggs. Add dry ingredients, raisins and coconut. Mix well. Drop on cookie sheets and bake at 350 degrees for 10-12 minutes.
Mrs. Ralph Garrett (Dottie)

OLD TIME TEA CAKES

1 cup sugar
½ cup oleo
1 egg
1 tablespoon baking powder
2 tablespoons milk
2¼ cups flour

Cream oleo and add sugar; then add well beaten egg. Add milk gradually. Sift the baking powder with one half of the flour, add to mixture; then add more flour, a little at a time. Beat and add flour until mixture leaves bowl (use all of other half of flour). Store in cool place for an hour or more to stiffen. Break off small pieces of dough, roll and cut on floured board. Bake on greased tins in hot oven, 400 degrees, for about 10 to 12 minutes, until light brown.

Mrs. Leonard Green, Jr. (June)

TEA CAKES

2 sticks oleo
1½ cups sugar
2 eggs
3 cups flour
½ teaspoon soda
1 teaspoon baking powder
1 tablespoon vanilla

Cream together oleo and sugar. Add all other ingredients. Mix well. Drop by teaspoon onto a greased cookie sheet. Bake at 375 degrees. Cool and store in tightly covered container.

Mrs. Clara Cummins, Bossier City, Louisiana

OLD FASHIONED TEA CAKES

1 cup butter or oleo
3 cups sugar
3 eggs
About 2 pounds of flour
⅓ cup buttermilk with 1 teaspoon soda
1 teaspoon vanilla

Mix ingredients in order given, using enough flour to make dough stiff enough to roll out on floured board or cloth. Bake at 325 degrees until lightly browned.

Mrs. Christine Waites

MAM-MAW'S OLD FASHIONED TEA CAKES

2 cups sugar
3 sticks butter or oleo
3 eggs
4 cups self-rising flour
1 teaspoon vanilla
¼ cup milk

Cream butter and sugar. Add eggs, beat well. Add flour and milk alternately. Add vanilla. Chill dough 3-4 hours. Divide mixture; flour hands and roll dough into balls. Flour work surface, roll dough to ¼ inch thickness and cut as desired. Bake on ungreased cookie sheet at 325 degrees 8 to 10 minutes. Dough can be mixed, rolled into balls, and refrigerated a few days or frozen until ready to bake.
Mrs. Elsie Wren

BAPTIST COOKIES

½ stick oleo, softened
⅔ cup sugar
1 cup chopped dates
1 cup chopped nuts (or more)
1 egg, beaten
2½ cups Rice Krispies
Coconut

Melt oleo in skillet over low fire. Stir in sugar, dates and beaten egg. Heat thoroughly. Stir in Rice Krispies and nuts. Form into balls and roll in coconut. Cool. Store in covered container.
Mrs. Art Ogletree, Jr. (Ann)

CHOCOLATE CRINKLES

½ cup shortening
1⅔ cups sugar
2 teaspoons vanilla
2 eggs
2 squares unsweetened chocolate (melted)
2 cups all-purpose flour
2 teaspoons baking powder
½ teaspoon salt
⅓ cup milk
½ cup chopped nuts

Cream shortening and sugar. Add vanilla. Beat in eggs and melted chocolate. Add dry ingredients alternately with milk. Add chopped nuts. Form in small balls; roll in powdered sugar. Bake on greased cookie sheet 15 minutes in 350 degree oven. Makes 48 cookies.
Mrs. Dale Ward (Renee)

FRUIT CAKE COOKIES

1 cup brown sugar
½ stick margarine or butter
2 eggs
1½ cups flour
¼ teaspoon nutmeg
½ teaspoon cinnamon
1 pound white candied pineapple, cut in pieces
1 pound candied cherries cut in half
1½ teaspoons soda
1 tablespoon buttermilk
3 cups pecans (chopped)
⅓ cup bourbon

Cream sugar and butter together. Add eggs one at a time. Add ½ cup flour and mix well. Add spices. In separate bowl place nuts, cut up fruit and add ½ cup flour, blend. Fold fruit mixture into creamed mixture. Add milk, soda, bourbon and balance of flour. Mix well. Drop by spoonfuls onto greased pan or into tiny paper cups for a miniature cake. Bake at 325 degrees for 10 to 12 minutes.
Mrs. Lois Mambourg

SPICY BANANA BARS

1 cup flour
¾ cup sugar
½ teaspoon baking powder
½ teaspoon salt
¼ teaspoon soda
¾ teaspoon cinnamon
¼ teaspoon cloves
¼ teaspoon allspice
¼ cup butter
⅓ cup mashed ripe bananas
1 egg, unbeaten
¼ cup milk
⅓ cup chopped pecans

Sift together the flour, sugar, baking powder, salt, soda, cinnamon, cloves and allspice. Cream butter and add bananas, blend thoroughly. Add egg and then add dry ingredients alternately with milk. Stir in pecans. Spread in a well greased and lightly floured pan (13x9x2-inch). Bake at 350 degrees for 22 to 25 minutes. Frost while warm with Lemon Frosting:

Lemon Frosting:
2 tablespoons melted butter
1 tablespoon hot water
2 teaspoons lemon juice
1 cup sifted confectioners' sugar

Combine melted butter, hot water and lemon juice. Blend in confectioners' sugar. If necessary to thin, add a few drops of hot water at a time.
Mrs. Leonard Green, Jr. (June)

CONGO SQUARES

1⅓ sticks oleo
1 pound light brown sugar
3 eggs
2¾ cups sifted flour
2½ teaspoons baking powder
½ teaspoon salt
½ teaspoon vanilla
1 6-ounce package chocolate chips

Combine all ingredients and pour into greased baking pan, 12x8-inch, and bake in preheated 350 degree oven for about 30 minutes. Cut in squares.
Mrs. Leonard Green, Jr. (June)

PUMPKINETTES

½ cup Crisco
1 cup sugar
½ cup brown sugar
2 unbeaten eggs
2 cups pumpkin
1 teaspoon lemon extract
2¾ cups sifted flour
1 teaspoon soda
½ teaspoon salt
2 teaspoons cinnamon
½ teaspoon nutmeg
1 cup chopped raisins
1 cup finely chopped nuts

Cream shortening and sugars, add eggs and pumpkin and mix well. Mix flour and all other dry ingredients together and add to sugar and pumpkin mixture and stir in raisins and nuts last; mix well and drop by rounded teaspoons onto greased cookie sheet and bake 15 minutes in 350 degree oven. Makes 5 dozen.

For glaze: Mix 2 tablespoons soft margarine, 2 cups sifted powdered sugar, 1 tablespoon lemon juice or 2 tablespoons sweet milk to make paste. As pumpkinettes come out of oven top with glaze — Good! Good!
Mrs. F. A. Kihneman (Tora)

LEMON SQUARES

1 cup oleo, melted
2 cups flour
½ cup powdered sugar
2 cups sugar
4 eggs
5 tablespoons lemon juice

Mix well the oleo, flour and powdered sugar. Pack in baking pan. Bake 20 minutes at 350 degrees. Beat until fluffy, sugar, eggs and lemon juice. Pour over first ingredients and bake again 25 minutes. Sprinkle with powdered sugar. Cool and cut in squares.
Mrs. Leonard Green, Jr. (June)

DROP DOUGHNUT BALLS

½ cup sugar
½ cup milk
1 egg
2 tablespoons shortening
1½ cups sifted flour
½ teaspoon salt
2 teaspoons baking powder
½ teaspoon nutmeg
½ teaspoon cinnamon
Crisco for deep frying

Mix sugar, milk and egg. Add shortening. Add flour, salt, baking powder and spices which have been sifted together. Combine lightly. Drop from teaspoon into Crisco at 365 degrees. Cook until brown.
Mrs. Ronny Goodman (Janice)

RAISIN DROP COOKIES

2 cups brown sugar
1 cup shortening
2 eggs
2 teaspoons soda
½ teaspoon salt
½ teaspoon ginger
1 teaspoon cinnamon
1 teaspoon nutmeg
4½ cups flour

Cream brown sugar and shortening. Beat eggs. Then add to sugar mix. Sift together soda, salt, ginger, cinnamon, nutmeg, and flour. Cook one box of raisins in water until cooked down to 1 cup of liquid. Alternate flour mixture and liquid. Stir in raisins. Drop cookies. Bake 15 minutes at 350 degree oven.
Mrs. Ann Ferrara

DATE BARS

3 eggs
1 cup sugar
1½ package dates, chopped
1 cup chopped pecans
¾ cup flour
1 teaspoon baking powder
1 teaspoon vanilla

Beat eggs. Add sugar slowly; add dates and pecans. Stir well and add flour and baking powder; stir. Add vanilla. Pour in baking pan and cook at 325 degrees for 30 to 40 minutes. Cut in squares.
Mrs. Leonard Green, Jr. (June)

SNICKERDOODLES

1 cup shortening (part butter)
1½ cups sugar
2 eggs
2⅔ cups flour
2 teaspoons cream of tartar
1 teaspoon soda
¼ teaspoon salt
2 tablespoons sugar
2 tablespoons cinnamon

Preheat oven to 400 degrees. Mix shortening, sugar and eggs thoroughly. Mix flour, cream of tartar, soda and salt. Stir into mixture. Mix well. Roll into balls the size of small walnuts. Roll the balls in a mixture of 2 tablespoons sugar and 2 tablespoons cinnamon. Place 2 inches apart on greased cookie sheet. Yield: 5 dozen cookies.

Mrs. Bill Alexander (Mary Lynn)

FORGOTTEN COOKIES

2 egg whites
Pinch of salt
½ teaspoon vanilla
⅔ cup sugar
1 6-ounce package semi-sweet miniature chocolate chips
1 cup chopped nuts

Beat the egg whites with the pinch of salt and the vanilla. Gradually add the sugar, while beating, and beat until stiff. Add the chocolate chips and the chopped nuts. Drop by teaspoons onto the shiny side of a sheet of foil. Heat oven to 350 degrees for 5 minutes. Turn oven off. Place cookies in oven and leave overnight.

Mrs. A. H. Otto (Marjorie)

POTATO CHIP COOKIES

1 pound oleo
1 cup sugar
1 teaspoon vanilla
3½ cups flour
1 to 1½ cups crushed potato chips

Cream oleo and sugar together. Add vanilla, flour and potato chips. Using a teaspoon, drop on dry cookie sheet. Bake 10 to 15 minutes at 375 degrees. Sprinkle or roll in powdered sugar.

Mrs. Ella McNeil
Mrs. J. Kent Colvin (Yvonne)

LIZZIES

½ cup butter or margarine
4 eggs
2⅔ teaspoons soda
⅔ cup whiskey
1½ pounds nuts (6 cups)
1 pound white raisins
½ pound candied green pineapple
1 cup brown sugar
3 tablespoons milk
3 cups flour
1 teaspoon each cloves, nutmeg and cinnamon
1 pound red cherries

Mix fruit with ½ cup flour. Cream butter and sugar, add eggs, flour and other ingredients. Mix well and drop by teaspoons on ungreased cookie sheet. Cook at 350 degrees until light brown, about 16 to 20 minutes.
Mrs. A. H. Otto (Marjorie)

RHONDA'S COOKIES

6-ounce can frozen orange juice (do not dilute)
½ cup pecans (chopped)
½ cup coconut
1 pound crushed vanilla wafers
1 stick butter
1 pound confectioners' sugar

Melt butter. Combine all ingredients. Roll into little balls and place on waxed paper to set.
Miss Rhonda Berry

CHRISTMAS HOLLY CORN FLAKES

30 large marshmallows
1 stick oleo
1 teaspoon green food color
1 teaspoon peppermint extract
4 cups corn flakes
1 large package candy red hots

In a sauce pan over low heat, cook marshmallows and oleo to a syrup. Add food color and extract and blend thoroughly. Remove from heat. Stir in corn flakes until well coated with syrup. Drop by tablespoonfuls onto waxed paper or greased cookie sheet. Decorate with red hots to resemble holly berries.
Mrs. J. W. Adcox (Mary)

SEVEN LAYER COOKIES

- ½ cup butter or margarine
- 1 cup graham cracker crumbs
- 1 cup moist coconut
- 1 6-ounce package butterscotch morsels
- 1 6-ounce package chocolate morsels
- 1 14-ounce can condensed milk
- 1½ cups nuts, finely chopped

Melt butter in 9x12x2-inch pan. Spread graham cracker crumbs over melted butter. Sprinkle coconut over crumbs; sprinkle chocolate morsels over coconut and next, sprinkle butterscotch morsels over the chocolate morsels. Drizzle condensed milk evenly over everything and top with nuts.

Bake in preheated oven at 350 degrees for 30 minutes. Cut into squares while still warm.

Mrs. Art Ogletree, Jr. (Ann)

UNCOOKED CHOCOLATE COOKIES

- 1¾ cups sugar
- ½ cup cocoa
- 1 stick oleo
- ½ cup milk
- 3 cups quick oatmeal
- 1 cup nuts
- 1 teaspoon vanilla
- ½ cup coconut

Mix together sugar, cocoa, oleo and milk. Bring to rolling boil and pour over oatmeal, nuts, vanilla and coconut. Mix together ingredients. Drop by teaspoons on waxed paper.

Mrs. A. H. Otto (Marjorie)

NO COOK COOKIES

- 1 stick oleo
- ½ cup milk
- 4 tablespoons cocoa
- 2 cups sugar
- ½ cup peanut butter
- 1 teaspoon vanilla
- 3 cups oatmeal, uncooked
- 1 can angel flake coconut

Cook oleo, milk, cocoa and sugar in rolling boil for 1 minute. Blend rest of ingredients in. Drop in cookie size by a teaspoon on waxed paper. Yields 5-6 dozen.

Mrs. H. Russell Maddox (Tommie Lue)

FLOREINE'S COOKIES

2 sticks oleo
1 cup brown sugar
1 cup chopped nuts
24 (12 double) graham crackers

Boil oleo and brown sugar for 2 minutes. Add nuts. Pour over graham crackers. Bake 5 minutes at 350 degrees.
Mrs. O. W. Bradley (Floreine)

PECAN PRALINES

2 cups brown sugar
½ teaspoon baking soda
¾ cup milk
2 cups pecans
1 tablespoon butter
1 teaspoon vanilla

In a saucepan, put the brown sugar, baking soda and milk over low heat. Bring to soft ball stage. Add pecans, butter and vanilla. Beat until slightly creamy.

Put a damp towel on the table or countertop. On top of damp towel, put waxed paper sprinkled with salt. Pour the mixture onto the waxed paper to cool.

This is very rich and delicious — not for dieters!
Mrs. Floyd Cunningham (Nell)

EASY PECAN PRALINES

1 cup buttermilk
2 cups sugar
1 teaspoon soda
1 teaspoon vanilla
2 cups pecans (chopped)

Combine buttermilk, sugar, and soda and cook over low flame until the mixture forms a soft ball in water. Watch mixture constantly and stir often. After soft ball forms add vanilla and pecans. Stir until mixture begins to cool and then drop by tablespoons onto waxed paper. Allow to cool and set. Will store well in a tightly closed container.
Mrs. Wallace Mills (Jean)

PRALINES I

1 pound box light brown sugar
¼ cup margarine
½ pint heavy cream
¼ teaspoon cinnamon
Pinch of salt
1 teaspoon vanilla
2 cups nuts (chopped)

Mix all ingredients except flavoring and nuts. Cook until it forms a soft ball in water. Take off heat; add vanilla and nuts. Beat well and pour into small plastic cups or onto well greased cookie sheet. If you use a cookie sheet cut into 2 inch squares or less if desired. If cups are used, when completely cooled and set, pralines will pop out of cup with a little pressure applied to the bottom of cup.

Mrs. F. A. Kihneman (Tora)

PRALINES II

1½ cups white sugar
1½ cups dark brown sugar
3 tablespoons Karo syrup
1 5.33-ounce can evaporated milk
⅛ teaspoon salt
⅓ stick margarine
1 teaspoon vanilla
4 cups pecans

Mix sugars, syrup, milk, salt, and margarine together. Cook in heavy sauce pan, stirring constantly. As mixture comes to a boil, test drop in cold water for soft ball. Put pan in cold water and cool for 10 minutes. Add vanilla, beat 5 minutes and add pecans. Mix well. Drop by tablespoons onto waxed paper or marble slab.

Mrs. Lois Mambourg

PRALINES III

1 stick oleo
1 pound box light brown sugar
⅓ cup water
2 cups pecans

Dissolve on the stove the first three ingredients. Add 2 cups of pecans. Cook to soft ball stage then beat lightly. Spread on waxed buttered paper or in paper cups.

Mrs. C. A. Waites (Christine)

CHOCOLATE FUDGE

2 cups sugar
2 tablespoons flour
3 tablespoons cocoa
¼ teaspoon salt
1 cup nuts (chopped)
2 tablespoons Karo
1 stick margarine
⅔ cup evaporated milk
1 teaspoon vanilla

Mix sugar, flour, cocoa, salt, Karo, margarine, and milk. Cook on moderate heat until mixture forms soft ball in cool water. Cool for 15 minutes; add vanilla and nuts . Beat until creamy and pour into buttered pan. When cool cut into squares.

Mrs. F. A. Kihneman (Tora)

MILLION DOLLAR FUDGE

3 4½-ounce plain Hershey bars
2 6-ounce packages chocolate chips
1 pint marshmallow creme
1 teaspoon butter or margarine
1 pound pecans (chopped coarsely)
1 teaspoon vanilla
4½ cups sugar
1 large can evaporated milk (13 ounces)

Mix in 6 to 8-quart pan — Hershey bars (broken into pieces), chocolate chips and butter. Add sugar and milk. Bring to boil and cook 6 minutes, stirring constantly. Remove from heat and add all other ingredients except pecans. Beat until smooth and creamy. Add pecans. Drop in small balls on waxed paper. Let stand 4 to 6 hours.

Mrs. Jo Whittaker

QUICKIE FUDGE

¾ cup butter or oleo
⅔ cup evaporated milk
3 cups sugar
1 12-ounce package chocolate bits
1 7-ounce jar marshmallow creme
1 teaspoon vanilla flavoring
1 cup chopped pecans

Mix oleo, evaporated milk and sugar and stir over low heat and bring to full boil, stirring continually. Boil 5 minutes, stirring to avoid scorching. Remove from heat and add remaining ingredients. Stir until chocolate bits and creme are dissolved. Pour into 9x13-inch buttered pan. Cut into squares.

Ms. Sherry Anderson

PEANUT BUTTER CHOCOLATE CANDY

1 stick margarine
2 cups sugar
⅔ cup condensed milk
2 tablespoons cocoa
½ cup peanut butter (crunchy is great)
2 cups uncooked Quaker oats
1 teaspoon vanilla

Melt butter, add sugar, milk and cocoa. Bring to boil, cook for 5 minutes. Remove from heat, add peanut butter, blend well, add vanilla and oats. Spoon onto waxed paper. Yields approximately 50 pieces.

Do not over cook. If this should happen, make another batch, not cooking as long and mix with the over cooked batch. It works.

Mrs. L. R. Jaudon (Betty)

COCOA PEANUT CLUSTERS

2 cups sugar
1 heaping tablespoon butter
1 teaspoon vanilla
½ cup sweet milk
1 heaping tablespoon cocoa
1 cup roasted peanuts

Mix sugar, cocoa and milk. Boil 6 minutes, counting from time bubbling begins. Add butter, nuts and vanilla, take from heat, stir just enough to mix in nuts. Drop from spoon on waxed paper.

Mrs. Louis R. Jaudon (Betty)

PEANUT BUTTER BALLS

1 cup margarine, softened
1½ cups peanut butter
4 cups powdered sugar
4 ounces paraffin
24 ounces German sweet chocolate

Combine margarine, peanut butter and powdered sugar thoroughly. Roll into one inch balls; refrigerate approximately 30 minutes. Melt chocolate and paraffin in top of double boiler. Using toothpick, dip each ball into chocolate to coat. Place on waxed paper to harden. Store in refrigerator. Makes approximately 100 balls.

Mrs. R. W. Fletcher (Sue)

PEANUT BRITTLE

- 2 cups sugar
- 1 cup Karo
- ½ cup water
- 1½ teaspoons soda
- ½ teaspoon salt
- ¼ cup margarine
- 3 cups raw peanuts (heat)

Mix sugar, Karo, and water. Cook until it spins a hair. Add nuts; cook until syrup turns light gold color. Mix salt, soda, and margarine and fold into syrup mixture. This will become foamy. Pour onto slightly greased cookie sheet. Let cool for 45 minutes to an hour. Then crack into pieces.
Mrs. F. A. Kihneman (Tora)

MARTHA WASHINGTON CANDY

- 1 pound box confectioners' sugar
- 1 14-ounce can sweetened condensed milk
- 1 4-ounce can coconut
- 2 12-ounce packages chocolate chips
- ¾ bar of paraffin
- 1 quart finely chopped pecans
- 1 10-ounce bottle maraschino cherries (chopped finely)

Mix all ingredients. Place in freezer until cold. Shape into balls about 1 inch in diameter. Dip in mixture made of chocolate and paraffin melted over hot water and low heat. Place on wire rack to cool and set.
Mrs. Jo Whittaker

BOURBON BALLS

- 1 cup vanilla wafer crumbs
- 1 cup of chopped pecans
- 1 cup of powdered sugar
- 2 tablespoons cocoa
- ¼ cup rum or bourbon
- 1½ tablespoons corn syrup or honey

Mix bourbon and corn syrup together. Then mix with combined vanilla wafer crumbs, pecans, and cocoa. Roll into balls about the size of a pecan (large ones) and then roll in powdered sugar. These keep well if you can save any!
Mrs. Gladys Poore

DIVINITY

3 cups sugar
1 cup Karo syrup
1 cup water
2 egg whites
¼ teaspoon cream of tartar

Mix sugar, syrup, and water. Cook until it spins a hair. Beat egg whites until very stiff and add the cream of tartar. Pour ½ of syrup mixture over whites while beating. Cook the balance of syrup a little longer. Add this to the egg mixture, beating continuously until the glaze leaves; then drop by tablespoons on waxed paper or on buttered platter and cut into squares.
Mrs. F. A. Kihneman (Tora)

POTATO CANDY

2 packages butterscotch morsels
1 can shoestring potatoes (large)
½ cup chopped pecans

Melt butterscotch morsels over boiling water. Slightly chop potatoes and add to melted butterscotch. Add pecans and mix thoroughly. Drop by teaspoonful onto greased surface and let cool.
Mrs. A. R. Snider (Frances)

BON BONS

2 1-pound boxes powdered sugar
1 stick butter
1 14-ounce can condensed milk
1 teaspoon vanilla
2 cups chopped pecans
2 cups coconut
1 6-ounce package chocolate chips
¾ block paraffin

Cream powdered sugar, butter, condensed milk and vanilla. Add nuts and coconut. Roll this mixture into small balls. Melt chocolate and paraffin together in a double boiler over low heat. Stick a toothpick into each ball and dip into chocolate-paraffin mixture and place on waxed paper.
Mrs. Ann Ferrara

DATE LOAF DELIGHT

3 cups sugar
4 tablespoons syrup
1 pinch salt
½ stick butter
1½ cups milk
1 8-ounce package pitted dates, chopped
1 teaspoon vanilla
1½ cups pecans, broken

In medium-sized (3-quart) heavy pan, mix sugar, salt, syrup, butter and milk. Over medium-high heat, stirring, cook to 234 degrees or until mixture forms soft ball in the fingers after being dropped in a cup of cool water. Add the chopped dates and recook to 234 degrees or the soft ball stage. Remove and let cool for about ten minutes. Add vanilla and pecans; beat until candy loses gloss and thickens. Place on damp dishtowel and form with buttered hands several rolls about 1½ inches in diameter. Roll up in towel and refrigerate. Keep chilled until ready to slice and serve.
Mrs. Floyd Cunningham (Nell)

JEWEL CANDY

1 cup granulated sugar
½ cup light Karo syrup
⅓ cup water
¼ teaspoon flavoring oil*
Food color oil
Powdered sugar

Line 8x8x2-inch pan with foil, extending up sides, and butter well.

Butter sides of 1-quart saucepan. Combine sugar, syrup and water in pan. Bring to boil stirring constantly until sugar is dissolved. Cook to hard crack stage — 300 degrees. Remove from heat, add flavoring and coloring. Pour into foil lined pan. When just beginning to set around edges, lift out of pan. Candy should still be runny in center and hot. Cut with scissors into 1-inch strips, beginning with outside edges. Cut strips into irregular shaped pieces. Work fast — one batch at a time.

Sprinkle cut pieces with powdered sugar to prevent sticking together.

**Available in peppermint, wintergreen, chocolate and fruit flavors.*

Mrs. Floyd Cunningham (Nell)

Desserts

For many years after the discovery of oil, kerosene was the main product and gasoline was dumped as waste. As gas and electric lights replaced the kerosene lamps, the future looked dark for the petroleum industry. Although automobiles used gasoline, there were only about 8,000 in the United States in 1900. It was not until 1910, when automobiles had increased to 500,000, that the demand for gasoline began to grow. It was during this year that Louisiana passed regulations limiting speed of automobiles to 15 miles-per-hour on curves and only four miles-per-hour on crossing a bridge, passing a buggy, a rider on horseback, or in front of a church.

There were very few automobiles in Shreveport until this time, and the Louisiana State Fair made no provisions for admission of automobiles back in 1907. However, by 1912 the fair planned an opening day parade of 100 automobiles. One of the earliest automobiles here after 1900 was a small electric one owned by Dr. T. E. Schumpert.

Shreveporters were quick to realize the horseless carriage had made one man equal to 25 on horseback and by 1915 nearly 500 automobiles were registered with the Caddo Parish sheriff, who collected a fee of $10.

The Louisiana Motor Company, located in Cedar Grove, assembled Bour-Davis autos. Three or four of these six-cylinder automobiles with Red Seal Continental engines were assembled here weekly between 1918-1922.

INTERESTING FACTS ABOUT SHREVEPORT

Outstanding in World War II was fighter pilot ace William T. Whisner, Jr., a Byrd High School graduate and student of Centenary College. His many feats included the thrilling rescue of his squadron leader, Major Peddy, who had bailed out in the English Channel; his battles with German planes at tree-top levels; destruction of enemy ammunition locomotives, trains, and truck convoys; air raids on Dusseldorf, Berlin, Paris and Vienna; and a record fighter bag of six Nazi planes in one day! Major Whisner was also featured on the Coco-Cola Spotlight Band program as the "G.I. of the Week" on June 2, 1944. This program, which was broadcast from England, was carried on radio station KRMD. At war's end he won the equivalent of 23 medals, a Presidential Citation and four battle stars, including the Distinguished Flying Cross with two clusters, Silver Star, Air Medal with 12 clusters, a European Theatre ribbon with four battle stars, a Distinguished Unit Citation medal and letters of commendation.

BANANA SPLIT DESSERT

- 1 cup flour
- ½ cup chopped walnuts
- ¼ cup brown sugar
- 2 cups powdered sugar
- 2 sticks butter or margarine, room temperature
- 1 20-ounce can crushed pineapple, well drained
- 1 10-ounce package frozen strawberries, well drained
- 3 sliced bananas
- 2 eggs
- 1 4½-ounce container of Cool Whip
- 1 prepared package Dream Whip

In bowl put the flour, nuts and brown sugar. Mix well and cut in 1 stick of butter. Press into 9x9-inch square greased pan and bake at 400 degrees for 12 to 15 minutes, or until brown. Cool.

Mix powdered sugar, eggs and 1 stick butter and beat until fluffy; spoon onto cooled crust. Top with sliced bananas, pineapple and strawberries.

Combine the Cool Whip and the prepared Dream Whip. Spread onto fruit and top with chopped walnuts.

Mrs. Barbara Parnell

PEACH COBBLER

- 9 fresh peaches
- 1¾ cups sugar
- 2 tablespoons flour
- 1 stick oleo
- Pinch of salt

Pastry:

- 1 cup flour
- ½ teaspoon salt
- ⅓ cup shortening
- 4 tablespoons milk
- 1 stick oleo

Cook peaches until tender. Mix flour with sugar. Add to peaches; add oleo. Mix and pour into baking dish (9x13-inch).

Blend flour, salt and shortening with pastry blender or two knives until it is the texture of coarse meal. Add milk gradually. Chill dough. Roll on floured board. Cut in strips; place on top of peaches (as lattice). Melt oleo and pour or brush on top of the pastry strips. Bake in oven 350 degrees for 40-45 minutes until light brown.

Mrs. J. Kent Colvin (Yvonne)

FRUIT COBBLER

1 cup sugar
2 teaspoons baking powder
1/8 teaspoon salt (scant)
1 cup fruit (your choice)
1 stick butter
3/4 cup flour
3/4 cup milk

Place butter in deep dish and put into 350 degree oven to melt. Make batter of flour, sugar, baking powder, salt and milk. Pour over melted butter, but do not stir. Pour fruit on top of batter and bake at 350 degrees until cake batter is done — about 30 minutes.
Mrs. Edward Robinson, Keithville, Louisiana

POOR BOY COBBLER

6 slices bread (buttered)
2 16-ounce cans blackberries
1 1/2 cups sugar
1 stick margarine
2 tablespoons cornstarch
1/4 teaspoon salt

Toast bread and cut in 1/2-inch squares. Drain juice from berries. Mix sugar with cornstarch and set aside. Put 1/2 of bread squares in bottom of 2-quart casserole, pour in the berries without juice, chop butter over this. Put other bread squares on top. Mix sugar, cornstarch and juice from berries together and pour over the top. Push bread under juice and bake for 1 hour at 350 degrees. Very good.
Mrs. F. A. Kihneman (Tora)

FRESH STRAWBERRY COBBLER

1 cup sugar
1/4 cup flour
Dash of salt
4 cups fresh strawberries
2 tablespoons butter
Single crust pastry

Wash and hull strawberries. Combine sugar, flour and salt. Toss this mixture lightly with strawberries. Fill 1-quart baking dish with fruit and dot with butter. Top with your favorite single crust pastry. Press pastry firmly to edges of dish; flute edges and cut gashes in pastry. Bake at 425 degrees for 25 minutes until crust is brown. Serve with ice cream or whipped cream, if desired.
Mrs. Hubert L. Joyner (Virginia)

CHERRY DESSERT

1 21-ounce can cherry pie filling (Wilderness Brand)
1 8-ounce can Del Monte crushed pineapple
1 14-ounce can Eagle Brand milk
1 9-ounce carton Cool Whip
1 cup chopped pecans

In large mixing bowl, mix cherry pie filling, pineapple with juice, Eagle Brand milk, Cool Whip and pecans. Mix ingredients until mixture is a deep pink color. Cover and refrigerate. Since this dessert has Cool Whip and Eagle Brand milk, it will stay for several days without getting watery and will not spoil easily. Delicious served with ham and turkey, but goes well with any meal you have planned. It will fill the large Tupperware salad bowl and will easily serve 16-20 people.
Mrs. Sherry Anderson

CHERRY DELIGHT

Crust:
2 cups flour
½ cup brown sugar
1 cup oleo
1 cup chopped nuts

Filling:
2 9-ounce packages Cool Whip
1 8-ounce package cream cheese
1 cup powdered sugar
1 teaspoon vanilla
2 cans cherry pie filling

Crust: Mix like regular pie crust only do not use any water. Press into 9x13-inch pan and bake 15 minutes at 400 degrees. Use fork to crumble the crust into pieces and leave in pan.
Filling: Mix powdered sugar, cream cheese and vanilla. Fold into Cool Whip. Spread over crumb crust. Pour cherry pie filling over mixture. Refrigerate at least 12 hours before serving. Cut into squares for serving. Will keep for several days.
Mrs. Art Ogletree, Jr. (Ann)

HOT FUDGE SAUCE

3 cups sugar
3 squares chocolate
1 13-ounce can evaporated milk

Mix all ingredients in top of double boiler; cook slowly until thick and smooth. Stir occasionally to keep smooth. Cook about one hour.
Mrs. John E. Ewing (Helen)

CREAM PUFFS

1 cup water
½ cup butter or margarine
¼ teaspoon salt
4 eggs
1 cup sifted flour

Mix water, margarine, and salt. Put on stove and let come to a boil. Remove from stove while boiling and put all of flour into mixture. Stir until mixture leaves side of pan. Beat in eggs one at a time until well mixed. Beat well. Cover cookie sheet with greased foil. Spoon large amounts onto cookie sheet and bake in 450 degree oven for 15 minutes then reduce heat to 350 degrees and cook for 25 more minutes. Remove from oven and let cool. Cut open and fill with your favorite cream filling or they may be filled with creamed chicken or veal or perhaps any good salad mixture. Makes 8 puffs.
Mrs. F. A. Kihneman (Tora)

MAMA'S CREAM FILLING

1½ cups sugar
¾ cup milk
4 tablespoons margarine
1 teaspoon vanilla
¼ teaspoon salt

Mix all ingredients and cook slowly until well blended. Continue to cook over low heat until it begins to thicken or form a soft ball in water. Remove from heat and beat until creamy, not too long. Very good.
Mrs. F. A. Kihneman (Tora)

CREAM FILLING

½ cup flour
¾ cup sugar
2 cups scalded milk
1 teaspoon vanilla
½ tablespoon butter or margarine
1 egg
¼ teaspoon salt

Mix flour and sugar together. Slowly add the hot milk. Pour mixture into a double boiler and cook for 20 minutes. Remove from heat. Beat the egg, add the egg and butter to the flour and milk mixture. Return to the fire and cook over water until the egg is coagulated; then add the salt. Cool, and add flavoring.

Chocolate filling may be made by following the recipe for Cream Filling, increasing the sugar to 1 cup and adding a paste made by cooking 1 square or 1 ounce of chocolate with ¼ cup of boiling water. Stir and heat until smooth and thoroughly blended. This filling is good in cream puffs.
Mrs. C. D. Attaway (Margie)

PISTACHIO DELIGHT

1 cup flour
2 tablespoons sugar
1 stick butter or margarine
1 cup chopped pecans
1 8-ounce package cream cheese
2 cups powdered sugar
1 13½-ounce Cool Whip
2 3¾ ounce packages instant pistachio pudding
2½ cups milk

First Layer: Melt butter, mix sugar, flour and ½ cup chopped pecans, press into glass dish 9x13-inch (3-quart Pyrex dish) and bake at 375 degrees for 15 minutes. Cool

Second Layer: Soften cream cheese, mix in ½ of Cool Whip, and add 2 cups powdered sugar. Spread this on top of first layer.

Third Layer: Mix 2 packages instant pistachio pudding mix with the milk. Mix until thick. Pour over second layer. Chill.

Fourth Layer: Spread other ½ of Cool Whip over third layer and sprinkle with remaining pecans.

This Delight works well using different flavors of pudding for the third layer. You can also use two different flavors, by using only one box of pudding and 1¼ cups of milk for each side. A table knife down the center of dish will divide your flavors until the pudding is set. Remove knife before adding fourth layer.

Mrs. Louis R. Jaudon (Betty)

SWEET POTATO PUDDING

3 eggs
¾ cup sugar
1 cup milk
3 tablespoons margarine
½ teaspoon salt
½ teaspoon ground cinnamon
½ teaspoon ground ginger
¼ teaspoon ground cloves
2 cups raw sweet potato (coarsely grated)
½ cup walnuts (chopped)
2 tablespoons grated orange rind

Beat eggs well. Add sugar, milk, butter, and spices. Gradually add to the sweet potato and orange rind. Fold in walnuts and cook for 30 minutes. At end of 30 minutes stir mixture and cook 30 more minutes or until pudding is done.

Mrs. C. D. Attaway (Margie)

BLUEBERRY CHEESE CAKE

Graham cracker crust for 12x12-inch pan
2 eggs, beaten well
2 8-ounce packages cream cheese
1 teaspoon vanilla
2 cups sugar

Prepare graham cracker crust according to package directions. Combine softened cream cheese, sugar, eggs and vanilla. Mix well and spread on crust in 12x12-inch pan and bake 15 minutes in 325 degree oven.

Blueberry Topping:
1 15-ounce can blueberries (reserve juice)
¼ cup sugar
¼ cup water
2 tablespoons cornstarch
1 tablespoon lemon juice
½ pint whipping cream or 9-ounce carton Cool Whip

Drain blueberries, reserving juice. Add sugar, water, cornstarch and lemon juice to all of the blueberry juice. Cook until thick. Allow to cool thoroughly. Fold in berries. Spread this on top of cream cheese mixture. Chill 24 hours. Put whipping cream (or Cool Whip) on top. (Add some sugar and vanilla to whipping cream.) Cut in squares. Very rich.
Mrs. Watson G. Hodges (June)

CHEESE CAKE

1 3-ounce package lemon Jello
1 8-ounce package cream cheese
1 8-ounce can crushed pineapple
1 cup hot water
2 teaspoons vanilla
1 cup sugar
1 13-ounce can Pet milk (chilled)
Graham crackers to cover bottom of dish or pan

Dissolve Jello in 1 cup hot water and set aside to cool. Have cheese at room temperature. Cream with sugar, add vanilla and pineapple. Add to Jello. Whip Pet milk and blend into other ingredients.

Sprinkle graham cracker crumbs on the bottom of a square dish or pan. Pour in cheese cake and sprinkle crumbs on top. Refrigerate until firm. (Cheese cake may also be poured into 2 graham cracker pie crusts.)
Mrs. Jo Whittaker

CHOCOLATE CHEESE CAKE

Crust:

- 1 stick butter
- 1 cup flour
- ½ cup crumbled nuts

Bottom layer:

- 8 ouncc package cream cheese
- ½ large size Cool Whip (13½ ounces)
- 1 cup powdered sugar

Pudding layer:

- 2 4½-ounce instant pudding mix (chocolate)
- 3 cups milk

Crust: Melt butter and add flour and nuts. Pat into pan. Brown in 325 degree oven until *very light* brown (not golden).

Bottom layer: Mix and put in cooled crust.

Pudding layer: Mix pudding mix with milk; beat and pour on top of cream cheese.

Before serving: Put remaining Cool Whip on top of pie.

Mrs. Russell Smith (Liz)

PEACH PUDDING

- 1 5⅝-ounce package instant vanilla pudding
- 1 8-ounce carton sour cream
- 2 cups sliced fresh (or canned) peaches

Crunch Mix:

- 1 cup sugar
- 1 egg
- 1 cup chopped nuts

Mix vanilla pudding according to directions on box. Fold in sour cream. For Crunch Mix combine sugar, egg and nuts. Spread on buttered foil and bake for 18 minutes at 350 degrees. In a 9x13-inch baking dish put a layer of Crunch Mix, then layer of pudding, then layer of sliced peaches; repeat layers, ending with Crunch Mix on top. Chill.

Mrs. Ellis M. Bush (Juanita)

APPLE COMPOTE

6 cooking apples (Jonathan or Winesap)
½ cup sugar
1 cup water
4 tablespoons Red Hots

Boil sugar, water and Red Hots until dissolved. Add peeled and quartered apples; cook over low heat until apples are tender. Chill. May be served with whipped cream but are good without it. Serves 6.
Mrs. Dale Ward (Renee)

EASY BAVARIAN

1 3-ounce package gelatin (any red flavor)
¼ cup sugar
1 cup boiling water
1 cup cold water
1½ cups thawed whipped topping

Dissolve red gelatin and sugar in boiling water. Add cold water. Chill in refrigerator until slightly thickened. Blend whipped topping into gelatin. Chill until set in one quart or six to eight individual molds. Unmold and garnish with additional thawed whipped topping. A single cherry or mint leaf makes a pretty garnish. Yield: Six to eight servings.
Miss Patsy Ogletree

STRAWBERRY VELVET

½ cup mayonnaise
1 8-ounce package cream cheese, softened
¼ cup orange juice
1 10-ounce package frozen strawberries
1 3-ounce package strawberry gelatin
1 cup boiling water
½ cup syrup from thawed strawberries

Blend mayonnaise and cream cheese. Mix well. Gradually blend in orange juice. Then dissolve gelatin in boiling water and syrup from strawberries. Stir gelatin into mayonnaise mixture. Chill until slightly thickened. Fold in drained strawberries. Pour into one quart mold. Chill until firm. Yield: four to six servings.
Mrs. W. D. Sandifer, Jr. (Evelyn)

CHOCOLATE CRUNCH DELIGHT

1½ sticks butter
1½ cups flour
2 teaspoons sugar
½ cup chopped pecans
Pinch salt
1 8-ounce package cream cheese
1 teaspoon vanilla
1 cup unsifted powdered sugar
1 large (13½-ounce) carton Cool Whip
2 4½-ounce boxes instant chocolate pudding
4 cups milk
Pecans

Beat butter until fluffy. To this add flour, pecans, sugar, and salt. Spread into greased 13x9-inch pan. Bake at 350 degrees for 18 to 20 minutes. Set aside until cool.

Beat cream cheese until fluffy. To this add vanilla and powdered sugar. Fold in ½ of the Cool Whip. Spread on top of crust. Sprinkle with chopped pecans.

In a separate bowl combine instant chocolate pudding, instant vanilla pudding and milk. Beat mixture until stiff with electric mixer. Spread over cream cheese mixture. Sprinkle with chopped pecans.

Top with remaining ½ bowl of Cool Whip and pecans.

Mrs. Sue Wilcox

COCONUT DELIGHT

1 stick soft oleo
1 cup plain flour
½ cup chopped pecans
1 8-ounce package cream cheese
1 9-ounce carton Cool Whip
1 cup confectioners' sugar
Angel Flake Coconut
2 small packages instant coconut pudding
3 cups milk

Mix oleo, flour and pecans and pat into bottom of 13x9-inch pan and bake twenty minutes at 350 degrees. Let this cool real well. Mix well the cream cheese, 1 cup of Cool Whip and the confectioners' sugar and spread over the first layer. Sprinkle with coconut. Mix the instant pudding and milk until thickened and spread over second layer. Spread the remainder of Cool Whip over the third layer and sprinkle with coconut and more chopped nuts for garnish.

Mrs. Ralph Garrett (Dottie)

LEMON FRUIT FREEZE

⅔ cup butter or margarine
⅓ cup sugar
7 cups Rice or Corn Chex Cereal, crushed to 3 cups
1 can (14 ounces) Eagle Brand sweetened condensed milk
½ cup lemon juice
1 can (21 ounces) lemon pie filling
1 can (17 ounces) fruit cocktail, well drained
2 cups whipped topping

In medium saucepan, melt butter, stir in sugar, then crumbs. Reserving ⅓ cup for garnish, pat crumbs firmly on bottom of 13x9-inch baking pan. Bake at 300 degrees for 12 minutes. Cool. In large bowl, mix condensed milk and lemon juice. Stir in pie filling and fruit cocktail, pour over crust. Top with whipped topping and crumbs. Freeze 4 hours. Remove from freezer 20 minutes before cutting. If desired, garnish with lemon slices.

NOTE: Do not substitute evaporated milk for sweetened condensed milk in this recipe.

Mrs. Art Ogletree, Jr. (Ann)

MOCHA FREEZE

2 packages Nabisco Famous Chocolate Wafers
5 teaspoons sugar
6 tablespoons butter or oleo
½ cup chopped pecans (optional)
½ gallon coffee ice cream
1 9-ounce container Cool Whip
Semi-sweet chocolate (shaved)

Crush chocolate wafers finely. Mix with sugar, butter, and pecans. Press ¾ of the mixture into bottom of a buttered 11¾x7½-inch baking dish. Bake at 350 degrees for approximately 10 minutes. Remove from oven and cool thoroughly. Spread slightly softened ice cream over crust. Place in freezer until firm. Sprinkle remaining crumb mixture over ice cream layer and return to freezer. Before serving top with Cool Whip and shaved chocolate. Cut into squares. Serves 8 to 10.

NOTE: If coffee ice cream is not available make in following manner:

½ gallon vanilla ice cream
4 tablespoons instant coffee
2 teaspoons hot water

Dissolve coffee in hot water to make a paste. Using electric mixer blend paste into ice cream to taste depending on coffee strength desired.

Mrs. Robert Snead (Shirley)

CRANBERRY FREEZE

- **2 3-ounce packages cream cheese, softened**
- **2 tablespoons mayonnaise**
- **1 cup whole cranberry sauce**
- **1 cup crushed pineapple, in heavy syrup, drained**
- **½ cup pecans, thinly sliced**
- **½ pint whipping cream**
- **1 cup confectioners' sugar**
- **1 teaspoon vanilla**
- **Red food coloring (optional)**

Mash together cream cheese, mayonnaise, cranberry sauce, drained pineapple and pecans. Set aside. Whip one half of the carton of whipping cream to yield one cup. Fold in confectioners' sugar and vanilla. Add that to cream cheese mixture. Blend completely and freeze. If desired, before serving, whip remaining whipping cream and garnish top. If Freeze is not pink enough, add 1 or 2 drops of red food coloring before putting it in the freezer.

NOTE: Use a container suitable for freezing.

Mrs. Ed Ferguson (Margaret)

FRUIT SHERBET

- **½ gallon fruit juices**
- **2 cups water**
- **3 cups sugar**

Boil sugar and water until sugar is thoroughly dissolved. Cool and add chilled juices. Freeze according to directions of freezer (hand crank or with electric motor).

Variation: Use 1⅞ cups water and ⅔ cup nonfat dry milk and artificial sweetener instead of sugar. Juices for this recipe comes from cans of fruit used for other things. The juice is saved in a half gallon milk carton or plastic container and frozen until ready to make the sherbet. If the container is not full add enough orange juice (made from frozen concentrate), a little lemon juice and/or grapefruit juice.

Mrs. Lawrence A. McKinley, Magnolia Springs, Alabama

FRUIT FREEZE

- **1 can (13 ounces) crushed pineapple**
- **1 large package frozen strawberries**
- **2 large bananas, mashed**
- **1 large bag frozen mixed fruit**
- **1 cup sugar**
- **2 cups gingerale**

Mix all ingredients and freeze. Serve slushy as a breakfast fruit, or as a light cold dessert with a Mexican or Italian meal.

Mrs. John H. Lenard, Jr. (Carol), Lenexa, Kansas

PUDDING CAKE

1 stick (plus 2 tablespoons) butter or margarine
1 cup all-purpose flour
1 cup (or more) chopped pecans
1 8-ounce package cream cheese
1 cup powdered sugar
1 9-ounce carton frozen whipped topping
1 4½-ounce package instant chocolate pudding
1 3¾-ounce package instant vanilla pudding
2¾ cups cold milk
1 plain milk chocolate candy bar
1 teaspoon vanilla

Allow butter and cream cheese to soften to room temperature and whipped topping to thaw. Combine butter, flour and pecans. Press into 13x9x2-inch pan or glass baking dish on *bottom only.* Bake at 350 degrees for 20 minutes. Do not let it get too done. Cool thoroughly. Blend cream cheese, powdered sugar, and 1 cup of topping. Spread this mixture over *cooled* crust. Blend instant pudding mixes with milk and add vanilla. Pour this mixture over cream cheese layer. Put remainder of topping on top of these layers. Grate candy bar over top. Refrigerate. Yield: 15 ample servings or more small servings. This may be frozen ahead and it makes it even firmer and easier to cut.
Mrs. J. Leon Fortson (Hellon)

THREE LAYER DELIGHT

1 cup flour
1 cup chopped nuts
1 stick margarine
1 8-ounce package cream cheese
1 cup powdered sugar
2 cups milk
2 cups Cool Whip
1 4½-ounce package chocolate instant pudding
1 3¾-ounce package vanilla instant pudding
½ cup shaved chocolate

Melt margarine and combine with flour and nuts. Mix well and pat into bottom of an oblong 3-quart baking dish. Bake at 325 degrees for 20 minutes. Cool. Combine cream cheese, powdered sugar and 1 cup Cool Whip and spread evenly over baked crust. Prepare instant puddings with milk according to package directions and beat together until thick. Spread evenly over second layer. Spread last cup of Cool Whip over top and sprinkle with shaved chocolate. Chill thoroughly and serve.
Mrs. Vincent Demmel (Erby)

SAUCE FOR A PLAIN CAKE

⅔ cup water
1 cup sugar
1 stick margarine
½ teaspoon flavoring, using any flavor desired

Place all ingredients in a sauce pan and bring to a slow boil. Allow to simmer for three minutes. In the meantime, use a toothpick to punch small holes about the top of a plain cake. Then pour the sauce mixture slowly over the cake, allowing it to penetrate the cake as you pour, thus giving the sauce time to get into the cake rather than pouring down the sides.
Mrs. Marvin Kines (Ora)

GRAHAM CRACKER LOAF

1 pound graham crackers, rolled fine
1 pound miniature marshmallows
1 pound chopped dates
1 cup chopped nuts
1 cup thick cream
Whipped cream

Mix all ingredients, except ½ cup cracker crumbs, together and form into a loaf. Dust loaf in remaining crumbs. Let stand over night. Slice and serve with whipped cream.
Mrs. Ruth Glenn
Ms. Lena Jones

LEMON FLUFF

1 13-ounce can Pet milk
Pinch of cream of tartar
¼ cup lemon juice
Grated rind of 1 lemon
½ cup sugar
1 sack vanilla wafers (approximately 7 ounces)

Whip can of cold Pet milk. Add cream of tartar, lemon juice, grated rind and sugar. Roll vanilla wafers into crumbs. Spread half of milk mixture into 8x16-inch pan. Cover this with vanilla wafer crumbs and top with remainder of milk mixture. Sprinkle a few crumbs on top and place in refrigerator overnight.
Mrs. James Harris (Cora)

VANILLA ICE CREAM I

1 can condensed milk (14-ounces)
4 or 6 eggs
1 cup sugar
2 teaspoons vanilla
3 quarts homogenized milk

Beat milk, eggs, sugar and vanilla with electric mixer until slightly thick, then add your favorite fruit. Pour into ice cream freezer with the homogenized milk and freeze according to your freezer instructions.
Mrs. A. L. Belluomini (Verda), Kerrville, Texas

VANILLA ICE CREAM II

5 eggs
1½ cups sugar
1 package Junket
1 13-ounce can evaporated milk
1 teaspoon vanilla
1 14-ounce condensed milk
Approximately ½ gallon sweet milk

Mix in ice cream maker and fill to line with milk (sweet). Yields 4 quarts.
Mrs. Gladys Poore

ICE CREAM FOR HOME FREEZER

1 gallon size:
4 eggs
2½ cups sugar
6 cups milk
4 cups light cream
1½ tablespoons vanilla
½ teaspoon salt

1½ gallon size:
6 eggs
3¾ cups sugar
9 cups milk
3 13-ounce cans evaporated milk
2 tablespoons vanilla

Beat eggs until light. Add sugar gradually, beating until mixture thickens. Add remaining ingredients; mix thoroughly. Freeze in ice-cream freezer.
Mrs. Floyd Cunningham (Nell)

PEANUT BUTTER ICE CREAM

- 6 eggs
- 2½ cups sugar
- 1 13-ounce can of evaporated milk
- 1 pint whipping cream
- 1 cup peanut butter (plain or crunchy)
- 1½ teaspoons vanilla
- Approximately ½ gallon sweet milk

Beat well. Pour into ice cream maker. Fill the rest of the way with milk (sweet). Yields 4 quarts.

Mrs. Gladys Poore

EASY HOMEMADE ICE CREAM

- 6 eggs
- 2 cups sugar
- 1 6-ounce can of evaporated milk
- ½ gallon milk
- 1 teaspoon vanilla
- 1 box ice cream salt

Beat eggs and add sugar. Mix well. Add rest of ingredients. Pour into crank type or electric freezer. Use ½ to ¾ box ice cream salt in ice to freeze. Makes 4-5 quarts.

Mrs. Thomas A. Powell (Anna), Jackson, Mississippi

COFFEE SYRUP

- 1 cup sugar
- ¾ cup water
- 1 teaspoon instant coffee
- ¼ cup boiling water

Mix sugar and ¾ cup water together in sauce pan. Stir over low heat until sugar is dissolved. Cover, bring to boiling, boil five minutes. Remove from heat. Put coffee in small cup, add boiling water and mix until blended. Stir into sugar mixture. Cool; store covered in refrigerator. Makes 1 cup. Good topping for ice cream.

Mrs. John E. Ewing (Helen)

ANNA'S HUSBAND DELIGHT

Crust:

1 stick oleo (melted)
1 cup flour
½ cup chopped pecans

First Layer:

1 8-ounce cream cheese (softened)
2 cups of (13½-ounce) Cool Whip
1 cup confectioners' sugar

Second Layer:

2 4½-ounce boxes instant chocolate Jello pudding
3½ cups milk

Mix crust ingredients together in 9x13-inch Pyrex dish. Bake 10-12 minutes at 350 degrees.

Cream together ingredients for first layer and spread over cooled crust.

For second layer, mix Jello and milk together; spread over first layer.

Top with layer of Cool Whip and a few chopped nut meats.

Mrs. Thomas A. Powell (Anna), Jackson, Mississippi

Accompaniments · Beverages

The Shriners Hospital for Crippled Children located in Shreveport in 1922 was the first of its kind in the world.

The idea of the hospitals for crippled children was credited to Noble W. Freeland Kendrick who, in 1919, proposed that the Order of the Nobles of the Mystic Shrine of North America should undertake, as an organization, to do something for friendless, orphaned, and crippled children. The Shreveport unit was opened on September 16, 1922.

The Shriners organization was founded by an actor, Billy Florence, and a Civil War surgeon, Dr. Walter M. Flemin who, the official history says, "could have earned a good livelihood as a juggler and magician."

Florence stumbled across a vehicle for the new society in Marseilles, France, when he was invited to a party given by an Arabian diplomat. The entertainment was an elaborately staged musical comedy at the end of which guests were initiated into a secret society.

Florence concocted his own version of the ceremony, told Dr. Fleming about it and the two created the Shrine. Its members wear ornate oriental robes, gowns and medals at rituals. Its rituals are carefully and colorfully staged with Shriners wearing robes of purple, gold, red and green. Trained make up men, also Shriners, apply beards and stage makeup to make the participants look like the romantic Arabs of old.

Beyond the ritual and parades and clowning is a serious side to the Shrine. It operates 22 hospitals for burned and crippled children throughout North America. Since 1922, Shriners Hospitals for Crippled Children Orthopedic Units have offered the finest possible care for children afflicted with deformities, diseases and injuries involving the bones, joints and muscles. In addition, these hospitals treat patients with "healed burns," including the loss of function of any part of the body, such as deformities or excessive scarring.

Shriners Hospitals for Crippled Children are open to any child, regardless of race or religion, under 16 years old, whose parents or guardians are unable to pay for the type of medical care offered. There is no charge to the patient, parent or any third party for anything received at a Shriners Hospital.

All surgery, medical care, casts, braces, artificial limbs, x-rays, therapy, recreation, clothing and in-hospital schooling are provided free of charge. Application forms can be obtained by writing to SHRINERS HOSPITALS FOR CRIPPLED CHILDREN, 323 North Michigan Avenue, Chicago, Illinois 60601.

FRUIT COMPOTE

¼ cup butter
3 tablespoons flour
½ teaspoon curry powder
1-pound, 13-ounce can peach halves, undrained
1-pound, 4-ounce can pineapple spears, undrained
1-pound can pear halves, drained
¼ pound firmly packed brown sugar

Melt butter in oven proof, 2-quart casserole while oven is heating to 375 degrees. Remove from oven; stir in flour and curry powder. Add fruit and juice; stir gently. Sprinkle with brown sugar and ginger. Bake for 20 to 25 minutes and serve warm. Yield: 6 servings.
Mrs. W. D. Sandifer, Jr. (Evelyn)

SPICED PEACHES

1 large can cling peach halves
½ cup brown sugar
2 tablespoons butter
½ teaspoon cardamon
⅛ cup sherry
¼ cup grenadine syrup
Pinch of salt
1 teaspoon lemon juice

Drain peaches and save ½ cup of juice. In baking dish combine the juice with all of the other ingredients and place peach halves in it. Spoon the liquid over the peach halves well. Bake uncovered in 400 degree oven for 30 minutes. Serve warm.
Mrs. James A. Richardson, Jr. (Margie), Baton Rouge, Louisiana

BRANDIED CRANBERRIES

4 cups cranberries
4 tablespoons brandy (or more)
2 cups sugar

Spread cranberries on cookie sheet and pour sugar over them. Cover tightly with foil and bake 1 hour at 350 degrees. Pour brandy over the baked berries. Cool and store in covered container. Will keep several weeks.
Mrs. Gladys Poore

TWELVE MINUTE CRANBERRY SAUCE

4 cups fresh cranberries
2 cups sugar
1½ cups water

Combine sugar, water and berries in sauce pan. Heat to boiling point. Stir until sugar is dissolved, then boil rapidly until berries pop open (about 5 minutes). Makes 1 quart sauce.

Mrs. F. A. Kihneman (Tora)

SPICED CRANBERRIES

4 cups cranberries
3 cups sugar
2 sticks cinnamon
5 whole cloves
5 whole allspice
2 blades mace

Pick over and wash the berries. Place in a saucepan and cover with cold water. Tie spices in a cheese cloth bag and drop in with the berries. Cook until the berries burst. Remove spices, add sugar and cook until mixture is clear. Chill.

Mrs. Myrtle Collins
Mrs. Ruth V. Glenn

FIG PRESERVES

1 pound fresh figs
½ pound sugar or a bit more
2 slices of lemon

Figs may be peeled but not necessary. Leave them whole or they can be sliced. Wash figs thoroughly and put layer of figs and sugar with cut up lemon over them. Let stand overnight. The juice will be plenty for cooking the next morning without adding any water. Cook slowly until figs turn a golden color and the juice drops heavily from a spoon. Cut out fire and immediately put into sterilized jars and fill ¼ inch from top. Add the juice until it just covers the fruit. Seal tightly.

NOTE: If you want to make peach preserves use 1 pound peaches, ¾ or 1 pound sugar and no lemon and prepare the same as figs.

Mrs. Alfred Otto Sr. (Thekla), Taylor, Texas

STRAWBERRY FIG PRESERVES

4 cups peeled figs (small)
2 3-ounce packages strawberry or raspberry gelatin
3 cups sugar

First, be sure figs are not too soft and watery. Place dry gelatin on top of peeled figs, and then the sugar on top of that. Let stand (marinate) for 45 minutes; this brings all the juice up to the top.

Put on a low fire and cook 5 minutes. Raise fire gradually, cooking for about 15 minutes more. You can bring almost to a boil, but not to a fiery boil, as this will make the preserves turn dark.

Test small amount in saucer, to be sure figs are cooked and mixture is thick enough. You want the figs to be cooked, but not so well done that they break apart.

When figs have finished cooking, seal in sterile jars.

Preserves will be pretty strawberry color with delicious flavor. Excellent served over ice cream or on morning toast.

Mrs. C. D. Attaway (Margie)
Mrs. P. W. Woodruff (Beulah)

MAYHAW JELLY

3 cups juice from mayhaws
2 cups sugar
Paraffin

Wash mayhaws well until free of leaves and trash. Place berries in deep bucket or pan in kitchen sink and turn water on them while holding berries down with hands. Fill with water until your hands are completely covered. Cook over medium heat until berries lose their color and water is bright pink. Strain juice through double layer of cheese cloth; then take berries in cloth and let cool enough to handle with hands. Crush berries in the cloth and squeeze all the juice that you can get out of the berries. This substance is cloudy. Combine the two juices and mix. Using a deep kettle combine 3 cups of juice and 2 cups sugar. Cook until 210 degrees register on candy thermometer. Let temperature stay on 210 degrees for 2 or 3 minutes *only*. Pour into sterilized jelly glasses and let cool completely. Seal with paraffin.

NOTE: Juice may be stored in refrigerator for 2 weeks or frozen indefinitely. This recipe is best when made in small quantities — no more than 6 cups of juice.

Mrs. Beynon S. Cheesman (Katherine)

PEACH MARMALADE

8 pounds fresh peaches
3 large oranges
4 large lemons
5 pounds and 2½ cups sugar
1 tablespoon allspice

Peel peaches, remove pits and knife-chop finely. Cut oranges and lemons in quarters and remove seeds; put through coarse blade of food chopper. There should be 3 quarts chopped peaches and about 6 cups ground orange and lemons. Place peaches and ground fruit in a large kettle; add sugar and allspice. Over moderate heat, bring slowly to a boil, stirring often. Boil gently for 45 minutes, stirring often, until fruit is translucent and the mixture sheets from a metal spoon. Remove from heat.

Skim off foam and ladle at once into hot wide-mouth jars or jars of your choice. Fill to within ⅛ inch of top; add caps and screw on bands evenly and tightly. Invert for a few seconds and stand jars upright to cool. Makes 20 8-ounce jars.

NOTE: To make the sheet test to determine whether marmalade is ready, dip a cold metal spoon into the boiling mixture. When two or three drops form together and sheet off the spoon, the marmalade should be done.

Mrs. A. H. Otto (Marjorie)

PEACH MARMALADE

8 cups (4 pounds) ground peaches
14 cups (6 pounds) sugar
1 bottle Certo

Grind peaches and mix in sugar. Let come to a full boil, cook hard about 3 minutes. Turn out fire, stir in Certo and then stir off and on for 5 minutes so fruit will settle. Seal in sterile jars.

Mrs. C. D. Attaway (Margie)

PEACH-CANTALOUPE CONSERVE

3 cups chopped cantaloupe
3 cups chopped peaches
4½ cups sugar
3 tablespoons lemon juice
½ teaspoon nutmeg
¼ teaspoon salt
¼ teaspoon grated orange peel
⅓ cup slivered almonds (toasted)

In large kettle, mix chopped fruit; bring to a full rolling boil, stirring constantly. Add the sugar and lemon juice and return to a full rolling boil. Boil 12 minutes. Add nutmeg, salt, orange peel and almonds; boil 4 to 5 minutes or until it reaches jelly stage (use jelly thermometer). Pour into scalded jars and seal. Makes 3 pints.

Mrs. A. H. Otto (Marjorie)

PEACH HONEY

2½ cups water
2 cups sugar
1 package (12 ounces) dried peaches

Combine all ingredients in a large saucepan. Bring to boiling over high heat; reduce heat; simmer 45 minutes or until the peaches are soft. Puree in a blender or food processor and pour into sterilized jars and seal. Makes about 3 half pints.
Mrs. Court Crow (Jeanne)

PEAR CHUTNEY

30 cups chopped pears
3 boxes dark raisins
6 boxes dark brown sugar
6 cloves garlic, pressed
6 lemons, sliced thin
6 tablespoons salt
1½ teaspoons cayenne pepper
1 piece crystallized ginger
6 hot peppers, minced
½ gallon plus 4 cups vinegar
6 onions, chopped
1 tablespoon curry
1 teaspoon each cinnamon, cloves, allspice and nutmeg
2 packages dried apricots

Peel and chop pears into bite size pieces. Cut lemons in quarters lengthwise, remove seeds, slice thin. Chop ginger and onion. Put vinegar in large kettle, add sugar, spices, salt, etc. Press garlic and add to liquid. Cook for about ten minutes, add all other ingredients and cook until pears are tender to a fork but not soft. Remove from fire and let set overnight. Reheat and bottle in jars. This should ripen several weeks before using.
Mrs. Charles T. McCord, Jr. (Mary)

PINEAPPLE PEAR HONEY

2 quarts pears
5 cups sugar
Juice of 2 lemons
1 8-ounce can crushed pineapple

Grind pears with coarse blade, mix together with sugar, lemon juice and crushed pineapple. Cook one-half hour in cast iron skillet, stirring often. Put in hot sterilized jars and seal.
Mrs. A. H. Otto (Marjorie)

WINTER JAM

3 cups fresh cranberries
1½ cups water
1 cup crushed pineapple
1 cup peeled diced apple
1 medium lemon
3 cups sugar

Cook cranberries and apple in water until tender. Press fruits and juices through strainer to remove skins. Add juice and grated rind of 1 lemon, crushed pineapple and sugar. Mix thoroughly in deep kettle. Bring rapidly to a boil and continue boiling, stirring constantly, until jam becomes thick and clear. Pour into hot jars and seal. Makes 4 8-ounce jars.
Mrs. A. R. Snider (Frances)

TOMATO RELISH

½ gallon ripe tomatoes, peeled
½ cup hot peppers, chopped fine
2½ cups onion, chopped
2 cups vinegar
2 cups sugar
2 teaspoons salt

Mix and cook all ingredients until medium thick. Put into jars. Great with peas, cabbage, and other vegetables.
Mrs. Fran Lorant Moore

GREEN TOMATO RELISH

⅔ dishpan (aluminum type) of hard green tomatoes chopped in large pieces
½ gallon chopped onions
1 quart chopped hot green peppers
6 cups sugar
1 cup salt
Black pepper to season
½ gallon red vinegar

Mix all ingredients and put in large cooking vessel and bring to boil. Stir while heating. Put in sterilized jars while hot and seal tightly.

NOTE: 1 bushel green tomatoes makes approximately 24 quarts.
Mrs. Jo Whittaker

90 PROOF RELISH

(Very Very Hot)

1 quart apple cider vinegar
1 cup plain salt
6 large onions
6-8 red peppers
2 quarts water
1 gallon hot peppers
2 large bell peppers
6-8 banana peppers

Chop all peppers and onions in blender; filling blender ½ full with peppers and covering to top with water. Drain each batch, using the drained liquid over and over; add more water if liquid gets low after chopping several batches.

Bring to a boil, vinegar, water and plain salt. Add chopped peppers and onions and the liquid that remained after all was chopped. Simmer until relish cooks down. If relish looks too dry, add 1 or 2 cups of water and stir well. Pack in ½ pint or pint jars, seal. Let set for 4 to 6 weeks.
Mrs. Louis R. Jaudon (Betty)

PEAR RELISH

4 quarts pears
8 bell peppers (4 red and 4 green)
3 hot red peppers
2 quarts onions ground (about 4 pounds)
12 dill pickles
2 quarts vinegar
4 cups sugar
8 tablespoons flour
6 tablespoons dry mustard
4 tablespoons salt
2 tablespoons tumeric

Grind and drain pears, bell peppers, hot red peppers, onions and dill pickles. Mix and add to this sugar, flour, dry mustard, salt and tumeric. Add vinegar and cook ten minutes after this comes to a boil. Put in hot sterilized pint jars and seal.
Mrs. A. H. Otto (Marjorie)

SWEET PICKLES

48 ounce jar of dill pickles drained and sliced
1 cup vinegar
3 cups sugar
1 tablespoon pickling spice

Bring to rolling boil and pour over sliced pickles which were put back in the original jar after slicing. Let cool and then refrigerate.
Mrs. Porter J. Crow (Ellie)

BREAD & BUTTER PICKLES

12 large cucumbers
5 cups sliced onions
2 teaspoons salt
4 cups sugar
4 sticks cinnamon
1 quart vinegar
2½ teaspoons tumeric
1 red pepper or ¼ teaspoon cayenne pepper

Slice cucumbers and onions, sprinkle in 2 teaspoons salt, let stand one hour, drain. Place in deep kettle with sugar, vinegar, tumeric, red pepper and cinnamon. Cook slowly over simmer burner until sugar is dissolved. Turn flame on full and boil rapidly until slices begin to shine (about 30 minutes). Pack in hot jars, fill to overflowing with hot syrup and seal.
Mrs. A. H. Otto (Marjorie)

FREEZER BREAD AND BUTTER PICKLES

2 quarts sliced cucumbers
2 teaspoons coarse salt
1 cup vinegar
1 medium onion sliced
1½ cups white sugar

Mix cucumbers, onion and salt and place in refrigerator for 3 hours. Take them out and drain them for 1 hour. Mix sugar with vinegar, stirring until sugar dissolves. Pour this sugar solution over the drained cucumbers, cover and refrigerate over night, stirring occasionally. Put in freezer containers and freeze. Eat as is, or mix with sour cream.
Mrs. John H. Lenard, Jr. (Carol), Lenexa, Kansas

PICKLED SQUASH

8 cups fresh yellow squash, thinly sliced
2 cups onion, sliced thinly
1 tablespoon salt
½ cup diced bell pepper
1 cup vinegar (and a little more)
1¾ cups sugar
½ teaspoon celery seed
½ teaspoon mustard seed

Combine squash and onions. Sprinkle salt over top of squash and onions and let sit for one hour. Combine bell pepper, vinegar, sugar, celery seed and mustard seed and bring to boil. Add squash and onions, return to boiling point. Pack pickles with juice in sterile jars. Seal. Makes two quarts.
Mrs. Hal Johnson, Jr. (Shirley)

FIG PICKLES

¼ gallon figs with stems
¼ cup soda
Water
1 teaspoon powdered alum
4 cups sugar
1 tablespoon cloves, spices or cinnamon
White vinegar

Sprinkle soda over figs and cover with water. Let stand 15 minutes. Wash in clear water.

Mix powdered alum in 1 gallon water and pour over figs and let stand 15 minutes. Drain.

Make syrup of sugar, 2 cups water, cloves, spices tied in cloth and white vinegar. Pour boiling syrup mixture over figs and cook until figs are light brown or transparent. Pour hot into sterilized jars and seal.

Mrs. James H. Worley, Sr. (Wincie)

SWEET AND SPICY MUSTARD

5 tablespoons dry mustard
½ cup sugar
1 tablespoon all purpose flour
½ teaspoon salt
Dash of red pepper
2 eggs, beaten
½ cup vinegar
1 tablespoon butter or margarine

Combine mustard, sugar, flour, salt and red pepper in top of double boiler. Add eggs and vinegar, blending thoroughly. Cook over boiling water, stirring constantly until thickened. Add butter; stir until melted. Cool. Store in jar in refrigerator. Makes 1⅓ cups.

Sweet and Spicy Mustard is a little sweet, a little hot and a little spicy. It's great on sandwiches, in potato salad or on meat.

Mrs. R. W. Fletcher (Sue)

BETTY'S EVERYTHING NICE SPICE

1 box salt (26 ounce)
1 ½-ounce box black ground pepper
1 ounce bottle chili powder
2 ounce bottle ground red pepper
1 ounce bottle pure garlic powder
1 ounce of Accent

Mix the above ingredients together, stirring well. Place in shakers or spice containers.

This spice is tasty when used in out-door cooking, direct from the table or in any dish when being prepared.

Mrs. Louis R. Jaudon (Betty)

CHILI SAUCE I

14 pounds ripe tomatoes
1 pound sweet green peppers
1 pound sweet red peppers
¾ pound onions
1 teaspoon cinnamon
3 tablespoons salt
1 cup sugar
1 teaspoon ground cloves
1 teaspoon allspice

Wash vegetables. Peel tomatoes and onions and chop all vegetables separately. Measure. Put vegetables, salt and sugar in large kettle and simmer until mixture begins to thicken. Add vinegar and spices; continue cooking until mixture is thick, stirring occasionally to prevent burning. Put in hot jars and seal.
Mrs. A. H. Otto (Marjorie)

CHILI SAUCE II

4 gallons chopped and peeled tomatoes
2 cups chopped onions
1 cup chopped sweet red pepper
1 small hot red pepper
2½ cups vinegar
3 tablespoons salt
½ cup sugar
1 tablespoon white mustard seed
1 teaspoon allspice
1 teaspoon cinnamon

Combine the vegetables, salt, and sugar and cook until the mixture is done . . . boil for approximately 5 to 10 minutes.
Mrs. Court Crow (Jeanne)

CHILI SAUCE III

2 cups bell pepper
2 cups onion
6 cups tomato
2 pods hot pepper
½ cup water
1 cup sugar
1 cup vinegar
1 tablespoon salt
1 stick pickling spice (optional)

Finely chop all four vegetables, keeping bell peppers and onions separated from tomatoes and hot peppers. Simmer onions and bell peppers in ½ cup water until tender. Add tomatoes, hot peppers, sugar, vinegar and salt. If desired, place pickling spice in cheesecloth. Add to mixture after all of the other ingredients are well mixed. Remove pickling spice before storing. Be sure to use proper sterilization and canning procedures. Makes approximately 3 pints, depending upon desired thickness.
Mrs. Ed Ferguson (Margaret)

HOT SAUCE

2 gallons chopped peeled tomatoes
6 teaspoons salt
5 cups white vinegar
20 pods long green peppers
1 large bell pepper (optional)
2 cups sugar
1 2-ounce box mustard seed
6 large chopped onions
4 teaspoons celery seed
3 stalks of celery (optional)

Mix all tomatoes, peppers, sugar, vinegar and seasonings; bring to boil and cook to desired consistency. Seal in jars.
Mrs. Louis R. Jaudon (Betty)

HOT SPICED TEA I

6 cups water
3-3½ quarts apple cider
1 cup fresh lemon juice
3 teaspoons tea or 3 tea bags
1½ cups brown sugar
2 sticks cinnamon
¼ teaspoon nutmeg
¼ teaspoon allspice

Put water and cider in 32 cup percolator. Put other ingredients in the basket. Go through the entire perk cycle. This may also be done in a kettle on the stove.
Mrs. Onnie B. Cross (Maree)

HOT SPICED TEA II

1¼ cups Tang
½ cup sugar
⅓ cup instant tea
½ teaspoon cinnamon
¼ teaspoon cloves
Dash of salt

Mix all ingredients together and store in sealed container. To one cup of hot water add 2 teaspoons of mixture. This is a delightful winter drink.
Mrs. F. A. Kihneman (Tora)

SPICED TEA

1 medium size jar of Tang
½ cup plus 2 tablespoons regular instant tea
1 teaspoon cinnamon
½ teaspoon cloves
1¼ cups sugar

Combine Tang, tea, cinnamon, cloves, and sugar in a large container. Mix 2 tablespoons per cup hot water.
Mrs. C. A. Waites (Christine)

RUSSIAN TEA

1¼ cups or 1 9-ounce jar of Tang
½ cup sugar
⅓ cup instant tea
½ teaspoon ground cinnamon
¼ teaspoon ground cloves
Dash of salt

To prepare mix, combine instant tea, Tang, sugar, spices and salt. Stir well. Store in tightly covered labeled jar. For each serving of hot tea place 2 well rounded teaspoons of mix in a cup, add boiling water, stir until dissolved. Serve immediately, garnished with cinnamon stick stirrers if desired.

For one quart of tea combine ½ cup of mix to one quart of boiling water in a heat proof pitcher.
Mrs. John L. Hoppe (Jo)

INSTANT RUSSIAN TEA

2 cups Tang
½ cup instant tea
1⅓ cups sugar
1 envelope lemonade mix
1 tablespoon cinnamon
1½ teaspoons cloves

Mix all ingredients together and store in air tight jar. When ready to serve, use 2 heaping teaspoons to 1 cup boiling water.
Mrs. Mary Wells

INSTANT HOT CHOCOLATE

1 pound of Hershey's Plain Chocolate or Nestles Quick
1 8-quart box powdered milk
1 6-ounce jar of Coffeemate
2 cups powdered sugar
Boiling water

Mix all of the above ingredients well. To serve, fill cup half way full of chocolate mixture and add water to fill the remainder of the cup.
Mrs. Ann Ferrara

OLD FASHIONED EGG NOG

6 eggs (separated)
6 tablespoons sugar
Dash of nutmeg
8 tablespoons whiskey
½ pint whipping cream

Break eggs and separate. Beat yolks of eggs until light yellow and creamy. Add sugar and mix thoroughly. Gradually add the whiskey, stirring constantly. Fold in your stiffly beaten egg whites and the whipped cream. It is ready to drink. It is best served from a cup. Sprinkle with a dash of nutmeg.
C. D. Attaway (Don)

WASSAIL BOWL

1 gallon sweet apple cider
1 cup light or dark brown sugar
1 6-ounce can frozen lemonade
1 12-ounce can frozen orange juice
1 tablespoon whole cloves
1 tablespoon allspice (whole)
1 teaspoon nutmeg
12 cinnamon sticks

In a large pot combine all liquids. Put spices in cheese cloth, add to cider. Simmer covered 20 minutes. Remove and discard bag. Serve hot. Put cinnamon stick in each cup. (Good holiday drink)
Billy W. Kelly, LaPorte, Texas

BANANA PUNCH

4 cups sugar
6 cups water
1 46-ounce can pineapple juice
Juice of 5 oranges or 1 6-ounce can frozen orange juice, undiluted
5 very ripe bananas
Juice of 2 lemons
2 quarts ginger ale

Combine sugar and water; heat and boil 3 minutes. Set aside to cool. When cooled, add to it the pineapple juice and orange juice. Mash the bananas and pour the lemon juice over them. Add bananas to juice mixture. Mix. Freeze some of the mixture in ice trays and some in milk cartons. Set out of freezer to soften at least 1 hour before serving. Place large chunks in punch bowl and mash; add the ginger ale. Let the frozen cubes float in bowl.
Mrs. John E. Ewing (Helen)

CHRISTMAS PUNCH

2 8-ounce bottles green maraschino cherries
2 10-ounce boxes frozen strawberries
Sugar to taste
12 6-ounce cans frozen pink lemonade
2 quarts ginger ale

Mix together, chill and serve.
Marteal Merrett

CHAMPAGNE PUNCH

2 6¾-ounce cans frozen pink lemonade
2 10-ounce packages frozen strawberries
2 8-ounce cans crushed pineapple
4 bottles ginger ale or
2 bottles ginger ale and 2 bottles of champagne

Mix first three ingredients in blender, then add ginger ale and/or ginger ale and champagne. When ready to serve add crushed ice.
Mrs. John L. Hoppe (Jo)

HAWAIIAN PUNCH

- **1 46-ounce can red berry fruit flavor Hawaiian punch**
- **1 46-ounce can pineapple juice**
- **1 quart ginger ale**
- **1 12-ounce can pink lemonade (frozen)**

Mix pink lemonade according to the directions on the can. Add all other juices and stir well. Put in punch bowl with ice cubes and just before serving add the ginger ale.

Mrs. Art Ogletree, Jr. (Ann)

3 WAY HOLIDAY PUNCH

- **2 cans (6 ounces each) or**
- **1 can (12 ounces) frozen fruit juicy red punch concentrate, thawed, and undiluted**
- **1 cup unsweetened pineapple juice**
- **1 cup orange juice**
- **1½ cups water**
- **1 32-ounce bottle ginger ale (optional)**
- **1 bottle rosé wine (optional)**

Combine ingredients in 2 quart container. Refrigerate. For toyland punch, add 1 bottle (32 ounces) chilled ginger ale.

For rosy wine cooler, add 1 bottled chilled rosé wine.

For Christmas Spirit, add 1½ cups light rum or vodka and 2 bottles (12 ounces each) chilled lemon-lime carbonated beverage.

Mrs. A. R. Snider (Frances)

PUNCH FOR 50 PEOPLE

- **3 3-ounce boxes Jello (any flavor)**
- **3 cups boiling water**
- **4 cups sugar**
- **4 cups boiling water**
- **2 48-ounce cans pineapple juice**
- **1 8-ounce bottle ReaLemon Juice**
- **4 quarts ginger ale**

Mix the first two ingredients together and set aside to cool. Mix the next two ingredients together and set aside to cool. Mix the last two ingredients together and after all other mixes are cool, mix everything together and pour into containers and freeze. When you are ready to serve, remove from freezer (about 1 to 2 hours before ready to serve) pour 4 quarts of ginger ale over this mix and serve.

Mrs. James T. Kelly (Mercille)

KAHLÚA
(Home Brew)

¾ cup water
1 cup sugar
2 cups vodka
7 teaspoons of instant coffee
1 cup white Karo syrup

Bring ¾ cup water to boil, add instant coffee, stir; add sugar. Slowly boil the syrup for 8 minutes. DO NOT STIR. Let cool.

In glass bottle, mix white Karo syrup and vodka. Add the coffee syrup and shake to mix. It's ready to drink. If you prefer a weaker or stronger coffee flavor, vary the amount of instant coffee. If you prefer your Kahlúa not so sweet, decrease the amount of Karo syrup.

Kahlúa is good on the rocks as well as mixed half Kahlúa and half milk, over ice.

Mrs. Benita Swan, Panama City Beach, Florida

PARADISE FRUIT CUBES

Pineapple cubes:
1 large can pineapple chunks
1 46-ounce can pineapple-grapefruit drink or pineapple-orange drink

Cherry cubes:
1 large bottle maraschino cherries or 2 10-ounce jars
1 46-ounce can pineapple-grapefruit drink or pineapple-orange drink

Using 6 ice-cube trays, place a chunk of pineapple or cherry in each section. After all trays are filled, pour juice from the pineapple chunks along with 1 can of pineapple-grapefruit drink over fruit. Cherry syrup should be mixed with the second can of drink mix making the cherry cubes a pretty pink color while the pineapple cubes will be golden color. Freeze all 6 trays of pineapple cubes, loosen; place in plastic zip-lock bags. Then mix cherry cubes, freeze; loosen; place in bags. Keep in freezer until ready to use. Great in punch mix or place several cubes of each flavor in glass and pour 7-Up over them. For an alcoholic drink, add 1 ounce of vodka or gin.

Mrs. Louis R. Jaudon (Betty)

HELPFUL HINTS

A small crochet hook will make an easy job of deveining shrimp.

★ ★ ★

To get onion off your hands wash in milk and rinse in cold water.

★ ★ ★

To remove ink stains wet tip of a match and rub on ink with finger and it will disappear.

★ ★ ★

To polish brass mix 2 pounds salt, 1 cup vinegar and enough flour to make paste. Rub brass with polish until stains are gone. Rinse with cold water and dry.

★ ★ ★

To remove black marks on floors use finger nail polish remover and sponge to clean.

★ ★ ★

To remove rust stains dampen spot with equal parts cream of tartar and salt.

★ ★ ★

To remove discoloration from aluminum cooking utensils add 2 tablespoons cream of tartar to each quart of water and boil 8 minutes.

★ ★ ★

If the vegetable grows beneath ground it grows covered in the cold earth; then start it in cold water, and cover pot with lid.

★ ★ ★

If a vegetable grows above ground it grows uncovered in the hot sun; then start it in boiling water and leave pot uncovered.

★ ★ ★

Brush the top of your double crust pie with a beaten egg. You will have a nice glazed crust when baked.

★ ★ ★

Baking soda makes a very good fire extinguisher.

★ ★ ★

Add a little boiling water to cloudy tea to restore its clear amber color.

Nut meats will come out in halves if soaked overnight in water before cracking.

★ ★ ★

If butter is rubbed around the top of the pan when making fudge, it will not boil over.

★ ★ ★

Your muffin tins are excellent for baking apples, stuffed peppers, etc.

★ ★ ★

When to beat fudge: Never beat fudge as soon as it is taken from the fire. Set in pan of cold water until cool, then beat.

★ ★ ★

To make carrots curl, slice very thin lengthwise. Drop in ice water. The curl is natural and permanent.

★ ★ ★

Use a regular size ice cream scoop when a recipe calls for one quarter cup of shortening.

★ ★ ★

To freshen wilted greens, douse quickly in hot and then ice water with a little vinegar added.

★ ★ ★

Use yogurt or buttermilk instead of oil or sour cream for salad dressings and dips.

★ ★ ★

Add 1 tablespoon oil, butter or margarine to rice before boiling. Makes grains separate and glossy and rice will never stick to pot.

★ ★ ★

When cutting marshmallows or chopping dates, dip your scissors in water and cut them wet; they won't stick.

★ ★ ★

Add 1/8 teaspoon salt to flour before mixing with water for thickening to a smoother consistency.

★ ★ ★

When scalding milk in a sauce pan, add a spoonful of sugar to eliminate milk sticking to bottom of pan.

Vinegar and salt makes fine cleaner for crystal or bottles that are stained. Let stand over night and rinse in cold water.

★ ★ ★

If you get something too salty while cooking add 1 teaspoon vinegar and 1 teaspoon sugar and reheat.

★ ★ ★

A pinch of salt will make cream whip more easily and rapidly.

★ ★ ★

Baking apples — prick the skin and they will cook without bursting.

★ ★ ★

For even consistency, when making pie crust: Add water with clothes sprinkler.

★ ★ ★

Do not grease the sides of cake pans. How would you like to climb a greased pole?

★ ★ ★

When icing a cake, the icing will not run off if a little flour is dusted on the surface of the cake.

★ ★ ★

To successfully cut angel food cake or sunshine cake, use a hot sharp knife.

★ ★ ★

For a nice decoration on white frosting, shave colored gum drops very thin and stick on. They will curl like little roses.

★ ★ ★

To remove onion or garlic odors from hands rub with fresh parsley or to remove from breath chew fresh parsley.

★ ★ ★

Grease the spout of pitcher with butter or margarine — prevents dripping.

★ ★ ★

Cooking at high temperature reduces potency of spices.

★ ★ ★

Put a heel of bread on top of cabbage before putting the lid on the pot and cooking it; there will be no odor. Also good for cooking broccoli and brussel sprouts.

To prevent mildew on refrigerator gaskets and also inside, wipe with pure vinegar.

★ ★ ★

When freezing fresh water fish put in empty milk cartons and fill with water and seal. Keeps fish fresher tasting longer.

★ ★ ★

A few drops of ammonia will help wonderfully in the dishwater if the dishes are unusually greasy.

★ ★ ★

A little salt sprinkled in the frying pan will keep fat or shortening from spattering.

METRIC SYSTEM

250 degrees Fahrenheit = 106 degrees Centigrade
350 degrees Fahrenheit = 162 degrees Centigrade
450 degrees Fahrenheit = 218 degrees Centigrade

1 teaspoon		5 cubic centimeters
1 tablespoon	3 teaspoons	15 cubic centimeters
¼ cup	4 tablespoons	59.1 cubic centimeters
1 cup		236.5 cubic centimeters
1 pint	2 cups	473 cubic centimeters
1 quart	2 pints	946 cubic centimeters
1 gallon	4 quarts	3.785 liters
1 pound	16 ounces	454 grams

TABLE OF EQUIVALENTS

STANDARD EQUIVALENTS:

A few grains	less than 1/8 teaspoon
1 coffee spoon	1/4 teaspoon
60 drops	1 teaspoon
3 teaspoons	1 tablespoon
2 tablespoons	1 fluid ounce
16 fluid ounces	1 pint
16 ounces	1 pound
16 tablespoons	1 cup
1 cup	1/2 pint
2 pints	1 quart
4 cups	1 quart
4 quarts	1 gallon
8 quarts	1 peck
4 pecks	1 bushel

NUT EQUIVALENTS:

ALMONDS

1 lb. in shell	1 cup shelled
1 c. whole	about 5 1/2 oz.
1 c. grated	about 2 1/2 oz.
1 c. chopped	about 4 1/2 oz.
2 1/2 c. ground	about 8 oz.
1 c. blanched	about 6 oz.
1 c. blanched, ground	about 1 1/3 c.
1 c. blanched	about 1 1/3 c. sliced

COCONUT

1 c. dry shredded	about 2 oz.
1 1/2 c. moist shredded	about 4 oz.
3 1/2 c. grated	about 8 oz.
5 c. fresh	about 1 lb.

PEANUTS

1 lb. in shell	about 1/2 lb. shelled
1 c. peanut meats	1 1/3 c. ground
1 1/2 lb. peanut meats	3 c. chopped

PECANS

1 c. pecan meats	about 4 oz.
1 c. pecan meats	about 1 c. ground
1 c. pecan meats	about 1 2/3 c. grated

WALNUTS

1 lb. in shell	2 c. shelled
1 c. grated	about 3 1/2 oz.
1 c. ground	about 6 oz.
1 c. chopped	about 4 oz.

TABLE OF EQUIVALENTS

FOOD EQUIVALENTS:

Apples	3 pounds	= about 2 quarts, sliced
Baking Powder	1 t. single-acting	= ¾ t. double-acting
Cheese	1 pound	= 4½ cups
Cottage Cheese	1 pound	= 2 cups
Chocolate, unsweetened	1 square (1 oz.)	= 3-4 T. grated chocolate
Cornstarch	1 T.	= 2 T. flour
Crackers, graham	3 cups crumbs	= 30-36 crackers
Crackers, salted	1 cup fine crumbs	= 20 crackers
Dates, pitted	1 pound	= 2 cups
Eggs		
Whole	1 egg	= about 3 T.
	1 cup	= 5-6 eggs
Whites	1 white	= about 2 T.
	1 cup	= 8-10 whites
Yolks	1 yolk	= about 1 T.
	1 cup	= 14-16 yolks
Figs, chopped	1 pound	= 3 cups
Flour, unsifted	1 pound	= 3 cups
All-purpose, sifted once	1 pound	= 3¾ cups
Cake, sifted once	1 pound	= 2 cups
Gelatin, unflavored	1 envelope (Knox)	= 1 T.
Lemon	1 average size	= 2-3 T. juice, 3 T. rind
Lentils	1 cup dry	= 2 cups cooked
Macaroni	1-1¼ cups dry (4 oz.)	= 2¼ cups cooked
Marshmallows	½ pound	= 30 standard size
	1 standard size	= 10 miniature
Noodles	1½-2 cups dry (4 oz.)	= 2¼ cups cooked
Prunes, dried	1 pound, dried	= 2½ cups
	1 pound, cooked	= 4 cups
Punch	1 gallon	= serves approx. 20
	12 quarts	= 96 punch glasses
Raisins	1 pound seeded	= 2½ cups
	1 pound seedless	= 3 cups
Rice	1 cup raw	= 3-3½ cups cooked
	1 cup pre-cooked	= 2 cups
Shortening, Butter	1 pound	= 2 cups
	½ pound	= 2 sticks
	1 stick	= ½ cup or 8 T.
Spaghetti	1-1¼ cups raw (4 oz.)	= 2½ cups cooked
Sugar		
Brown, sieved and packed	1 pound	= 2⅛ cups
Confectioners' sifted	1 pound	= about 4 cups
Granulated	1 pound	= 2⅛ cups
Yeast	1 cake yeast	= 1 level T. active dry
	1 pkg. dry yeast	= 1 level T. active dry
Vanilla Wafers	1 cup crumbs	= about 22 wafers
Zwieback	1 cup crumbs	= 8-9 slices

Index

SHREVE'S LANDING
P. O. Box 2022
Shreveport, Louisiana 71166

Please send me _______ copies of SHREVE'S LANDING at $7.50 plus $1.00 postage and handling, per book. (Louisiana residents add 3% sales tax.)

Enclosed is my check or money order for $ ______________________.
NAME ______________________________________
ADDRESS ____________________________________
CITY ________________ STATE ______________ ZIP ______________

Proceeds from the sale of SHREVE'S LANDING will be used to sponsor scholarships for deserving women students and for business women desiring further education.

SHREVE'S LANDING
P. O. Box 2022
Shreveport, Louisiana 71166

Please send me _______ copies of SHREVE'S LANDING at $7.50 plus $1.00 postage and handling, per book. (Louisiana residents add 3% sales tax.)

Enclosed is my check or money order for $ ______________________.
NAME ______________________________________
ADDRESS ____________________________________
CITY ________________ STATE ______________ ZIP ______________

Proceeds from the sale of SHREVE'S LANDING will be used to sponsor scholarships for deserving women students and for business women desiring further education.

SHREVE'S LANDING
P. O. Box 2022
Shreveport, Louisiana 71166

Please send me _______ copies of SHREVE'S LANDING at $7.50 plus $1.00 postage and handling, per book. (Louisiana residents add 3% sales tax.)

Enclosed is my check or money order for $ ______________________.
NAME ______________________________________
ADDRESS ____________________________________
CITY ________________ STATE ______________ ZIP ______________

Proceeds from the sale of SHREVE'S LANDING will be used to sponsor scholarships for deserving women students and for business women desiring further education.

Re-Order Additional Copies